United Nations Convention
on the Law of the Sea

Selected Treaty Series:

Vienna Convention on Diplomatic Relations
with Optional Protocols
S.T.S. No. 1961/MULT/DIPL

Vienna Convention on Consular Relations
with Optional Protocols
S.T.S. No. 1963/MULT/CONS

Vienna Convention on the Law of Treaties
S.T.S. No. 1969/MULT/TREATIES

United Nations Convention on the Law of the Sea
S.T.S. No. 1982/MULT/SEA

Vienna Convention on the Law of Treaties
between States and International Organizations
or between International Organizations
S.T.S. No. 1986/MULT/TREATIES

Additional treaties forthcoming

Selected Case Series:

Judgment of the International Military Tribunal at
Nuremberg for the Trial of German Major War Criminals
S.C.S. No. IMT/GoeringH/1946

Additional cases forthcoming

United Nations Convention on the Law of the Sea

Selected Treaty Series
William Thomas Worster, Editor

Uitgeverij Nieuwe Rijn

United Nations Convention on the Law of the Sea

Table of Contents[*]

[*] Table of contents added for the reader's reference. It does not constitute a part of the Final Act of the Conference.

United Nations Convention
on the Law of the Sea

Final Act of the Third United Nations
Conference on the Law of the Sea, Montego Bay, Jamaica
Convened pursuant to
UN General Assembly Resolution 3067 (XXVIII) (16 November 1973)
Final Part of the Eleventh Session** 6 to 10 December 1982
Convention adopted on 10 December 1982
Opened for signature on 10 December 1982
Entered into force 16 November 1994

** The prior sessions were as follows:
- First session held at UN Headquarters, New York, New York, USA from 3 to 15 December 1973
- Second session held at Parque Central, Caracas, Venezuela from 20 June to 29 August 1974
- Third session held at UN Office at Geneva, Switzerland from 17 March to 9 May 1975
- Fourth session held at UN Headquarters, New York, New York, USA from 15 March to 7 May 1976
- Fifth session held at UN Headquarters, New York, New York, USA from 2 August to 17 September 1976
- Sixth session held at UN Headquarters, New York, New York, USA from 23 May to 15 July 1977
- Seventh session held at UN Office at Geneva, Switzerland from 28 March to 19 May 1978; resumed at UN Headquarters, New York, New York, USA from 21 August to 15 September 1978
- Eighth session held at UN Office at Geneva, Switzerland from 19 March to 27 April 1979; resumed at UN Headquarters, New York, New York, USA from 19 July to 24 August 1979
- Ninth session held at UN Headquarters, New York, New York, USA from 3 March to 4 April 1980; resumed at UN Office at Geneva, Switzerland from 28 July to 29 August 1980
- Tenth session held at UN Headquarters, New York, New York, USA from 9 March to 24 April 1981; resumed at UN Office at Geneva, Switzerland from 3 to 28 August 1981
- Eleventh session held at UN Headquarters, New York, New York, USA from 8 March to 30 April 1982; resumed at UN Headquarters, New York, New York, USA from 22 to 24 September 1982; resumed at Montego Bay, Jamaica from 6 to 10 December 1982

The States Parties to this Convention,

Prompted by the desire to settle, in a spirit of mutual understanding and cooperation, all issues relating to the law of the sea and aware of the historic significance of this Convention as an important contribution to the maintenance of peace, justice and progress for all peoples of the world,

Noting that developments since the United Nations Conferences on the Law of the Sea held at Geneva in 1958 and 1960 have accentuated the need for a new and generally acceptable Convention on the law of the sea,

Conscious that the problems of ocean space are closely interrelated and need to be considered as a whole,

Recognizing the desirability of establishing through this Convention, with due regard for the sovereignty of all States, a legal order for the seas and oceans which will facilitate international communication, and will promote the peaceful uses of the seas and oceans, the equitable and efficient utilization of their resources, the conservation of their living resources, and the study, protection and preservation of the marine environment,

Bearing in mind that the achievement of these goals will contribute to the realization of a just and equitable international economic order which takes into account the interests and needs of mankind as a whole and, in particular, the special interests and needs of developing countries, whether coastal or land-locked,

Desiring by this Convention to develop the principles embodied in resolution 2749 (XXV) of 17 December 1970 in which the General Assembly of the United Nations solemnly declared *inter alia* that the area of the seabed and ocean floor and the subsoil thereof, beyond the limits of national jurisdiction, as well as its resources, are the common heritage of mankind, the exploration and exploitation of which shall be carried out for the benefit of mankind as a whole, irrespective of the geographical location of States,

Believing that the codification and progressive development of the law of the sea achieved in this Convention will contribute to the strengthening of peace, security, cooperation and friendly relations among all nations in conformity with the principles of justice and equal rights and will promote the economic and social advancement of all peoples of the world, in accordance with the Purposes and Principles of the United Nations as set forth in the Charter,

Affirming that matters not regulated by this Convention continue to be governed by the rules and principles of general international law,

Have agreed as follows:

PART I INTRODUCTION

Article 1 Use of terms and scope

1. For the purposes of this Convention:

(1) "Area" means the seabed and ocean floor and subsoil thereof, beyond the limits of national jurisdiction;

(2) "Authority" means the International Seabed Authority;

(3) "activities in the Area" means all activities of exploration for, and exploitation of, the resources of the Area;

(4) "pollution of the marine environment" means the introduction by man, directly or indirectly, of substances or energy into the marine environment, including estuaries, which results or is likely to result in such deleterious effects as harm to living resources and marine life, hazards to human health, hindrance to marine activities, including fishing and other legitimate uses of the sea, impairment of quality for use of sea water and reduction of amenities;

(5) (a) "dumping" means:

(i) any deliberate disposal of wastes or other matter from vessels, aircraft, platforms or other man-made structures at sea;

(ii) any deliberate disposal of vessels, aircraft, platforms or other man-made structures at sea;

(b) "dumping" does not include:

(i) the disposal of wastes or other matter incidental to, or derived from the normal operations of vessels, aircraft, platforms or other man-made structures at sea and their equipment, other than wastes or other matter transported by or to vessels, aircraft, platforms or other man-made structures at sea, operating for the purpose of disposal of such matter or derived from the treatment of such wastes or other matter on such vessels, aircraft, platforms or structures;

(ii) placement of matter for a purpose other than the mere disposal thereof, provided that such placement is not contrary to the aims of this Convention.

2. (1) "States Parties" means States which have consented to be bound by this Convention and for which this Convention is in force.

(2) This Convention applies *mutatis mutandis* to the entities referred to in article 305, paragraph l(b), (c), (d), (e) and (f), which become Parties to this Convention in accordance with the conditions relevant to each, and to that extent "States Parties" refers to those entities.

PART II   TERRITORIAL SEA AND CONTIGUOUS ZONE

SECTION 1   GENERAL PROVISIONS

Article 2   Legal status of the territorial sea, of the air space over the territorial sea and of its bed and subsoil

1. The sovereignty of a coastal State extends, beyond its land territory and internal waters and, in the case of an archipelagic State, its archipelagic waters, to an adjacent belt of sea, described as the territorial sea.

2. This sovereignty extends to the air space over the territorial sea as well as to its bed and subsoil.

3. The sovereignty over the territorial sea is exercised subject to this Convention and to other rules of international law.

SECTION 2   LIMITS OF THE TERRITORIAL SEA

Article 3   Breadth of the territorial sea

Every State has the right to establish the breadth of its territorial sea up to a limit not exceeding 12 nautical miles, measured from baselines determined in accordance with this Convention.

Article 4   Outer limit of the territorial sea

The outer limit of the territorial sea is the line every point of which is at a distance from the nearest point of the baseline equal to the breadth of the territorial sea.

Article 5   Normal baseline

Except where otherwise provided in this Convention, the normal baseline for measuring the breadth of the territorial sea is the low-water line along the coast as marked on large-scale charts officially recognized by the coastal State.

Article 6   Reefs

In the case of islands situated on atolls or of islands having fringing reefs, the baseline for measuring the breadth of the territorial sea is the seaward low-water line of the reef, as shown by the appropriate symbol on charts officially recognized by the coastal State.

Article 7   Straight baselines

1. In localities where the coastline is deeply indented and cut into, or if there is a fringe of islands along the coast in its immediate vicinity, the method of straight baselines joining appropriate points may be employed in drawing the baseline from which the breadth of the territorial sea is measured.

2. Where because of the presence of a delta and other natural conditions the coastline is highly unstable, the appropriate points may be selected along the furthest seaward extent of the low-water line and, notwithstanding subsequent regression of the low-water line, the straight baselines shall remain effective until changed by the coastal State in accordance with this Convention.

3. The drawing of straight baselines must not depart to any appreciable extent from the general direction of the coast, and the sea areas lying within the lines must be sufficiently closely linked to the land domain to be subject to the regime of internal waters.

4. Straight baselines shall not be drawn to and from low-tide elevations, unless lighthouses or similar installations which are permanently above sea level have been built on them or except in instances where the drawing of baselines to and from such elevations has received general international recognition.

5. Where the method of straight baselines is applicable under paragraph 1, account may be taken, in determining particular baselines, of economic interests peculiar to the region concerned, the reality and the importance of which are clearly evidenced by long usage.

6. The system of straight baselines may not be applied by a State in such a manner as to cut off the territorial sea of another State from the high seas or an exclusive economic zone.

Article 8   Internal waters

1. Except as provided in Part IV, waters on the landward side of the baseline of the territorial sea form part of the internal waters of the State.

2. Where the establishment of a straight baseline in accordance with the method set forth in article 7 has the effect of enclosing as internal waters areas which had not previously been considered as such, a right of innocent passage as provided in this Convention shall exist in those waters.

Article 9   Mouths of rivers

If a river flows directly into the sea, the baseline shall be a straight line across the mouth of the river between points on the low-water line of its banks.

Article 10   Bays

1. This article relates only to bays the coasts of which belong to a single State.

2. For the purposes of this Convention, a bay is a well-marked indentation whose penetration is in such proportion to the width of its mouth as to contain land-locked waters and constitute more than a mere curvature of the coast. An indentation shall not, however, be regarded as a bay unless its area is as large as, or larger than, that of the semi-circle whose diameter is a line drawn across the mouth of that indentation.

3. For the purpose of measurement, the area of an indentation is that lying between the low-water mark around the shore of the indentation and a line joining the low-water mark of its natural entrance points. Where, because of the presence of islands, an indentation has more than one mouth, the semi-circle shall be drawn on a line as long as the sum total of the lengths of the lines across the different mouths. Islands within an indentation shall be included as if they were part of the water area of the indentation.

4. If the distance between the low-water marks of the natural entrance points of a bay does not exceed 24 nautical miles, a closing line may be

drawn between these two low-water marks, and the waters enclosed thereby shall be considered as internal waters.

5. Where the distance between the low-water marks of the natural entrance points of a bay exceeds 24 nautical miles, a straight baseline of 24 nautical miles shall be drawn within the bay in such a manner as to enclose the maximum area of water that is possible with a line of that length.

6. The foregoing provisions do not apply to so-called "historic" bays, or in any case where the system of straight baselines provided for in article 7 is applied.

Article 11   Ports

For the purpose of delimiting the territorial sea, the outermost permanent harbour works which form an integral part of the harbour system are regarded as forming part of the coast. Off-shore installations and artificial islands shall not be considered as permanent harbour works.

Article 12   Roadsteads

Roadsteads which are normally used for the loading, unloading and anchoring of ships, and which would otherwise be situated wholly or partly outside the outer limit of the territorial sea, are included in the territorial sea.

Article 13   Low-tide elevations

1. A low-tide elevation is a naturally formed area of land which is surrounded by and above water at low tide but submerged at high tide. Where a low-tide elevation is situated wholly or partly at a distance not exceeding the breadth of the territorial sea from the mainland or an island, the low-water line on that elevation may be used as the baseline for measuring the breadth of the territorial sea.

2. Where a low-tide elevation is wholly situated at a distance exceeding the breadth of the territorial sea from the mainland or an island, it has no territorial sea of its own.

Article 14   Combination of methods for determining baselines

The coastal State may determine baselines in turn by any of the methods provided for in the foregoing articles to suit different conditions.

Article 15   Delimitation of the territorial sea between States with opposite or adjacent coasts

Where the coasts of two States are opposite or adjacent to each other, neither of the two States is entitled, failing agreement between them to the contrary, to extend its territorial sea beyond the median line every point of which is equidistant from the nearest points on the baselines from which the breadth of the territorial seas of each of the two States is measured. The above provision does not apply, however, where it is necessary by reason of historic title or other special circumstances to delimit the territorial seas of the two States in a way which is at variance therewith.

Article 16   Charts and lists of geographical coordinates

1. The baselines for measuring the breadth of the territorial sea determined in accordance with articles 7, 9 and 10, or the limits derived therefrom, and the lines of delimitation drawn in accordance with articles 12 and 15 shall be shown on charts of a scale or scales adequate for ascertaining their position. Alternatively, a list of geographical coordinates of points, specifying the geodetic datum, may be substituted.

2. The coastal State shall give due publicity to such charts or lists of geographical coordinates and shall deposit a copy of each such chart or list with the Secretary-General of the United Nations.

SECTION 3   INNOCENT PASSAGE IN THE TERRITORIAL SEA

Subsection A   Rules applicable to all ships

Article 17   Right of innocent passage

Subject to this Convention, ships of all States, whether coastal or land-locked, enjoy the right of innocent passage through the territorial sea.

Article 18   **Meaning of passage**

1. Passage means navigation through the territorial sea for the purpose of:

    (a) traversing that sea without entering internal waters or calling at a roadstead or port facility outside internal waters; or

    (b) proceeding to or from internal waters or a call at such roadstead or port facility.

2. Passage shall be continuous and expeditious. However, passage includes stopping and anchoring, but only in so far as the same are incidental to ordinary navigation or are rendered necessary by *force majeure* or distress or for the purpose of rendering assistance to persons, ships or aircraft in danger or distress.

Article 19   **Meaning of innocent passage**

1. Passage is innocent so long as it is not prejudicial to the peace, good order or security of the coastal State. Such passage shall take place in conformity with this Convention and with other rules of international law.

2. Passage of a foreign ship shall be considered to be prejudicial to the peace, good order or security of the coastal State if in the territorial sea it engages in any of the following activities:

    (a) any threat or use of force against the sovereignty, territorial integrity or political independence of the coastal State, or in any other manner in violation of the principles of international law embodied in the Charter of the United Nations;

    (b) any exercise or practice with weapons of any kind;

    (c) any act aimed at collecting information to the prejudice of the defence or security of the coastal State;

    (d) any act of propaganda aimed at affecting the defence or security of the coastal State;

    (e) the launching, landing or taking on board of any aircraft;

    (f) the launching, landing or taking on board of any military device;

(g) the loading or unloading of any commodity, currency or person contrary to the customs, fiscal, immigration or sanitary laws and regulations of the coastal State;

(h) any act of wilful and serious pollution contrary to this Convention;

(i) any fishing activities;

(j) the carrying out of research or survey activities;

(k) any act aimed at interfering with any systems of communication or any other facilities or installations of the coastal State;

(l) any other activity not having a direct bearing on passage.

Article 20   Submarines and other underwater vehicles

In the territorial sea, submarines and other underwater vehicles are required to navigate on the surface and to show their flag.

Article 21   Laws and regulations of the coastal State relating to innocent passage

1. The coastal State may adopt laws and regulations, in conformity with the provisions of this Convention and other rules of international law, relating to innocent passage through the territorial sea, in respect of all or any of the following:

(a) the safety of navigation and the regulation of maritime traffic;

(b) the protection of navigational aids and facilities and other facilities or installations;

(c) the protection of cables and pipelines;

(d) the conservation of the living resources of the sea;

(e) the prevention of infringement of the fisheries laws and regulations of the coastal State;

(f) the preservation of the environment of the coastal State and the prevention, reduction and control of pollution thereof;

(g) marine scientific research and hydrographic surveys;

(h) the prevention of infringement of the customs, fiscal, immigration or sanitary laws and regulations of the coastal State.

2. Such laws and regulations shall not apply to the design, construction, manning or equipment of foreign ships unless they are giving effect to generally accepted international rules or standards.

3. The coastal State shall give due publicity to all such laws and regulations.

4. Foreign ships exercising the right of innocent passage through the territorial sea shall comply with all such laws and regulations and all generally accepted international regulations relating to the prevention of collisions at sea.

Article 22   **Sea lanes and traffic separation schemes in the territorial sea**

1. The coastal State may, where necessary having regard to the safety of navigation, require foreign ships exercising the right of innocent passage through its territorial sea to use such sea lanes and traffic separation schemes as it may designate or prescribe for the regulation of the passage of ships.

2. In particular, tankers, nuclear-powered ships and ships carrying nuclear or other inherently dangerous or noxious substances or materials may be required to confine their passage to such sea lanes.

3. In the designation of sea lanes and the prescription of traffic separation schemes under this article, the coastal State shall take into account:

(a) the recommendations of the competent international organization;

(b) any channels customarily used for international navigation;

(c) the special characteristics of particular ships and channels; and

(d) the density of traffic.

4. The coastal State shall clearly indicate such sea lanes and traffic separation schemes on charts to which due publicity shall be given.

Article 23 **Foreign nuclear-powered ships and ships carrying nuclear or other inherently dangerous or noxious substances**

Foreign nuclear-powered ships and ships carrying nuclear or other inherently dangerous or noxious substances shall, when exercising the right of innocent passage through the territorial sea, carry documents and observe special precautionary measures established for such ships by international agreements.

Article 24 **Duties of the coastal State**

1. The coastal State shall not hamper the innocent passage of foreign ships through the territorial sea except in accordance with this Convention.

In particular, in the application of this Convention or of any laws or regulations adopted in conformity with this Convention, the coastal State shall not:

(a) impose requirements on foreign ships which have the practical effect of denying or impairing the right of innocent passage; or

(b) discriminate in form or in fact against the ships of any State or against ships carrying cargoes to, from or on behalf of any State.

2. The coastal State shall give appropriate publicity to any danger to navigation, of which it has knowledge, within its territorial sea.

Article 25 **Rights of protection of the coastal State**

1. The coastal State may take the necessary steps in its territorial sea to prevent passage which is not innocent.

2. In the case of ships proceeding to internal waters or a call at a port facility outside internal waters, the coastal State also has the right to take the necessary steps to prevent any breach of the conditions to which admission of those ships to internal waters or such a call is subject.

3. The coastal State may, without discrimination in form or in fact among foreign ships, suspend temporarily in specified areas of its territorial sea the innocent passage of foreign ships if such suspension is essential for the protection of its security, including weapons exercises. Such suspension shall take effect only after having been duly published.

Article 26   Charges which may be levied upon foreign ships

1. No charge may be levied upon foreign ships by reason only of their passage through the territorial sea.

2. Charges may be levied upon a foreign ship passing through the territorial sea as payment only for specific services rendered to the ship. These charges shall be levied without discrimination.

Subsection B   Rules applicable to merchant ships and government ships operated for commercial purposes

Article 27   Criminal jurisdiction on board a foreign ship

1. The criminal jurisdiction of the coastal State should not be exercised on board a foreign ship passing through the territorial sea to arrest any person or to conduct any investigation in connection with any crime committed on board the ship during its passage, save only in the following cases:

(a) if the consequences of the crime extend to the coastal State;

(b) if the crime is of a kind to disturb the peace of the country or the good order of the territorial sea;

(c) if the assistance of the local authorities has been requested by the master of the ship or by a diplomatic agent or consular officer of the flag State; or

(d) if such measures are necessary for the suppression of illicit traffic in narcotic drugs or psychotropic substances.

2. The above provisions do not affect the right of the coastal State to take any steps authorized by its laws for the purpose of an arrest or investigation on board a foreign ship passing through the territorial sea after leaving internal waters.

3. In the cases provided for in paragraphs 1 and 2, the coastal State shall, if the master so requests, notify a diplomatic agent or consular officer of the flag State before taking any steps, and shall facilitate contact between such agent or officer and the ship's crew. In cases of emergency this notification may be communicated while the measures are being taken.

4. In considering whether or in what manner an arrest should be made, the local authorities shall have due regard to the interests of navigation.

5. Except as provided in Part XII or with respect to violations of laws and regulations adopted in accordance with Part V, the coastal State may not take any steps on board a foreign ship passing through the territorial sea to arrest any person or to conduct any investigation in connection with any crime committed before the ship entered the territorial sea, if the ship, proceeding from a foreign port, is only passing through the territorial sea without entering internal waters.

Article 28   Civil jurisdiction in relation to foreign ships

1. The coastal State should not stop or divert a foreign ship passing through the territorial sea for the purpose of exercising civil jurisdiction in relation to a person on board the ship.

2. The coastal State may not levy execution against or arrest the ship for the purpose of any civil proceedings, save only in respect of obligations or liabilities assumed or incurred by the ship itself in the course or for the purpose of its voyage through the waters of the coastal State.

3. Paragraph 2 is without prejudice to the right of the coastal State, in accordance with its laws, to levy execution against or to arrest, for the purpose of any civil proceedings, a foreign ship lying in the territorial sea, or passing through the territorial sea after leaving internal waters.

Subsection C   Rules applicable to warships and other governmental ships operated for non-commercial purposes

Article 29   Definition of warships

For the purposes of this Convention, "warship" means a ship belonging to the armed forces of a State bearing the external marks distinguishing such ships of its nationality, under the command of an officer duly commissioned by the government of the State and whose name appears in the appropriate service list or its equivalent, and manned by a crew which is under regular armed forces discipline.

Article 30   **Non-compliance by warships with the laws and regulations of the coastal State**

If any warship does not comply with the laws and regulations of the coastal State concerning passage through the territorial sea and disregards any request for compliance therewith which is made to it, the coastal State may require it to leave the territorial sea immediately.

Article 31   **Responsibility of the flag State for damage caused by a warship or other governmental ship operated for non-commercial purposes**

The flag State shall bear international responsibility for any loss or damage to the coastal State resulting from the non-compliance by a warship or other government ship operated for non-commercial purposes with the laws and regulations of the coastal State concerning passage through the territorial sea or with the provisions of this Convention or other rules of international law.

Article 32   **Immunities of warships and other government ships operated for non-commercial purposes**

With such exceptions as are contained in subsection A and in articles 30 and 31, nothing in this Convention affects the immunities of warships and other government ships operated for non-commercial purposes.

SECTION 4   CONTIGUOUS ZONE

Article 33   Contiguous zone

1. In a zone contiguous to its territorial sea, described as the contiguous zone, the coastal State may exercise the control necessary to:

(a) prevent infringement of its customs, fiscal, immigration or sanitary laws and regulations within its territory or territorial sea;

(b) punish infringement of the above laws and regulations committed within its territory or territorial sea.

2. The contiguous zone may not extend beyond 24 nautical miles from the baselines from which the breadth of the territorial sea is measured.

PART III   STRAITS USED FOR INTERNATIONAL NAVIGATION

SECTION 1   GENERAL PROVISIONS

Article 34   Legal status of waters forming straits used for international navigation

1. The regime of passage through straits used for international navigation established in this Part shall not in other respects affect the legal status of the waters forming such straits or the exercise by the States bordering the straits of their sovereignty or jurisdiction over such waters and their air space, bed and subsoil.

2. The sovereignty or jurisdiction of the States bordering the straits is exercised subject to this Part and to other rules of international law.

Article 35   Scope of this Part

Nothing in this Part affects:

(a) any areas of internal waters within a strait, except where the establishment of a straight baseline in accordance with the method set forth in article 7 has the effect of enclosing as internal waters areas which had not previously been considered as such;

(b) the legal status of the waters beyond the territorial seas of States bordering straits as exclusive economic zones or high seas; or

(c) the legal regime in straits in which passage is regulated in whole or in part by long-standing international conventions in force specifically relating to such straits.

Article 36   High seas routes or routes through exclusive economic zones through straits used for international navigation

This Part does not apply to a strait used for international navigation if there exists through the strait a route through the high seas or through an exclusive economic zone of similar convenience with respect to navigational and hydrographical characteristics; in such routes, the other relevant Parts of this Convention, including the provisions regarding the freedoms of navigation and overflight, apply.

SECTION 2   TRANSIT PASSAGE

Article 37   Scope of this section

This section applies to straits which are used for international navigation between one part of the high seas or an exclusive economic zone and another part of the high seas or an exclusive economic zone.

Article 38   Right of transit passage

1. In straits referred to in article 37, all ships and aircraft enjoy the right of transit passage, which shall not be impeded; except that, if the strait is formed by an island of a State bordering the strait and its mainland, transit passage shall not apply if there exists seaward of the island a route through the high seas or through an exclusive economic zone of similar convenience with respect to navigational and hydrographical characteristics.

2. Transit passage means the exercise in accordance with this Part of the freedom of navigation and overflight solely for the purpose of continuous and expeditious transit of the strait between one part of the high seas or an exclusive economic zone and another part of the high seas or an exclusive economic zone. However, the requirement of continuous and expeditious transit does not preclude passage through the strait for the purpose of entering, leaving or returning from a State bordering the strait, subject to the conditions of entry to that State.

3. Any activity which is not an exercise of the right of transit passage through a strait remains subject to the other applicable provisions of this Convention.

Article 39   Duties of ships and aircraft during transit passage

1. Ships and aircraft, while exercising the right of transit passage, shall:

(a) proceed without delay through or over the strait;

(b) refrain from any threat or use of force against the sovereignty, territorial integrity or political independence of States bordering the strait, or in any other manner in violation of the principles of international law embodied in the Charter of the United Nations;

(c) refrain from any activities other than those incident to their normal modes of continuous and expeditious transit unless rendered necessary by *force majeure* or by distress;

(d) comply with other relevant provisions of this Part.

2. Ships in transit passage shall:

(a) comply with generally accepted international regulations, procedures and practices for safety at sea, including the International Regulations for Preventing Collisions at Sea;

(b) comply with generally accepted international regulations, procedures and practices for the prevention, reduction and control of pollution from ships.

3. Aircraft in transit passage shall:

(a) observe the Rules of the Air established by the International Civil Aviation Organization as they apply to civil aircraft; state aircraft will normally comply with such safety measures and will at all times operate with due regard for the safety of navigation;

(b) at all times monitor the radio frequency assigned by the competent internationally designated air traffic control authority or the appropriate international distress radio frequency.

Article 40   Research and survey activities

During transit passage, foreign ships, including marine scientific research and hydrographic survey ships, may not carry out any research or survey activities without the prior authorization of the States bordering straits.

Article 41   Sea lanes and traffic separation schemes in straits used for international navigation

1. In conformity with this Part, States bordering straits may designate sea lanes and prescribe traffic separation schemes for navigation in straits where necessary to promote the safe passage of ships.

2. Such States may, when circumstances require, and after giving due publicity thereto, substitute other sea lanes or traffic separation schemes for any sea lanes or traffic separation schemes previously designated or prescribed by them.

3. Such sea lanes and traffic separation schemes shall conform to generally accepted international regulations.

4. Before designating or substituting sea lanes or prescribing or substituting traffic separation schemes, States bordering straits shall refer proposals to the competent international organization with a view to their adoption. The organization may adopt only such sea lanes and traffic separation schemes as may be agreed with the States bordering the straits, after which the States may designate, prescribe or substitute them.

5. In respect of a strait where sea lanes or traffic separation schemes through the waters of two or more States bordering the strait are being proposed, the States concerned shall cooperate in formulating proposals in consultation with the competent international organization.

6. States bordering straits shall clearly indicate all sea lanes and traffic separation schemes designated or prescribed by them on charts to which due publicity shall be given.

7. Ships in transit passage shall respect applicable sea lanes and traffic separation schemes established in accordance with this article.

Article 42   **Laws and regulations of States bordering straits relating to transit passage**

1. Subject to the provisions of this section, States bordering straits may adopt laws and regulations relating to transit passage through straits, in respect of all or any of the following:

(a) the safety of navigation and the regulation of maritime traffic, as provided in article 41;

(b) the prevention, reduction and control of pollution, by giving effect to applicable international regulations regarding the discharge of oil, oily wastes and other noxious substances in the strait;

(c) with respect to fishing vessels, the prevention of fishing, including the stowage of fishing gear;

(d) the loading or unloading of any commodity, currency or person in contravention of the customs, fiscal, immigration or sanitary laws and regulations of States bordering straits.

2. Such laws and regulations shall not discriminate in form or in fact among foreign ships or in their application have the practical effect of denying, hampering or impairing the right of transit passage as defined in this section.

3. States bordering straits shall give due publicity to all such laws and regulations.

4. Foreign ships exercising the right of transit passage shall comply with such laws and regulations.

5. The flag State of a ship or the State of registry of an aircraft entitled to sovereign immunity which acts in a manner contrary to such laws and regulations or other provisions of this Part shall bear international responsibility for any loss or damage which results to States bordering straits.

Article 43   **Navigational and safety aids and other improvements and the prevention, reduction and control of pollution**

User States and States bordering a strait should by agreement cooperate:

(a) in the establishment and maintenance in a strait of necessary navigational and safety aids or other improvements in aid of international navigation; and

(b) for the prevention, reduction and control of pollution from ships.

Article 44   **Duties of States bordering straits**

States bordering straits shall not hamper transit passage and shall give appropriate publicity to any danger to navigation or overflight within or over the strait of which they have knowledge. There shall be no suspension of transit passage.

SECTION 3   INNOCENT PASSAGE

Article 45   Innocent passage

1. The regime of innocent passage, in accordance with Part II, section 3, shall apply in straits used for international navigation:

(a) excluded from the application of the regime of transit passage under article 38, paragraph 1; or

(b) between a part of the high seas or an exclusive economic zone and the territorial sea of a foreign State.

2. There shall be no suspension of innocent passage through such straits.

PART IV ARCHIPELAGIC STATES

Article 46   Use of terms

For the purposes of this Convention:

(a) "archipelagic State" means a State constituted wholly by one or more archipelagos and may include other islands;

(b) "archipelago" means a group of islands, including parts of islands, interconnecting waters and other natural features which are so closely interrelated that such islands, waters and other natural features form an intrinsic geographical, economic and political entity, or which historically have been regarded as such.

Article 47   Archipelagic baselines

1. An archipelagic State may draw straight archipelagic baselines joining the outermost points of the outermost islands and drying reefs of the archipelago provided that within such baselines are included the main islands and an area in which the ratio of the area of the water to the area of the land, including atolls, is between 1 to 1 and 9 to 1.

2. The length of such baselines shall not exceed 100 nautical miles, except that up to 3 per cent of the total number of baselines enclosing any archipelago may exceed that length, up to a maximum length of 125 nautical miles.

3. The drawing of such baselines shall not depart to any appreciable extent from the general configuration of the archipelago.

4. Such baselines shall not be drawn to and from low-tide elevations, unless lighthouses or similar installations which are permanently above sea level have been built on them or where a low-tide elevation is situated wholly or partly at a distance not exceeding the breadth of the territorial sea from the nearest island.

5. The system of such baselines shall not be applied by an archipelagic State in such a manner as to cut off from the high seas or the exclusive economic zone the territorial sea of another State.

6. If a part of the archipelagic waters of an archipelagic State lies between two parts of an immediately adjacent neighbouring State, existing rights and all other legitimate interests which the latter State has traditionally exercised in such waters and all rights stipulated by agreement between those States shall continue and be respected.

7. For the purpose of computing the ratio of water to land under paragraph 1, land areas may include waters lying within the fringing reefs of islands and atolls, including that part of a steep-sided oceanic plateau which is enclosed or nearly enclosed by a chain of limestone islands and drying reefs lying on the perimeter of the plateau.

8. The baselines drawn in accordance with this article shall be shown on charts of a scale or scales adequate for ascertaining their position. Alternatively, lists of geographical coordinates of points, specifying the geodetic datum, may be substituted.

9. The archipelagic State shall give due publicity to such charts or lists of geographical coordinates and shall deposit a copy of each such chart or list with the Secretary-General of the United Nations.

Article 48   Measurement of the breadth of the territorial sea, the contiguous zone, the exclusive economic zone and the continental shelf

The breadth of the territorial sea, the contiguous zone, the exclusive economic zone and the continental shelf shall be measured from archipelagic baselines drawn in accordance with article 47.

Article 49 **Legal status of archipelagic waters, of the air space over archipelagic waters and of their bed and subsoil**

1. The sovereignty of an archipelagic State extends to the waters enclosed by the archipelagic baselines drawn in accordance with article 47, described as archipelagic waters, regardless of their depth or distance from the coast.

2. This sovereignty extends to the air space over the archipelagic waters, as well as to their bed and subsoil, and the resources contained therein.

3. This sovereignty is exercised subject to this Part.

4. The regime of archipelagic sea lanes passage established in this Part shall not in other respects affect the status of the archipelagic waters, including the sea lanes, or the exercise by the archipelagic State of its sovereignty over such waters and their air space, bed and subsoil, and the resources contained therein.

Article 50 **Delimitation of internal waters**

Within its archipelagic waters, the archipelagic State may draw closing lines for the delimitation of internal waters, in accordance with articles 9, 10 and 11.

Article 51 **Existing agreements, traditional fishing rights and existing submarine cables**

1. Without prejudice to article 49, an archipelagic State shall respect existing agreements with other States and shall recognize traditional fishing rights and other legitimate activities of the immediately adjacent neighbouring States in certain areas falling within archipelagic waters. The terms and conditions for the exercise of such rights and activities, including the nature, the extent and the areas to which they apply, shall, at the request of any of the States concerned, be regulated by bilateral agreements between them. Such rights shall not be transferred to or shared with third States or their nationals.

2. An archipelagic State shall respect existing submarine cables laid by other States and passing through its waters without making a landfall. An archipelagic State shall permit the maintenance and replacement of such cables upon receiving due notice of their location and the intention to repair or replace them.

Article 52   Right of innocent passage

1. Subject to article 53 and without prejudice to article 50, ships of all States enjoy the right of innocent passage through archipelagic waters, in accordance with Part II, section 3.

2. The archipelagic State may, without discrimination in form or in fact among foreign ships, suspend temporarily in specified areas of its archipelagic waters the innocent passage of foreign ships if such suspension is essential for the protection of its security. Such suspension shall take effect only after having been duly published.

Article 53   Right of archipelagic sea lanes passage

1. An archipelagic State may designate sea lanes and air routes thereabove, suitable for the continuous and expeditious passage of foreign ships and aircraft through or over its archipelagic waters and the adjacent territorial sea.

2. All ships and aircraft enjoy the right of archipelagic sea lanes passage in such sea lanes and air routes.

3. Archipelagic sea lanes passage means the exercise in accordance with this Convention of the rights of navigation and overflight in the normal mode solely for the purpose of continuous, expeditious and unobstructed transit between one part of the high seas or an exclusive economic zone and another part of the high seas or an exclusive economic zone.

4. Such sea lanes and air routes shall traverse the archipelagic waters and the adjacent territorial sea and shall include all normal passage routes used as routes for international navigation or overflight through or over archipelagic waters and, within such routes, so far as ships are concerned, all normal navigational channels, provided that duplication of routes of similar convenience between the same entry and exit points shall not be necessary.

5. Such sea lanes and air routes shall be defined by a series of continuous axis lines from the entry points of passage routes to the exit points. Ships and aircraft in archipelagic sea lanes passage shall not deviate more than 25 nautical miles to either side of such axis lines during passage, provided that such ships and aircraft shall not navigate closer to the coasts than 10 per cent of the distance between the nearest points on islands bordering the sea lane.

6. An archipelagic State which designates sea lanes under this article may also prescribe traffic separation schemes for the safe passage of ships through narrow channels in such sea lanes.

7. An archipelagic State may, when circumstances require, after giving due publicity thereto, substitute other sea lanes or traffic separation schemes for any sea lanes or traffic separation schemes previously designated or prescribed by it.

8. Such sea lanes and traffic separation schemes shall conform to generally accepted international regulations.

9. In designating or substituting sea lanes or prescribing or substituting traffic separation schemes, an archipelagic State shall refer proposals to the competent international organization with a view to their adoption. The organization may adopt only such sea lanes and traffic separation schemes as may be agreed with the archipelagic State, after which the archipelagic State may designate, prescribe or substitute them.

10. The archipelagic State shall clearly indicate the axis of the sea lanes and the traffic separation schemes designated or prescribed by it on charts to which due publicity shall be given.

11. Ships in archipelagic sea lanes passage shall respect applicable sea lanes and traffic separation schemes established in accordance with this article.

12. If an archipelagic State does not designate sea lanes or air routes, the right of archipelagic sea lanes passage may be exercised through the routes normally used for international navigation.

Article 54   **Duties of ships and aircraft during their passage, research and survey activities, duties of the archipelagic State and laws and regulations of the archipelagic State relating to archipelagic sea lanes passage**

Articles 39, 40, 42 and 44 apply *mutatis mutandis* to archipelagic sea lanes passage.

PART V EXCLUSIVE ECONOMIC ZONE

Article 55   Specific legal regime of the exclusive economic zone

The exclusive economic zone is an area beyond and adjacent to the territorial sea, subject to the specific legal regime established in this Part, under which the rights and jurisdiction of the coastal State and the rights and freedoms of other States are governed by the relevant provisions of this Convention.

Article 56   Rights, jurisdiction and duties of the coastal State in the exclusive economic zone

1. In the exclusive economic zone, the coastal State has:

(a) sovereign rights for the purpose of exploring and exploiting, conserving and managing the natural resources, whether living or non-living, of the waters superjacent to the seabed and of the seabed and its subsoil, and with regard to other activities for the economic exploitation and exploration of the zone, such as the production of energy from the water, currents and winds;

(b) jurisdiction as provided for in the relevant provisions of this Convention with regard to:

(i) the establishment and use of artificial islands, installations and structures;

(ii) marine scientific research;

(iii) the protection and preservation of the marine environment;

(c) other rights and duties provided for in this Convention.

2. In exercising its rights and performing its duties under this Convention in the exclusive economic zone, the coastal State shall have due regard to the rights and duties of other States and shall act in a manner compatible with the provisions of this Convention.

3. The rights set out in this article with respect to the seabed and subsoil shall be exercised in accordance with Part VI.

Article 57   **Breadth of the exclusive economic zone**

The exclusive economic zone shall not extend beyond 200 nautical miles from the baselines from which the breadth of the territorial sea is measured.

Article 58   **Rights and duties of other States in the exclusive economic zone**

1. In the exclusive economic zone, all States, whether coastal or land-locked, enjoy, subject to the relevant provisions of this Convention, the freedoms referred to in article 87 of navigation and overflight and of the laying of submarine cables and pipelines, and other internationally lawful uses of the sea related to these freedoms, such as those associated with the operation of ships, aircraft and submarine cables and pipelines, and compatible with the other provisions of this Convention.

2. Articles 88 to 115 and other pertinent rules of international law apply to the exclusive economic zone in so far as they are not incompatible with this Part.

3. In exercising their rights and performing their duties under this Convention in the exclusive economic zone, States shall have due regard to the rights and duties of the coastal State and shall comply with the laws and regulations adopted by the coastal State in accordance with the provisions of this Convention and other rules of international law in so far as they are not incompatible with this Part.

Article 59   **Basis for the resolution of conflicts regarding the attribution of rights and jurisdiction in the exclusive economic zone**

In cases where this Convention does not attribute rights or jurisdiction to the coastal State or to other States within the exclusive economic zone, and a conflict arises between the interests of the coastal State and any other State or States, the conflict should be resolved on the basis of equity and in the light of all the relevant circumstances, taking into account the respective importance of the interests involved to the parties as well as to the international community as a whole.

Article 60   **Artificial islands, installations and structures in the exclusive economic zone**

1. In the exclusive economic zone, the coastal State shall have the exclusive right to construct and to authorize and regulate the construction, operation and use of:

(a) artificial islands;

(b) installations and structures for the purposes provided for in article 56 and other economic purposes;

(c) installations and structures which may interfere with the exercise of the rights of the coastal State in the zone.

2. The coastal State shall have exclusive jurisdiction over such artificial islands, installations and structures, including jurisdiction with regard to customs, fiscal, health, safety and immigration laws and regulations.

3. Due notice must be given of the construction of such artificial islands, installations or structures, and permanent means for giving warning of their presence must be maintained. Any installations or structures which are abandoned or disused shall be removed to ensure safety of navigation, taking into account any generally accepted international standards established in this regard by the competent international organization. Such removal shall also have due regard to fishing, the protection of the marine environment and the rights and duties of other States. Appropriate publicity shall be given to the depth, position and dimensions of any installations or structures not entirely removed.

4. The coastal State may, where necessary, establish reasonable safety zones around such artificial islands, installations and structures in which it may take appropriate measures to ensure the safety both of navigation and of the artificial islands, installations and structures.

5. The breadth of the safety zones shall be determined by the coastal State, taking into account applicable international standards. Such zones shall be designed to ensure that they are reasonably related to the nature and function of the artificial islands, installations or structures, and shall not exceed a distance of 500 metres around them, measured from each point of their outer edge, except as authorized by generally accepted international standards or as recommended by the competent international organization. Due notice shall be given of the extent of safety zones.

6. All ships must respect these safety zones and shall comply with generally accepted international standards regarding navigation in the vicinity of artificial islands, installations, structures and safety zones.

7. Artificial islands, installations and structures and the safety zones around them may not be established where interference may be caused to the use of recognized sea lanes essential to international navigation.

8. Artificial islands, installations and structures do not possess the status of islands. They have no territorial sea of their own, and their presence does not affect the delimitation of the territorial sea, the exclusive economic zone or the continental shelf.

Article 61   Conservation of the living resources

1. The coastal State shall determine the allowable catch of the living resources in its exclusive economic zone.

2. The coastal State, taking into account the best scientific evidence available to it, shall ensure through proper conservation and management measures that the maintenance of the living resources in the exclusive economic zone is not endangered by over-exploitation. As appropriate, the coastal State and competent international organizations, whether subregional, regional or global, shall cooperate to this end.

3. Such measures shall also be designed to maintain or restore populations of harvested species at levels which can produce the maximum sustainable yield, as qualified by relevant environmental and economic factors, including the economic needs of coastal fishing communities and the special requirements of developing States, and taking into account fishing patterns, the interdependence of stocks and any generally recommended international minimum standards, whether subregional, regional or global.

4. In taking such measures the coastal State shall take into consideration the effects on species associated with or dependent upon harvested species with a view to maintaining or restoring populations of such associated or dependent species above levels at which their reproduction may become seriously threatened.

5. Available scientific information, catch and fishing effort statistics, and other data relevant to the conservation of fish stocks shall be contributed and exchanged on a regular basis through competent international organizations, whether subregional, regional or global, where appropriate and with participation by all States concerned, including States whose nationals are allowed to fish in the exclusive economic zone.

Article 62   Utilization of the living resources

1. The coastal State shall promote the objective of optimum utilization of the living resources in the exclusive economic zone without prejudice to article 61.

2. The coastal State shall determine its capacity to harvest the living resources of the exclusive economic zone. Where the coastal State does not have the capacity to harvest the entire allowable catch, it shall, through agreements or other arrangements and pursuant to the terms, conditions, laws and regulations referred to in paragraph 4, give other States access to the surplus of the allowable catch, having particular regard to the provisions of articles 69 and 70, especially in relation to the developing States mentioned therein.

3. In giving access to other States to its exclusive economic zone under this article, the coastal State shall take into account all relevant factors, including, *inter alia*, the significance of the living resources of the area to the economy of the coastal State concerned and its other national interests, the provisions of articles 69 and 70, the requirements of developing States in the subregion or region in harvesting part of the surplus and the need to minimize economic dislocation in States whose nationals have habitually fished in the zone or which have made substantial efforts in research and identification of stocks.

4. Nationals of other States fishing in the exclusive economic zone shall comply with the conservation measures and with the other terms and conditions established in the laws and regulations of the coastal State. These laws and regulations shall be consistent with this Convention and may relate, *inter alia*, to the following:

(a) licensing of fishermen, fishing vessels and equipment, including payment of fees and other forms of remuneration, which, in the case of developing coastal States, may consist of adequate compensation in the field of financing, equipment and technology relating to the fishing industry;

(b) determining the species which may be caught, and fixing quotas of catch, whether in relation to particular stocks or groups of stocks or catch per vessel over a period of time or to the catch by nationals of any State during a specified period;

(c) regulating seasons and areas of fishing, the types, sizes and amount of gear, and the types, sizes and number of fishing vessels that may be used;

(d) fixing the age and size of fish and other species that may be caught;

(e) specifying information required of fishing vessels, including catch and effort statistics and vessel position reports;

(f) requiring, under the authorization and control of the coastal State, the conduct of specified fisheries research programmes and regulating the conduct of such research, including the sampling of catches, disposition of samples and reporting of associated scientific data;

(g) the placing of observers or trainees on board such vessels by the coastal State;

(h) the landing of all or any part of the catch by such vessels in the ports of the coastal State;

(i) terms and conditions relating to joint ventures or other cooperative arrangements;

(j) requirements for the training of personnel and the transfer of fisheries technology, including enhancement of the coastal State's capability of undertaking fisheries research;
(k) enforcement procedures.

5. Coastal States shall give due notice of conservation and management laws and regulations.

| Article 63 | Stocks occurring within the exclusive economic zones of two or more coastal States or both within the exclusive economic zone and in an area beyond and adjacent to it |

1. Where the same stock or stocks of associated species occur within the exclusive economic zones of two or more coastal States, these States shall seek, either directly or through appropriate subregional or regional

organizations, to agree upon the measures necessary to coordinate and ensure the conservation and development of such stocks without prejudice to the other provisions of this Part.

2. Where the same stock or stocks of associated species occur both within the exclusive economic zone and in an area beyond and adjacent to the zone, the coastal State and the States fishing for such stocks in the adjacent area shall seek, either directly or through appropriate subregional or regional organizations, to agree upon the measures necessary for the conservation of these stocks in the adjacent area.

Article 64   Highly migratory species

1. The coastal State and other States whose nationals fish in the region for the highly migratory species listed in Annex I shall cooperate directly or through appropriate international organizations with a view to ensuring conservation and promoting the objective of optimum utilization of such species throughout the region, both within and beyond the exclusive economic zone. In regions for which no appropriate international organization exists, the coastal State and other States whose nationals harvest these species in the region shall cooperate to establish such an organization and participate in its work.

2. The provisions of paragraph 1 apply in addition to the other provisions of this Part.

Article 65   Marine mammals

Nothing in this Part restricts the right of a coastal State or the competence of an international organization, as appropriate, to prohibit, limit or regulate the exploitation of marine mammals more strictly than provided for in this Part. States shall cooperate with a view to the conservation of marine mammals and in the case of cetaceans shall in particular work through the appropriate international organizations for their conservation, management and study.

Article 66   Anadromous stocks

1. States in whose rivers anadromous stocks originate shall have the primary interest in and responsibility for such stocks.

2. The State of origin of anadromous stocks shall ensure their conservation by the establishment of appropriate regulatory measures for fishing in all waters landward of the outer limits of its exclusive

economic zone and for fishing provided for in paragraph 3(b). The State of origin may, after consultations with the other States referred to in paragraphs 3 and 4 fishing these stocks, establish total allowable catches for stocks originating in its rivers.

3. (a) Fisheries for anadromous stocks shall be conducted only in waters landward of the outer limits of exclusive economic zones, except in cases where this provision would result in economic dislocation for a State other than the State of origin. With respect to such fishing beyond the outer limits of the exclusive economic zone, States concerned shall maintain consultations with a view to achieving agreement on terms and conditions of such fishing giving due regard to the conservation requirements and the needs of the State of origin in respect of these stocks.

(b) The State of origin shall cooperate in minimizing economic dislocation in such other States fishing these stocks, taking into account the normal catch and the mode of operations of such States, and all the areas in which such fishing has occurred.

(c) States referred to in subparagraph (b), participating by agreement with the State of origin in measures to renew anadromous stocks, particularly by expenditures for that purpose, shall be given special consideration by the State of origin in the harvesting of stocks originating in its rivers.

(d) Enforcement of regulations regarding anadromous stocks beyond the exclusive economic zone shall be by agreement between the State of origin and the other States concerned.

4. In cases where anadromous stocks migrate into or through the waters landward of the outer limits of the exclusive economic zone of a State other than the State of origin, such State shall cooperate with the State of origin with regard to the conservation and management of such stocks.

5. The State of origin of anadromous stocks and other States fishing these stocks shall make arrangements for the implementation of the provisions of this article, where appropriate, through regional organizations.

Article 67   Catadromous species

1. A coastal State in whose waters catadromous species spend the greater part of their life cycle shall have responsibility for the management of these species and shall ensure the ingress and egress of migrating fish.

2. Harvesting of catadromous species shall be conducted only in waters landward of the outer limits of exclusive economic zones. When conducted in exclusive economic zones, harvesting shall be subject to this article and the other provisions of this Convention concerning fishing in these zones.

3. In cases where catadromous fish migrate through the exclusive economic zone of another State, whether as juvenile or maturing fish, the management, including harvesting, of such fish shall be regulated by agreement between the State mentioned in paragraph 1 and the other State concerned. Such agreement shall ensure the rational management of the species and take into account the responsibilities of the State mentioned in paragraph 1 for the maintenance of these species.

Article 68   Sedentary species

This Part does not apply to sedentary species as defined in article 77, paragraph 4.

Article 69   Right of land-locked States

1. Land-locked States shall have the right to participate, on an equitable basis, in the exploitation of an appropriate part of the surplus of the living resources of the exclusive economic zones of coastal States of the same subregion or region, taking into account the relevant economic and geographical circumstances of all the States concerned and in conformity with the provisions of this article and of articles 61 and 62.

2. The terms and modalities of such participation shall be established by the States concerned through bilateral, subregional or regional greements taking into account, *inter alia*:

(a) the need to avoid effects detrimental to fishing communities or fishing industries of the coastal State;

(b) the extent to which the land-locked State, in accordance with the provisions of this article, is participating or is entitled to participate under existing bilateral, subregional or regional agreements in the exploitation of living resources of the exclusive economic zones of other coastal States;

(c) the extent to which other land-locked States and geographically disadvantaged States are participating in the exploitation of the living resources of the exclusive economic zone of the coastal State and the consequent need to avoid a particular burden for any single coastal State or a part of it;

(d) the nutritional needs of the populations of the respective States.

3. When the harvesting capacity of a coastal State approaches a point which would enable it to harvest the entire allowable catch of the living resources in its exclusive economic zone, the coastal State and other States concerned shall cooperate in the establishment of equitable arrangements on a bilateral, subregional or regional basis to allow for participation of developing land-locked States of the same subregion or region in the exploitation of the living resources of the exclusive economic zones of coastal States of the subregion or region, as may be appropriate in the circumstances and on terms satisfactory to all parties. In the implementation of this provision the factors mentioned in paragraph 2 shall also be taken into account.

4. Developed land-locked States shall, under the provisions of this article, be entitled to participate in the exploitation of living resources only in the exclusive economic zones of developed coastal States of the same subregion or region having regard to the extent to which the coastal State, in giving access to other States to the living resources of its exclusive economic zone, has taken into account the need to minimize detrimental effects on fishing communities and economic dislocation in States whose nationals have habitually fished in the zone.

5. The above provisions are without prejudice to arrangements agreed upon in subregions or regions where the coastal States may grant to land-locked States of the same subregion or region equal or preferential rights for the exploitation of the living resources in the exclusive economic zones.

Article 70   Right of geographically disadvantaged States

1. Geographically disadvantaged States shall have the right to participate, on an equitable basis, in the exploitation of an appropriate part of the surplus of the living resources of the exclusive economic zones of coastal States of the same subregion or region, taking into

account the relevant economic and geographical circumstances of all the States concerned and in conformity with the provisions of this article and of articles 61 and 62.

2. For the purposes of this Part, "geographically disadvantaged States" means coastal States, including States bordering enclosed or semi-enclosed seas, whose geographical situation makes them dependent upon the exploitation of the living resources of the exclusive economic zones of other States in the subregion or region for adequate supplies of fish for the nutritional purposes of their populations or parts thereof, and coastal States which can claim no exclusive economic zones of their own.

3. The terms and modalities of such participation shall be established by the States concerned through bilateral, subregional or regional agreements taking into account, *inter alia*:

(a) the need to avoid effects detrimental to fishing communities or fishing industries of the coastal State;

(b) the extent to which the geographically disadvantaged State, in accordance with the provisions of this article, is participating or is entitled to participate under existing bilateral, subregional or regional agreements in the exploitation of living resources of the exclusive economic zones of other coastal States;

(c) the extent to which other geographically disadvantaged States and land-locked States are participating in the exploitation of the living resources of the exclusive economic zone of the coastal State and the consequent need to avoid a particular burden for any single coastal State or a part of it;

(d) the nutritional needs of the populations of the respective States.

4. When the harvesting capacity of a coastal State approaches a point which would enable it to harvest the entire allowable catch of the living resources in its exclusive economic zone, the coastal State and other States concerned shall cooperate in the establishment of equitable arrangements on a bilateral, subregional or regional basis to allow for participation of developing geographically disadvantaged States of the same subregion or region in the exploitation of the living resources of the exclusive economic zones of coastal States of the subregion or region, as may be appropriate in the circumstances and on terms satisfactory to all parties. In the implementation of this provision the factors mentioned in paragraph 3 shall also be taken into account.

5. Developed geographically disadvantaged States shall, under the provisions of this article, be entitled to participate in the exploitation of living resources only in the exclusive economic zones of developed coastal States of the same subregion or region having regard to the extent to which the coastal State, in giving access to other States to the living resources of its exclusive economic zone, has taken into account the need to minimize detrimental effects on fishing communities and economic dislocation in States whose nationals have habitually fished in the zone.

6. The above provisions are without prejudice to arrangements agreed upon in subregions or regions where the coastal States may grant to geographically disadvantaged States of the same subregion or region equal or preferential rights for the exploitation of the living resources in the exclusive economic zones.

Article 71 Non-applicability of articles 69 and 70

The provisions of articles 69 and 70 do not apply in the case of a coastal State whose economy is overwhelmingly dependent on the exploitation of the living resources of its exclusive economic zone.

Article 72 Restrictions on transfer of rights

1. Rights provided under articles 69 and 70 to exploit living resources shall not be directly or indirectly transferred to third States or their nationals by lease or licence, by establishing joint ventures or in any other manner which has the effect of such transfer unless otherwise agreed by the States concerned.

2. The foregoing provision does not preclude the States concerned from obtaining technical or financial assistance from third States or international organizations in order to facilitate the exercise of the rights pursuant to articles 69 and 70, provided that it does not have the effect referred to in paragraph 1.

Article 73 Enforcement of laws and regulations of the coastal State

1. The coastal State may, in the exercise of its sovereign rights to explore, exploit, conserve and manage the living resources in the exclusive economic zone, take such measures, including boarding, inspection, arrest and judicial proceedings, as may be necessary to ensure compliance with the laws and regulations adopted by it in conformity with this Convention.

2. Arrested vessels and their crews shall be promptly released upon the posting of reasonable bond or other security.

3. Coastal State penalties for violations of fisheries laws and regulations in the exclusive economic zone may not include imprisonment, in the absence of agreements to the contrary by the States concerned, or any other form of corporal punishment.

4. In cases of arrest or detention of foreign vessels the coastal State shall promptly notify the flag State, through appropriate channels, of the action taken and of any penalties subsequently imposed.

Article 74   Delimitation of the exclusive economic zone between States with opposite or adjacent coasts

1. The delimitation of the exclusive economic zone between States with opposite or adjacent coasts shall be effected by agreement on the basis of international law, as referred to in Article 38 of the Statute of the International Court of Justice, in order to achieve an equitable solution.

2. If no agreement can be reached within a reasonable period of time, the States concerned shall resort to the procedures provided for in Part XV.

3. Pending agreement as provided for in paragraph 1, the States concerned, in a spirit of understanding and cooperation, shall make every effort to enter into provisional arrangements of a practical nature and, during this transitional period, not to jeopardize or hamper the reaching of the final agreement. Such arrangements shall be without prejudice to the final delimitation.

4. Where there is an agreement in force between the States concerned, questions relating to the delimitation of the exclusive economic zone shall be determined in accordance with the provisions of that agreement.

Article 75   Charts and lists of geographical coordinates

1. Subject to this Part, the outer limit lines of the exclusive economic zone and the lines of delimitation drawn in accordance with article 74 shall be shown on charts of a scale or scales adequate for ascertaining their position. Where appropriate, lists of geographical coordinates of points, specifying the geodetic datum, may be substituted for such outer limit lines or lines of delimitation.

2. The coastal State shall give due publicity to such charts or lists of geographical coordinates and shall deposit a copy of each such chart or list with the Secretary-General of the United Nations.

PART VI   CONTINENTAL SHELF

Article 76   Definition of the continental shelf

1. The continental shelf of a coastal State comprises the seabed and subsoil of the submarine areas that extend beyond its territorial sea throughout the natural prolongation of its land territory to the outer edge of the continental margin, or to a distance of 200 nautical miles from the baselines from which the breadth of the territorial sea is measured where the outer edge of the continental margin does not extend up to that distance.

2. The continental shelf of a coastal State shall not extend beyond the limits provided for in paragraphs 4 to 6.

3. The continental margin comprises the submerged prolongation of the land mass of the coastal State, and consists of the seabed and subsoil of the shelf, the slope and the rise. It does not include the deep ocean floor with its oceanic ridges or the subsoil thereof.

4. (a) For the purposes of this Convention, the coastal State shall establish the outer edge of the continental margin wherever the margin extends beyond 200 nautical miles from the baselines from which the breadth of the territorial sea is measured, by either:

(i) a line delineated in accordance with paragraph 7 by reference to the outermost fixed points at each of which the thickness of sedimentary rocks is at least 1 per cent of the shortest distance from such point to the foot of the continental slope; or

(ii) a line delineated in accordance with paragraph 7 by reference to fixed points not more than 60 nautical miles from the foot of the continental slope.

(b) In the absence of evidence to the contrary, the foot of the continental slope shall be determined as the point of maximum change in the gradient at its base.

5. The fixed points comprising the line of the outer limits of the continental shelf on the seabed, drawn in accordance with paragraph 4 (a)(i) and (ii), either shall not exceed 350 nautical miles from the baselines from which the breadth of the territorial sea is measured or shall not exceed 100 nautical miles from the 2,500 metre isobath, which is a line connecting the depth of 2,500 metres.

6. Notwithstanding the provisions of paragraph 5, on submarine ridges, the outer limit of the continental shelf shall not exceed 350 nautical miles from the baselines from which the breadth of the territorial sea is measured.

This paragraph does not apply to submarine elevations that are natural components of the continental margin, such as its plateaux, rises, caps, banks and spurs.

7. The coastal State shall delineate the outer limits of its continental shelf, where that shelf extends beyond 200 nautical miles from the baselines from which the breadth of the territorial sea is measured, by straight lines not exceeding 60 nautical miles in length, connecting fixed points, defined by coordinates of latitude and longitude.

8. Information on the limits of the continental shelf beyond 200 nautical miles from the baselines from which the breadth of the territorial sea is measured shall be submitted by the coastal State to the Commission on the Limits of the Continental Shelf set up under Annex II on the basis of equitable geographical representation. The Commission shall make recommendations to coastal States on matters related to the establishment of the outer limits of their continental shelf. The limits of the shelf established by a coastal State on the basis of these recommendations shall be final and binding.

9. The coastal State shall deposit with the Secretary-General of the United Nations charts and relevant information, including geodetic data, permanently describing the outer limits of its continental shelf. The Secretary-General shall give due publicity thereto.

10. The provisions of this article are without prejudice to the question of delimitation of the continental shelf between States with opposite or adjacent coasts.

Article 77   **Rights of the coastal State over the continental shelf**

1. The coastal State exercises over the continental shelf sovereign rights for the purpose of exploring it and exploiting its natural resources.

2. The rights referred to in paragraph 1 are exclusive in the sense that if the coastal State does not explore the continental shelf or exploit its natural resources, no one may undertake these activities without the express consent of the coastal State.

3. The rights of the coastal State over the continental shelf do not depend on occupation, effective or notional, or on any express proclamation.

4. The natural resources referred to in this Part consist of the mineral and other non-living resources of the seabed and subsoil together with living organisms belonging to sedentary species, that is to say, organisms which, at the harvestable stage, either are immobile on or under the seabed or are unable to move except in constant physical contact with the seabed or the subsoil.

Article 78   **Legal status of the superjacent waters and airspace and the rights and freedoms of other States**

1. The rights of the coastal State over the continental shelf do not affect the legal status of the superjacent waters or of the air space above those waters.

2. The exercise of the rights of the coastal State over the continental shelf must not infringe or result in any unjustifiable interference with navigation and other rights and freedoms of other States as provided for in this Convention.

Article 79   **Submarine cables and pipelines on the continental shelf**

1. All States are entitled to lay submarine cables and pipelines on the continental shelf, in accordance with the provisions of this article.

2. Subject to its right to take reasonable measures for the exploration of the continental shelf, the exploitation of its natural resources and the prevention, reduction and control of pollution from pipelines, the coastal State may not impede the laying or maintenance of such cables or pipelines.

3. The delineation of the course for the laying of such pipelines on the continental shelf is subject to the consent of the coastal State.

4. Nothing in this Part affects the right of the coastal State to establish conditions for cables or pipelines entering its territory or territorial sea, or its jurisdiction over cables and pipelines constructed or used in connection with the exploration of its continental shelf or exploitation of its resources or the operations of artificial islands, installations and structures under its jurisdiction.

5. When laying submarine cables or pipelines, States shall have due regard to cables or pipelines already in position. In particular, possibilities of repairing existing cables or pipelines shall not be prejudiced.

Article 80   Artificial islands, installations and structures on the continental shelf

Article 60 applies *mutatis mutandis* to artificial islands, installations and structures on the continental shelf.

Article 81   Drilling on the continental shelf

The coastal State shall have the exclusive right to authorize and regulate drilling on the continental shelf for all purposes.

Article 82   Payments and contributions with respect to the exploitation of the continental shelf beyond 200 nautical miles

1. The coastal State shall make payments or contributions in kind in respect of the exploitation of the non-living resources of the continental shelf beyond 200 nautical miles from the baselines from which the breadth of the territorial sea is measured.

2. The payments and contributions shall be made annually with respect to all production at a site after the first five years of production at that site. For the sixth year, the rate of payment or contribution shall be 1 per cent of the value or volume of production at the site. The rate shall increase by 1 per cent for each subsequent year until the twelfth year and shall remain at 7 per cent thereafter. Production does not include resources used in connection with exploitation.

3. A developing State which is a net importer of a mineral resource produced from its continental shelf is exempt from making such payments or contributions in respect of that mineral resource.

4. The payments or contributions shall be made through the Authority, which shall distribute them to States Parties to this Convention, on the basis of equitable sharing criteria, taking into account the interests and needs of developing States, particularly the least developed and the land-locked among them.

Article 83   Delimitation of the continental shelf between States with opposite or adjacent coasts

1. The delimitation of the continental shelf between States with opposite or adjacent coasts shall be effected by agreement on the basis of international law, as referred to in Article 38 of the Statute of the International Court of Justice, in order to achieve an equitable solution.

2. If no agreement can be reached within a reasonable period of time, the States concerned shall resort to the procedures provided for in Part XV.

3. Pending agreement as provided for in paragraph 1, the States concerned, in a spirit of understanding and cooperation, shall make every effort to enter into provisional arrangements of a practical nature and, during this transitional period, not to jeopardize or hamper the reaching of the final agreement. Such arrangements shall be without prejudice to the final delimitation.

4. Where there is an agreement in force between the States concerned, questions relating to the delimitation of the continental shelf shall be determined in accordance with the provisions of that agreement.

Article 84   Charts and lists of geographical coordinates

1. Subject to this Part, the outer limit lines of the continental shelf and the lines of delimitation drawn in accordance with article 83 shall be shown on charts of a scale or scales adequate for ascertaining their position. Where appropriate, lists of geographical coordinates of points, specifying the geodetic datum, may be substituted for such outer limit lines or lines of delimitation.

2. The coastal State shall give due publicity to such charts or lists of geographical coordinates and shall deposit a copy of each such chart or list with the Secretary-General of the United Nations and, in the case of

those showing the outer limit lines of the continental shelf, with the Secretary-General of the Authority.

Article 85   Tunnelling

This Part does not prejudice the right of the coastal State to exploit the subsoil by means of tunnelling, irrespective of the depth of water above the subsoil.

PART VII   HIGH SEAS

SECTION 1   GENERAL PROVISIONS

Article 86   Application of the provisions of this Part

The provisions of this Part apply to all parts of the sea that are not included in the exclusive economic zone, in the territorial sea or in the internal waters of a State, or in the archipelagic waters of an archipelagic State. This article does not entail any abridgement of the freedoms enjoyed by all States in the exclusive economic zone in accordance with article 58.

Article 87   Freedom of the high seas

1. The high seas are open to all States, whether coastal or land-locked. Freedom of the high seas is exercised under the conditions laid down by this Convention and by other rules of international law. It comprises, *inter alia*, both for coastal and land-locked States:

(a) freedom of navigation;

(b) freedom of overflight;

(c) freedom to lay submarine cables and pipelines, subject to Part VI;

(d) freedom to construct artificial islands and other installations permitted under international law, subject to Part VI;

(e) freedom of fishing, subject to the conditions laid down in section 2;

(f) freedom of scientific research, subject to Parts VI and XIII.

2. These freedoms shall be exercised by all States with due regard for the interests of other States in their exercise of the freedom of the high seas, and also with due regard for the rights under this Convention with respect to activities in the Area.

Article 88   Reservation of the high seas for peaceful purposes

The high seas shall be reserved for peaceful purposes.

Article 89   Invalidity of claims of sovereignty over the high seas

No State may validly purport to subject any part of the high seas to its sovereignty.

Article 90   Right of navigation

Every State, whether coastal or land-locked, has the right to sail ships flying its flag on the high seas.

Article 91   Nationality of ships

1. Every State shall fix the conditions for the grant of its nationality to ships, for the registration of ships in its territory, and for the right to fly its flag. Ships have the nationality of the State whose flag they are entitled to fly. There must exist a genuine link between the State and the ship.

2. Every State shall issue to ships to which it has granted the right to fly its flag documents to that effect.

Article 92   Status of ships

1. Ships shall sail under the flag of one State only and, save in exceptional cases expressly provided for in international treaties or in this Convention, shall be subject to its exclusive jurisdiction on the high seas. A ship may not change its flag during a voyage or while in a port of call, save in the case of a real transfer of ownership or change of registry.

2. A ship which sails under the flags of two or more States, using them according to convenience, may not claim any of the nationalities in question with respect to any other State, and may be assimilated to a ship without nationality.

Article 93   Ships flying the flag of the United Nations, its specialized agencies and the International Atomic Energy Agency

The preceding articles do not prejudice the question of ships employed on the official service of the United Nations, its specialized agencies or the International Atomic Energy Agency, flying the flag of the organization.

Article 94   Duties of the flag state

1. Every State shall effectively exercise its jurisdiction and control in administrative, technical and social matters over ships flying its flag.

2. In particular every State shall:

(a) maintain a register of ships containing the names and particulars of ships flying its flag, except those which are excluded from generally accepted international regulations on account of their small size; and

(b) assume jurisdiction under its internal law over each ship flying its flag and its master, officers and crew in respect of administrative, technical and social matters concerning the ship.

3. Every State shall take such measures for ships flying its flag as are necessary to ensure safety at sea with regard, *inter alia*, to:

(a) the construction, equipment and seaworthiness of ships;

(b) the manning of ships, labour conditions and the training of crews, taking into account the applicable international instruments;

(c) the use of signals, the maintenance of communications and the prevention of collisions.

4. Such measures shall include those necessary to ensure:

(a) that each ship, before registration and thereafter at appropriate intervals, is surveyed by a qualified surveyor of ships, and has on board such charts, nautical publications and navigational equipment and instruments as are appropriate for the safe navigation of the ship;

(b) that each ship is in the charge of a master and officers who possess appropriate qualifications, in particular in seamanship, navigation, communications and marine engineering, and that the crew is appropriate in qualification and numbers for the type, size, machinery and equipment of the ship;

(c) that the master, officers and, to the extent appropriate, the crew are fully conversant with and required to observe the applicable international regulations concerning the safety of life at sea, the prevention of collisions, the prevention, reduction and control of marine pollution, and the maintenance of communications by radio.

5. In taking the measures called for in paragraphs 3 and 4 each State is required to conform to generally accepted international regulations, procedures and practices and to take any steps which may be necessary to secure their observance.

6. A State which has clear grounds to believe that proper jurisdiction and control with respect to a ship have not been exercised may report the facts to the flag State. Upon receiving such a report, the flag State shall investigate the matter and, if appropriate, take any action necessary to remedy the situation.

7. Each State shall cause an inquiry to be held by or before a suitably qualified person or persons into every marine casualty or incident of navigation on the high seas involving a ship flying its flag and causing loss of life or serious injury to nationals of another State or serious damage to ships or installations of another State or to the marine environment. The flag State and the other State shall cooperate in the conduct of any inquiry held by that other State into any such marine casualty or incident of navigation.

Article 95   Immunity of warships on the high seas

Warships on the high seas have complete immunity from the jurisdiction of any State other than the flag State.

Article 96   Immunity of ships used only on government non-commercial service

Ships owned or operated by a State and used only on government non-commercial service shall, on the high seas, have complete immunity from the jurisdiction of any State other than the flag State.

Article 97 **Penal jurisdiction in matters of collision or any other incident of navigation**

1. In the event of a collision or any other incident of navigation concerning a ship on the high seas, involving the penal or disciplinary responsibility of the master or of any other person in the service of the ship, no penal or disciplinary proceedings may be instituted against such person except before the judicial or administrative authorities either of the flag State or of the State of which such person is a national.

2. In disciplinary matters, the State which has issued a master's certificate or a certificate of competence or licence shall alone be competent, after due legal process, to pronounce the withdrawal of such certificates, even if the holder is not a national of the State which issued them.

3. No arrest or detention of the ship, even as a measure of investigation, shall be ordered by any authorities other than those of the flag State.

Article 98 **Duty to render assistance**

1. Every State shall require the master of a ship flying its flag, in so far as he can do so without serious danger to the ship, the crew or the passengers:

(a) to render assistance to any person found at sea in danger of being lost;

(b) to proceed with all possible speed to the rescue of persons in distress, if informed of their need of assistance, in so far as such action may reasonably be expected of him;

(c) after a collision, to render assistance to the other ship, its crew and its passengers and, where possible, to inform the other ship of the name of his own ship, its port of registry and the nearest port at which it will call.

2. Every coastal State shall promote the establishment, operation and maintenance of an adequate and effective search and rescue service regarding safety on and over the sea and, where circumstances so require, by way of mutual regional arrangements cooperate with neighbouring States for this purpose.

Article 99   Prohibition of the transport of slaves

Every State shall take effective measures to prevent and punish the transport of slaves in ships authorized to fly its flag and to prevent the unlawful use of its flag for that purpose. Any slave taking refuge on board any ship, whatever its flag, shall *ipso facto* be free.

Article 100   Duty to cooperate in the repression of piracy

All States shall cooperate to the fullest possible extent in the repression of piracy on the high seas or in any other place outside the jurisdiction of any State.

Article 101   Definition of piracy

Piracy consists of any of the following acts:

(a) any illegal acts of violence or detention, or any act of depredation, committed for private ends by the crew or the passengers of a private ship or a private aircraft, and directed:

(i) on the high seas, against another ship or aircraft, or against persons or property on board such ship or aircraft;

(ii) against a ship, aircraft, persons or property in a place outside the jurisdiction of any State;

(b) any act of voluntary participation in the operation of a ship or of an aircraft with knowledge of facts making it a pirate ship or aircraft;

(c) any act of inciting or of intentionally facilitating an act described in subparagraph (a) or (b).

Article 102   Piracy by a warship, government ship or government aircraft whose crew has mutinied

The acts of piracy, as defined in article 101, committed by a warship, government ship or government aircraft whose crew has mutinied and taken control of the ship or aircraft are assimilated to acts committed by a private ship or aircraft.

Article 103   Definition of a pirate ship or aircraft

A ship or aircraft is considered a pirate ship or aircraft if it is intended by the persons in dominant control to be used for the purpose of committing one of the acts referred to in article 101. The same applies if the ship or aircraft has been used to commit any such act, so long as it remains under the control of the persons guilty of that act.

Article 104   Retention or loss of the nationality of a pirate ship or aircraft

A ship or aircraft may retain its nationality although it has become a pirate ship or aircraft. The retention or loss of nationality is determined by the law of the State from which such nationality was derived.

Article 105   Seizure of a pirate ship or aircraft

On the high seas, or in any other place outside the jurisdiction of any State, every State may seize a pirate ship or aircraft, or a ship or aircraft taken by piracy and under the control of pirates, and arrest the persons and seize the property on board. The courts of the State which carried out the seizure may decide upon the penalties to be imposed, and may also determine the action to be taken with regard to the ships, aircraft or property, subject to the rights of third parties acting in good faith.

Article 106   Liability for seizure without adequate grounds

Where the seizure of a ship or aircraft on suspicion of piracy has been effected without adequate grounds, the State making the seizure shall be liable to the State the nationality of which is possessed by the ship or aircraft for any loss or damage caused by the seizure.

Article 107   Ships and aircraft which are entitled to seize on account of piracy

A seizure on account of piracy may be carried out only by warships or military aircraft, or other ships or aircraft clearly marked and identifiable as being on government service and authorized to that effect.

Article 108   Illicit traffic in narcotic drugs or psychotropic substances

1. All States shall cooperate in the suppression of illicit traffic in narcotic drugs and psychotropic substances engaged in by ships on the high seas contrary to international conventions.

2. Any State which has reasonable grounds for believing that a ship flying its flag is engaged in illicit traffic in narcotic drugs or psychotropic substances may request the cooperation of other States to suppress such traffic.

Article 109   Unauthorized broadcasting from the high seas

1. All States shall cooperate in the suppression of unauthorized broadcasting from the high seas.

2. For the purposes of this Convention, "unauthorized broadcasting" means the transmission of sound radio or television broadcasts from a ship or installation on the high seas intended for reception by the general public contrary to international regulations, but excluding the transmission of distress calls.

3. Any person engaged in unauthorized broadcasting may be prosecuted before the court of:

  (a) the flag State of the ship;

  (b) the State of registry of the installation;

  (c) the State of which the person is a national;

  (d) any State where the transmissions can be received; or

  (e) any State where authorized radio communication is suffering interference.

4. On the high seas, a State having jurisdiction in accordance with paragraph 3 may, in conformity with article 110, arrest any person or ship engaged in unauthorized broadcasting and seize the broadcasting apparatus.

Article 110   Right of visit

1. Except where acts of interference derive from powers conferred by treaty, a warship which encounters on the high seas a foreign ship, other than a ship entitled to complete immunity in accordance with articles 95 and 96, is not justified in boarding it unless there is reasonable ground for suspecting that:

(a) the ship is engaged in piracy;

(b) the ship is engaged in the slave trade;

(c) the ship is engaged in unauthorized broadcasting and the flag State of the warship has jurisdiction under article 109;

(d) the ship is without nationality; or

(e) though flying a foreign flag or refusing to show its flag, the ship is, in reality, of the same nationality as the warship.

2. In the cases provided for in paragraph 1, the warship may proceed to verify the ship's right to fly its flag. To this end, it may send a boat under the command of an officer to the suspected ship. If suspicion remains after the documents have been checked, it may proceed to a further examination on board the ship, which must be carried out with all possible consideration.

3. If the suspicions prove to be unfounded, and provided that the ship boarded has not committed any act justifying them, it shall be compensated for any loss or damage that may have been sustained.

4. These provisions apply *mutatis mutandis* to military aircraft.

5. These provisions also apply to any other duly authorized ships or aircraft clearly marked and identifiable as being on government service.

Article 111   Right of hot pursuit

1. The hot pursuit of a foreign ship may be undertaken when the competent authorities of the coastal State have good reason to believe that the ship has violated the laws and regulations of that State. Such pursuit must be commenced when the foreign ship or one of its boats is within the internal waters, the archipelagic waters, the territorial sea or the contiguous zone of the pursuing State, and may only be continued outside the territorial sea or the contiguous zone if the pursuit has not been interrupted. It is not necessary that, at the time when the foreign ship within the territorial sea or the contiguous zone receives the order to stop, the ship giving the order should likewise be within the territorial sea or the contiguous zone. If the foreign ship is within a contiguous zone, as defined in article 33, the pursuit may only be undertaken if there has been a violation of the rights for the protection of which the zone was established.

2. The right of hot pursuit shall apply *mutatis mutandis* to violations in the exclusive economic zone or on the continental shelf, including safety zones around continental shelf installations, of the laws and regulations of the coastal State applicable in accordance with this Convention to the exclusive economic zone or the continental shelf, including such safety zones.

3. The right of hot pursuit ceases as soon as the ship pursued enters the territorial sea of its own State or of a third State.

4. Hot pursuit is not deemed to have begun unless the pursuing ship has satisfied itself by such practicable means as may be available that the ship pursued or one of its boats or other craft working as a team and using the ship pursued as a mother ship is within the limits of the territorial sea, or, as the case may be, within the contiguous zone or the exclusive economic zone or above the continental shelf. The pursuit may only be commenced after a visual or auditory signal to stop has been given at a distance which enables it to be seen or heard by the foreign ship.

5. The right of hot pursuit may be exercised only by warships or military aircraft, or other ships or aircraft clearly marked and identifiable as being on government service and authorized to that effect.

6. Where hot pursuit is effected by an aircraft:

(a) the provisions of paragraphs 1 to 4 shall apply *mutatis mutandis*;

(b) the aircraft giving the order to stop must itself actively pursue the ship until a ship or another aircraft of the coastal State, summoned by the aircraft, arrives to take over the pursuit, unless the aircraft is itself able to arrest the ship. It does not suffice to justify an arrest outside the territorial sea that the ship was merely sighted by the aircraft as an offender or suspected offender, if it was not both ordered to stop and pursued by the aircraft itself or other aircraft or ships which continue the pursuit without interruption.

7. The release of a ship arrested within the jurisdiction of a State and escorted to a port of that State for the purposes of an inquiry before the competent authorities may not be claimed solely on the ground that the ship, in the course of its voyage, was escorted across a portion of the exclusive economic zone or the high seas, if the circumstances rendered this necessary.

8. Where a ship has been stopped or arrested outside the territorial sea in circumstances which do not justify the exercise of the right of hot pursuit, it shall be compensated for any loss or damage that may have been thereby sustained.

Article 112   Right to lay submarine cables and pipelines

1. All States are entitled to lay submarine cables and pipelines on the bed of the high seas beyond the continental shelf.

2. Article 79, paragraph 5, applies to such cables and pipelines.

Article 113   Breaking or injury of a submarine cable or pipeline

Every State shall adopt the laws and regulations necessary to provide that the breaking or injury by a ship flying its flag or by a person subject to its jurisdiction of a submarine cable beneath the high seas done wilfully or through culpable negligence, in such a manner as to be liable to interrupt or obstruct telegraphic or telephonic communications, and similarly the breaking or injury of a submarine pipeline or high-voltage power cable, shall be a punishable offence. This provision shall apply also to conduct calculated or likely to result in such breaking or injury. However, it shall not apply to any break or injury caused by persons who acted merely with the legitimate object of saving their lives or their ships, after having taken all necessary precautions to avoid such break or injury.

Article 114   Breaking or injury by owners of a submarine cable
**   or pipeline of another submarine cable or pipeline**

Every State shall adopt the laws and regulations necessary to provide that, if persons subject to its jurisdiction who are the owners of a submarine cable or pipeline beneath the high seas, in laying or repairing that cable or pipeline, cause a break in or injury to another cable or pipeline, they shall bear the cost of the repairs.

Article 115   Indemnity for loss incurred in avoiding injury to a
**   submarine cable or pipeline**

Every State shall adopt the laws and regulations necessary to ensure that the owners of ships who can prove that they have sacrificed an anchor, a net or any other fishing gear, in order to avoid injuring a submarine cable or pipeline, shall be indemnified by the owner of the cable or pipeline, provided that the owner of the ship has taken all reasonable precautionary measures beforehand.

SECTION 2   CONSERVATION AND MANAGEMENT OF THE LIVING RESOURCES OF THE HIGH SEAS

Article 116   Right to fish on the high seas

All States have the right for their nationals to engage in fishing on the high seas subject to:

(a) their treaty obligations;

(b) the rights and duties as well as the interests of coastal States provided for, *inter alia*, in article 63, paragraph 2, and articles 64 to 67; and

(c) the provisions of this section.

Article 117   Duty of States to adopt with respect to their nationals measures for the conservation of the living resources of the high seas

All States have the duty to take, or to cooperate with other States in taking, such measures for their respective nationals as may be necessary for the conservation of the living resources of the high seas.

Article 118   Cooperation of States in the conservation and management of living resources

States shall cooperate with each other in the conservation and management of living resources in the areas of the high seas. States whose nationals exploit identical living resources, or different living resources in the same area, shall enter into negotiations with a view to taking the measures necessary for the conservation of the living resources concerned. They shall, as appropriate, cooperate to establish subregional or regional fisheries organizations to this end.

Article 119   Conservation of the living resources of the high seas

1. In determining the allowable catch and establishing other conservation measures for the living resources in the high seas, States shall:

(a) take measures which are designed, on the best scientific evidence available to the States concerned, to maintain or restore populations of harvested species at levels which can produce the maximum sustainable yield, as qualified by relevant environmental and economic factors, including the special requirements of developing States, and taking into account fishing patterns, the interdependence of stocks and any generally recommended international minimum standards, whether subregional, regional or global;

(b) take into consideration the effects on species associated with or dependent upon harvested species with a view to maintaining or restoring populations of such associated or dependent species above levels at which their reproduction may become seriously threatened.

2. Available scientific information, catch and fishing effort statistics, and other data relevant to the conservation of fish stocks shall be contributed and exchanged on a regular basis through competent international organizations, whether subregional, regional or global, where appropriate and with participation by all States concerned.

3. States concerned shall ensure that conservation measures and their implementation do not discriminate in form or in fact against the fishermen of any State.

Article 120   Marine mammals

Article 65 also applies to the conservation and management of marine mammals in the high seas.

PART VIII   REGIME OF ISLANDS

Article 121   Regime of islands

1. An island is a naturally formed area of land, surrounded by water, which is above water at high tide.

2. Except as provided for in paragraph 3, the territorial sea, the contiguous zone, the exclusive economic zone and the continental shelf of an island are determined in accordance with the provisions of this Convention applicable to other land territory.

3. Rocks which cannot sustain human habitation or economic life of their own shall have no exclusive economic zone or continental shelf.

PART IX   ENCLOSED OR SEMI-ENCLOSED SEAS

Article 122   Definition

For the purposes of this Convention, "enclosed or semi-enclosed sea" means a gulf, basin or sea surrounded by two or more States and connected to another sea or the ocean by a narrow outlet or consisting entirely or primarily of the territorial seas and exclusive economic zones of two or more coastal States.

Article 123   Cooperation of States bordering enclosed or semi-enclosed seas

States bordering an enclosed or semi-enclosed sea should cooperate with each other in the exercise of their rights and in the performance of their duties under this Convention. To this end they shall endeavour, directly or through an appropriate regional organization:

(a) to coordinate the management, conservation, exploration and exploitation of the living resources of the sea;

(b) to coordinate the implementation of their rights and duties with respect to the protection and preservation of the marine environment;

(c) to coordinate their scientific research policies and undertake where appropriate joint programmes of scientific research in the area;

(d) to invite, as appropriate, other interested States or international organizations to cooperate with them in furtherance of the provisions of this article.

PART X   RIGHT OF ACCESS OF LAND-LOCKED STATES TO AND FROM THE SEA AND FREEDOM OF TRANSIT

Article 124   Use of terms

1. For the purposes of this Convention:

(a) "land-locked State" means a State which has no sea-coast;

(b) "transit State" means a State, with or without a sea-coast, situated between a land-locked State and the sea, through whose territory traffic in transit passes;

(c) "traffic in transit" means transit of persons, baggage, goods and means of transport across the territory of one or more transit States, when the passage across such territory, with or without trans-shipment, warehousing, breaking bulk or change in the mode of transport, is only a portion of a complete journey which begins or terminates within the territory of the land-locked State;

(d) "means of transport" means:

(i) railway rolling stock, sea, lake and river craft and road vehicles;

(ii) where local conditions so require, porters and pack animals.

2. Land-locked States and transit States may, by agreement between them, include as means of transport pipelines and gas lines and means of transport other than those included in paragraph 1.

Article 125   Right of access to and from the sea and freedom of transit

1. Land-locked States shall have the right of access to and from the sea for the purpose of exercising the rights provided for in this Convention including those relating to the freedom of the high seas and the common heritage of mankind. To this end, land-locked States shall enjoy freedom of transit through the territory of transit States by all means of transport.

2. The terms and modalities for exercising freedom of transit shall be agreed between the land-locked States and transit States concerned through bilateral, subregional or regional agreements.

3. Transit States, in the exercise of their full sovereignty over their territory, shall have the right to take all measures necessary to ensure that the rights and facilities provided for in this Part for land-locked States shall in no way infringe their legitimate interests.

Article 126   Exclusion of application of the most-favoured-nation clause

The provisions of this Convention, as well as special agreements relating to the exercise of the right of access to and from the sea, establishing rights and facilities on account of the special geographical position of land-locked States, are excluded from the application of the most-favoured-nation clause.

Article 127   Customs duties, taxes and other charges

1. Traffic in transit shall not be subject to any customs duties, taxes or other charges except charges levied for specific services rendered in connection with such traffic.

2. Means of transport in transit and other facilities provided for and used by land-locked States shall not be subject to taxes or charges higher than those levied for the use of means of transport of the transit State.

Article 128   Free zones and other customs facilities

For the convenience of traffic in transit, free zones or other customs facilities may be provided at the ports of entry and exit in the transit States, by agreement between those States and the land-locked States.

Article 129   Cooperation in the construction and improvement of means of transport

Where there are no means of transport in transit States to give effect to the freedom of transit or where the existing means, including the port installations and equipment, are inadequate in any respect, the transit States and land-locked States concerned may cooperate in constructing or improving them.

Article 130   Measures to avoid or eliminate delays or other difficulties of a technical nature in traffic in transit

1. Transit States shall take all appropriate measures to avoid delays or other difficulties of a technical nature in traffic in transit.

2. Should such delays or difficulties occur, the competent authorities of the transit States and land-locked States concerned shall cooperate owards their expeditious elimination.

Article 131   Equal treatment in maritime ports

Ships flying the flag of land-locked States shall enjoy treatment equal to that accorded to other foreign ships in maritime ports.

Article 132   Grant of greater transit facilities

This Convention does not entail in any way the withdrawal of transit facilities which are greater than those provided for in this Convention and which are agreed between States Parties to this Convention or granted by a State Party. This Convention also does not preclude such grant of greater facilities in the future.

PART XI   THE AREA

SECTION 1   GENERAL PROVISIONS

Article 133   Use of terms

For the purposes of this Part:

(a) "resources" means all solid, liquid or gaseous mineral resources *in situ* in the Area at or beneath the seabed, including polymetallic nodules;

(b) resources, when recovered from the Area, are referred to as "minerals".

Article 134   Scope of this Part

1. This Part applies to the Area.

2. Activities in the Area shall be governed by the provisions of this Part.

3. The requirements concerning deposit of, and publicity to be given to, the charts or lists of geographical coordinates showing the limits referred to in article l, paragraph l(1), are set forth in Part VI.

4. Nothing in this article affects the establishment of the outer limits of the continental shelf in accordance with Part VI or the validity of agreements relating to delimitation between States with opposite or adjacent coasts.

Article 135   Legal status of the superjacent waters and air space

Neither this Part nor any rights granted or exercised pursuant thereto shall affect the legal status of the waters superjacent to the Area or that of the air space above those waters.

SECTION 2   PRINCIPLES GOVERNING THE AREA

Article 136   Common heritage of mankind

The Area and its resources are the common heritage of mankind.

Article 137   Legal status of the Area and its resources

1. No State shall claim or exercise sovereignty or sovereign rights over any part of the Area or its resources, nor shall any State or natural or juridical person appropriate any part thereof. No such claim or exercise of sovereignty or sovereign rights nor such appropriation shall be recognized.

2. All rights in the resources of the Area are vested in mankind as a whole, on whose behalf the Authority shall act. These resources are not subject to alienation. The minerals recovered from the Area, however, may only be alienated in accordance with this Part and the rules, regulations and procedures of the Authority.

3. No State or natural or juridical person shall claim, acquire or exercise rights with respect to the minerals recovered from the Area except in accordance with this Part. Otherwise, no such claim, acquisition or exercise of such rights shall be recognized.

Article 138   General conduct of States in relation to the Area

The general conduct of States in relation to the Area shall be in accordance with the provisions of this Part, the principles embodied in the Charter of the United Nations and other rules of international law in the interests of maintaining peace and security and promoting international cooperation and mutual understanding.

Article 139   Responsibility to ensure compliance and liability for damage

1. States Parties shall have the responsibility to ensure that activities in the Area, whether carried out by States Parties, or state enterprises or natural or juridical persons which possess the nationality of States Parties or are effectively controlled by them or their nationals, shall be carried out in conformity with this Part. The same responsibility applies to international organizations for activities in the Area carried out by such organizations.

2. Without prejudice to the rules of international law and Annex III, article 22, damage caused by the failure of a State Party or international organization to carry out its responsibilities under this Part shall entail liability; States Parties or international organizations acting together shall bear joint and several liability. A State Party shall not however be liable for damage caused by any failure to comply with this Part by a person whom it has sponsored under article 153, paragraph 2(b), if the State Party has taken all necessary and appropriate measures to secure effective compliance under article 153, paragraph 4, and Annex III, article 4, paragraph 4.

3. States Parties that are members of international organizations shall take appropriate measures to ensure the implementation of this article with respect to such organizations.

Article 140   Benefit of mankind

1. Activities in the Area shall, as specifically provided for in this Part, be carried out for the benefit of mankind as a whole, irrespective of the geographical location of States, whether coastal or land-locked, and taking into particular consideration the interests and needs of developing States and of peoples who have not attained full independence or other self-governing status recognized by the United Nations in accordance with General Assembly resolution 1514 (XV) and other relevant General Assembly resolutions.

2. The Authority shall provide for the equitable sharing of financial and other economic benefits derived from activities in the Area through any appropriate mechanism, on a non-discriminatory basis, in accordance with article 160, paragraph 2(f)(i).

Article 141   Use of the Area exclusively for peaceful purposes

The Area shall be open to use exclusively for peaceful purposes by all States, whether coastal or land-locked, without discrimination and without prejudice to the other provisions of this Part.

Article 142   Rights and legitimate interests of coastal States

1. Activities in the Area, with respect to resource deposits in the Area which lie across limits of national jurisdiction, shall be conducted with due regard to the rights and legitimate interests of any coastal State across whose jurisdiction such deposits lie.

2. Consultations, including a system of prior notification, shall be maintained with the State concerned, with a view to avoiding infringement of such rights and interests. In cases where activities in the Area may result in the exploitation of resources lying within national jurisdiction, the prior consent of the coastal State concerned shall be required.

3. Neither this Part nor any rights granted or exercised pursuant thereto shall affect the rights of coastal States to take such measures consistent with the relevant provisions of Part XII as may be necessary to prevent, mitigate or eliminate grave and imminent danger to their coastline, or related interests from pollution or threat thereof or from other hazardous occurrences resulting from or caused by any activities in the Area.

Article 143   Marine scientific research

1. Marine scientific research in the Area shall be carried out exclusively for peaceful purposes and for the benefit of mankind as a whole, in accordance with Part XIII.

2. The Authority may carry out marine scientific research concerning the Area and its resources, and may enter into contracts for that purpose. The Authority shall promote and encourage the conduct of marine scientific research in the Area, and shall coordinate and disseminate the results of such research and analysis when available.

3. States Parties may carry out marine scientific research in the Area. States Parties shall promote international cooperation in marine scientific research in the Area by:

(a) participating in international programmes and encouraging cooperation in marine scientific research by personnel of different countries and of the Authority;

(b) ensuring that programmes are developed through the Authority or other international organizations as appropriate for the benefit of developing States and technologically less developed States with a view to:

(i) strengthening their research capabilities;

(ii) training their personnel and the personnel of the Authority in the techniques and applications of research;

(iii) fostering the employment of their qualified personnel in research in the Area;

(c) effectively disseminating the results of research and analysis when available, through the Authority or other international channels when appropriate.

Article 144   Transfer of technology

1. The Authority shall take measures in accordance with this Convention:

(a) to acquire technology and scientific knowledge relating to activities in the Area; and

(b) to promote and encourage the transfer to developing States of such technology and scientific knowledge so that all States Parties benefit therefrom.

2. To this end the Authority and States Parties shall cooperate in promoting the transfer of technology and scientific knowledge relating to activities in the Area so that the Enterprise and all States Parties may benefit therefrom. In particular they shall initiate and promote:

(a) programmes for the transfer of technology to the Enterprise and to developing States with regard to activities in the Area, including, *inter alia*, facilitating the access of the Enterprise and of developing States to

the relevant technology, under fair and reasonable terms and
conditions;

(b) measures directed towards the advancement of the technology of
the Enterprise and the domestic technology of developing States,
particularly by providing opportunities to personnel from the
Enterprise and from developing States for training in marine science
and technology and for their full participation in activities in the Area.

Article 145   Protection of the marine environment

Necessary measures shall be taken in accordance with this Convention
with respect to activities in the Area to ensure effective protection for the
marine environment from harmful effects which may arise from such
activities. To this end the Authority shall adopt appropriate rules,
regulations and procedures for *inter alia*:

(a) the prevention, reduction and control of pollution and other
hazards to the marine environment, including the coastline, and of
interference with the ecological balance of the marine environment,
particular attention being paid to the need for protection from harmful
effects of such activities as drilling, dredging, excavation, disposal of
waste, construction and operation or maintenance of installations,
pipelines and other devices related to such activities;

(b) the protection and conservation of the natural resources of the Area
and the prevention of damage to the flora and fauna of the marine
environment.

Article 146   Protection of human life

With respect to activities in the Area, necessary measures shall be taken
to ensure effective protection of human life. To this end the Authority
shall adopt appropriate rules, regulations and procedures to supplement
existing international law as embodied in relevant treaties.

Article 147   Accommodation of activities in the Area and in the
marine environment

1. Activities in the Area shall be carried out with reasonable regard for
other activities in the marine environment.

2. Installations used for carrying out activities in the Area shall be subject to the following conditions:

(a) such installations shall be erected, emplaced and removed solely in accordance with this Part and subject to the rules, regulations and procedures of the Authority. Due notice must be given of the erection, emplacement and removal of such installations, and permanent means for giving warning of their presence must be maintained;

(b) such installations may not be established where interference may be caused to the use of recognized sea lanes essential to international navigation or in areas of intense fishing activity;

(c) safety zones shall be established around such installations with appropriate markings to ensure the safety of both navigation and the installations. The configuration and location of such safety zones shall not be such as to form a belt impeding the lawful access of shipping to particular maritime zones or navigation along international sea lanes;

(d) such installations shall be used exclusively for peaceful purposes;

(e) such installations do not possess the status of islands. They have no territorial sea of their own, and their presence does not affect the delimitation of the territorial sea, the exclusive economic zone or the continental shelf.

3. Other activities in the marine environment shall be conducted with reasonable regard for activities in the Area.

Article 148   Participation of developing States in activities in the Area

The effective participation of developing States in activities in the Area shall be promoted as specifically provided for in this Part, having due regard to their special interests and needs, and in particular to the special need of the land-locked and geographically disadvantaged among them to overcome obstacles arising from their disadvantaged location, including remoteness from the Area and difficulty of access to and from it.

Article 149   Achaeological and historical objects

All objects of an archaeological and historical nature found in the Area shall be preserved or disposed of for the benefit of mankind as a whole, particular regard being paid to the preferential rights of the State or country of origin, or the State of cultural origin, or the State of historical and archaeological origin.

SECTION 3   DEVELOPMENT OF RESOURCES OF THE AREA

Article 150   Policies relating to activities in the Area

Activities in the Area shall, as specifically provided for in this Part, be carried out in such a manner as to foster healthy development of the world economy and balanced growth of international trade, and to promote international cooperation for the over-all development of all countries, especially developing States, and with a view to ensuring:

(a) the development of the resources of the Area;

(b) orderly, safe and rational management of the resources of the Area, including the efficient conduct of activities in the Area and, in accordance with sound principles of conservation, the avoidance of unnecessary waste;

(c) the expansion of opportunities for participation in such activities consistent in particular with articles 144 and 148;

(d) participation in revenues by the Authority and the transfer of technology to the Enterprise and developing States as provided for in this Convention;

(e) increased availability of the minerals derived from the Area as needed in conjunction with minerals derived from other sources, to ensure supplies to consumers of such minerals;

(f) the promotion of just and stable prices remunerative to producers and fair to consumers for minerals derived both from the Area and from other sources, and the promotion of long-term equilibrium between supply and demand;

(g) the enhancement of opportunities for all States Parties, irrespective of their social and economic systems or geographical location, to participate in the development of the resources of the Area and the prevention of monopolization of activities in the Area;

(h) the protection of developing countries from adverse effects on their economies or on their export earnings resulting from a reduction in the price of an affected mineral, or in the volume of exports of that mineral, to the extent that such reduction is caused by activities in the Area, as provided in article 151;

(i) the development of the common heritage for the benefit of mankind as a whole; and

(j) conditions of access to markets for the imports of minerals produced from the resources of the Area and for imports of commodities produced from such minerals shall not be more favourable than the most favourable applied to imports from other sources.

Article 151   Production policies

1. (a) Without prejudice to the objectives set forth in article 150 and for the purpose of implementing subparagraph (h) of that article, the Authority, acting through existing forums or such new arrangements or agreements as may be appropriate, in which all interested parties, including both producers and consumers, participate, shall take measures necessary to promote the growth, efficiency and stability of markets for those commodities produced from the minerals derived from the Area, at prices remunerative to producers and fair to consumers. All States Parties shall cooperate to this end.

(b) The Authority shall have the right to participate in any commodity conference dealing with those commodities and in which all interested parties including both producers and consumers participate. The Authority shall have the right to become a party to any arrangement or agreement resulting from such conferences. Participation of the Authority in any organs established under those arrangements or agreements shall be in respect of production in the Area and in accordance with the relevant rules of those organs.

(c) The Authority shall carry out its obligations under the arrangements or agreements referred to in this paragraph in a manner which assures a uniform and non-discriminatory implementation in respect of all production in the Area of the minerals concerned. In doing so, the Authority shall act in a manner consistent with the terms of existing contracts and approved plans of work of the Enterprise.

2. (a) During the interim period specified in paragraph 3, commercial production shall not be undertaken pursuant to an approved plan of work until the operator has applied for and has been issued a production authorization by the Authority. Such production authorizations may not be applied for or issued more than five years prior to the planned commencement of commercial production under the plan of work unless, having regard to the nature and timing of project development, the rules, regulations and procedures of the Authority prescribe another period.

(b) In the application for the production authorization, the operator shall specify the annual quantity of nickel expected to be recovered under the approved plan of work. The application shall include a schedule of expenditures to be made by the operator after he has received the authorization which are reasonably calculated to allow him to begin commercial production on the date planned.

(c) For the purposes of subparagraphs (a) and (b), the Authority shall establish appropriate performance requirements in accordance with Annex III, article 17.

(d) The Authority shall issue a production authorization for the level of production applied for unless the sum of that level and the levels already authorized exceeds the nickel production ceiling, as calculated pursuant to paragraph 4 in the year of issuance of the authorization, during any year of planned production falling within the interim period.

(e) When issued, the production authorization and approved application shall become a part of the approved plan of work.

(f) If the operator's application for a production authorization is denied pursuant to subparagraph (d), the operator may apply again to the Authority at any time.

3. The interim period shall begin five years prior to 1 January of the year in which the earliest commercial production is planned to commence under an approved plan of work. If the earliest commercial production is delayed beyond the year originally planned, the beginning of the interim period and the production ceiling originally calculated shall be adjusted

accordingly. The interim period shall last 25 years or until the end of the Review Conference referred to in article 155 or until the day when such new arrangements or agreements as are referred to in paragraph 1 enter into force, whichever is earliest. The Authority shall resume the power provided in this article for the remainder of the interim period if the said arrangements or agreements should lapse or become ineffective for any reason whatsoever.

4. (a) The production ceiling for any year of the interim period shall be the sum of:

(i) the difference between the trend line values for nickel consumption, as calculated pursuant to subparagraph (b), for the year immediately prior to the year of the earliest commercial production and the year immediately prior to the commencement of the interim period; and

(ii) sixty per cent of the difference between the trend line values for nickel consumption, as calculated pursuant to subparagraph (b), for the year for which the production authorization is being applied for and the year immediately prior to the year of the earliest commercial production.

(b) For the purposes of subparagraph (a):

(i) trend line values used for computing the nickel production ceiling shall be those annual nickel consumption values on a trend line computed during the year in which a production authorization is issued. The trend line shall be derived from a linear regression of the logarithms of actual nickel consumption for the most recent 15-year period for which such data are available, time being the independent variable. This trend line shall be referred to as the original trend line;

(ii) if the annual rate of increase of the original trend line is less than 3 per cent, then the trend line used to determine the quantities referred to in subparagraph (a) shall instead be one passing through the original trend line at the value for the first year of the relevant 15-year period, and increasing at 3 per cent annually; provided however that the production ceiling established for any year of the interim period may not in any case exceed the difference between the original trend line value for that year and the original trend line value for the year immediately prior to the commencement of the interim period.

5. The Authority shall reserve to the Enterprise for its initial production a quantity of 38,000 metric tonnes of nickel from the available production ceiling calculated pursuant to paragraph 4.

6. (a) An operator may in any year produce less than or up to 8 per cent more than the level of annual production of minerals from polymetallic nodules specified in his production authorization, provided that the over-all amount of production shall not exceed that specified in the authorization. Any excess over 8 per cent and up to 20 per cent in any year, or any excess in the first and subsequent years following two consecutive years in which excesses occur, shall be negotiated with the Authority, which may require the operator to obtain a supplementary production authorization to cover additional production.

(b) Applications for such supplementary production authorizations shall be considered by the Authority only after all pending applications by operators who have not yet received production authorizations have been acted upon and due account has been taken of other likely applicants. The Authority shall be guided by the principle of not exceeding the total production allowed under the production ceiling in any year of the interim period. It shall not authorize the production under any plan of work of a quantity in excess of 46,500 metric tonnes of nickel per year.

7. The levels of production of other metals such as copper, cobalt and manganese extracted from the polymetallic nodules that are recovered pursuant to a production authorization should not be higher than those which would have been produced had the operator produced the maximum level of nickel from those nodules pursuant to this article. The Authority shall establish rules, regulations and procedures pursuant to Annex III, article 17, to implement this paragraph.

8. Rights and obligations relating to unfair economic practices under relevant multilateral trade agreements shall apply to the exploration for and exploitation of minerals from the Area. In the settlement of disputes arising under this provision, States Parties which are Parties to such multilateral trade agreements shall have recourse to the dispute settlement procedures of such agreements.

9. The Authority shall have the power to limit the level of production of minerals from the Area, other than minerals from polymetallic nodules, under such conditions and applying such methods as may be appropriate by adopting regulations in accordance with article 161, paragraph 8.

10. Upon the recommendation of the Council on the basis of advice from the Economic Planning Commission, the Assembly shall establish a system of compensation or take other measures of economic adjustment assistance including cooperation with specialized agencies and other international organizations to assist developing countries which suffer serious adverse effects on their export earnings or economies resulting from a reduction in the price of an affected mineral or in the volume of exports of that mineral, to the extent that such reduction is caused by activities in the Area. The Authority on request shall initiate studies on the problems of those States which are likely to be most seriously affected with a view to minimizing their difficulties and assisting them in their economic adjustment.

Article 152   Exercise of powers and functions by the Authority

1. The Authority shall avoid discrimination in the exercise of its powers and functions, including the granting of opportunities for activities in the Area.

2. Nevertheless, special consideration for developing States, including particular consideration for the land-locked and geographically disadvantaged among them, specifically provided for in this Part shall be permitted.

Article 153   System of exploration and exploitation

1. Activities in the Area shall be organized, carried out and controlled by the Authority on behalf of mankind as a whole in accordance with this article as well as other relevant provisions of this Part and the relevant Annexes, and the rules, regulations and procedures of the Authority.

2. Activities in the Area shall be carried out as prescribed in paragraph 3:

   (a) by the Enterprise, and

(b) in association with the Authority by States Parties, or state enterprises or natural or juridical persons which possess the nationality of States Parties or are effectively controlled by them or their nationals, when sponsored by such States, or any group of the foregoing which meets the requirements provided in this Part and in Annex III.

3. Activities in the Area shall be carried out in accordance with a formal written plan of work drawn up in accordance with Annex III and approved by the Council after review by the Legal and Technical Commission. In the case of activities in the Area carried out as authorized by the Authority by the entities specified in paragraph 2(b), the plan of work shall, in accordance with Annex III, article 3, be in the form of a contract. Such contracts may provide for joint arrangements in accordance with Annex III, article 11.

4. The Authority shall exercise such control over activities in the Area as is necessary for the purpose of securing compliance with the relevant provisions of this Part and the Annexes relating thereto, and the rules, regulations and procedures of the Authority, and the plans of work approved in accordance with paragraph 3. States Parties shall assist the Authority by taking all measures necessary to ensure such compliance in accordance with article 139.

5. The Authority shall have the right to take at any time any measures provided for under this Part to ensure compliance with its provisions and the exercise of the functions of control and regulation assigned to it thereunder or under any contract. The Authority shall have the right to inspect all installations in the Area used in connection with activities in the Area.

6. A contract under paragraph 3 shall provide for security of tenure. Accordingly, the contract shall not be revised, suspended or terminated except in accordance with Annex III, articles 18 and 19.

Article 154   Periodic review

Every five years from the entry into force of this Convention, the Assembly shall undertake a general and systematic review of the manner in which the international regime of the Area established in this Convention has operated in practice. In the light of this review the Assembly may take, or recommend that other organs take, measures in accordance with the provisions and procedures of this Part and the

Annexes relating thereto which will lead to the improvement of the operation of the regime.

Article 155   The Review Conference

1. Fifteen years from 1 January of the year in which the earliest commercial production commences under an approved plan of work, the Assembly shall convene a conference for the review of those provisions of this Part and the relevant Annexes which govern the system of exploration and exploitation of the resources of the Area. The Review Conference shall consider in detail, in the light of the experience acquired during that period:

(a) whether the provisions of this Part which govern the system of exploration and exploitation of the resources of the Area have achieved their aims in all respects, including whether they have benefited mankind as a whole;

(b) whether, during the 15-year period, reserved areas have been exploited in an effective and balanced manner in comparison with non-reserved areas;

(c) whether the development and use of the Area and its resources have been undertaken in such a manner as to foster healthy development of the world economy and balanced growth of international trade;

(d) whether monopolization of activities in the Area has been prevented;

(e) whether the policies set forth in articles 150 and 151 have been fulfilled; and

(f) whether the system has resulted in the equitable sharing of benefits derived from activities in the Area, taking into particular consideration the interests and needs of the developing States.

2. The Review Conference shall ensure the maintenance of the principle of the common heritage of mankind, the international regime designed to ensure equitable exploitation of the resources of the Area for the benefit of all countries, especially the developing States, and an Authority to organize, conduct and control activities in the Area. It shall also ensure the maintenance of the principles laid down in this Part with regard to the exclusion of claims or exercise of sovereignty over any part

of the Area, the rights of States and their general conduct in relation to the Area, and their participation in activities in the Area in conformity with this Convention, the prevention of monopolization of activities in the Area, the use of the Area exclusively for peaceful purposes, economic aspects of activities in the Area, marine scientific research, transfer of technology, protection of the marine environment, protection of human life, rights of coastal States, the legal status of the waters superjacent to the Area and that of the air space above those waters and accommodation between activities in the Area and other activities in the marine environment.

3. The decision-making procedure applicable at the Review Conference shall be the same as that applicable at the Third United Nations Conference on the Law of the Sea. The Conference shall make every effort to reach agreement on any amendments by way of consensus and there should be no voting on such matters until all efforts at achieving consensus have been exhausted.

4. If, five years after its commencement, the Review Conference has not reached agreement on the system of exploration and exploitation of the resources of the Area, it may decide during the ensuing 12 months, by a three-fourths majority of the States Parties, to adopt and submit to the States Parties for ratification or accession such amendments changing or modifying the system as it determines necessary and appropriate. Such amendments shall enter into force for all States Parties 12 months after the deposit of instruments of ratification or accession by three fourths of the States Parties.

5. Amendments adopted by the Review Conference pursuant to this article shall not affect rights acquired under existing contracts.

SECTION 4   THE AUTHORITY

Subsection A   General provisions

Article 156   Establishment of the Authority

1. There is hereby established the International Seabed Authority, which shall function in accordance with this Part.

2. All States Parties are *ipso facto* members of the Authority.

3. Observers at the Third United Nations Conference on the Law of the Sea who have signed the Final Act and who are not referred to in article 305, paragraph 1(c), (d), (e) or (f), shall have the right to participate in the Authority as observers, in accordance with its rules, regulations and procedures.

4. The seat of the Authority shall be in Jamaica.

5. The Authority may establish such regional centres or offices as it deems necessary for the exercise of its functions.

Article 157   Nature and fundamental principles of the Authority

1. The Authority is the organization through which States Parties shall, in accordance with this Part, organize and control activities in the Area, particularly with a view to administering the resources of the Area.

2. The powers and functions of the Authority shall be those expressly conferred upon it by this Convention. The Authority shall have such incidental powers, consistent with this Convention, as are implicit in and necessary for the exercise of those powers and functions with respect to activities in the Area.

3. The Authority is based on the principle of the sovereign equality of all its members.

4. All members of the Authority shall fulfil in good faith the obligations assumed by them in accordance with this Part in order to ensure to all of them the rights and benefits resulting from membership.

Article 158   Organs of the Authority

1. There are hereby established, as the principal organs of the Authority, an Assembly, a Council and a Secretariat.

2. There is hereby established the Enterprise, the organ through which the Authority shall carry out the functions referred to in article 170, paragraph 1.

3. Such subsidiary organs as may be found necessary may be established in accordance with this Part.

4. Each principal organ of the Authority and the Enterprise shall be responsible for exercising those powers and functions which are conferred upon it. In exercising such powers and functions each organ shall avoid taking any action which may derogate from or impede the exercise of specific powers and functions conferred upon another organ.

Subsection B   The Assembly

Article 159   Composition, procedure and voting

1. The Assembly shall consist of all the members of the Authority. Each member shall have one representative in the Assembly, who may be accompanied by alternates and advisers.

2. The Assembly shall meet in regular annual sessions and in such special sessions as may be decided by the Assembly, or convened by the Secretary-General at the request of the Council or of a majority of the members of the Authority.

3. Sessions shall take place at the seat of the Authority unless otherwise decided by the Assembly.

4. The Assembly shall adopt its rules of procedure. At the beginning of each regular session, it shall elect its President and such other officers as may be required. They shall hold office until a new President and other officers are elected at the next regular session.

5. A majority of the members of the Assembly shall constitute a quorum.

6. Each member of the Assembly shall have one vote.

7. Decisions on questions of procedure, including decisions to convene special sessions of the Assembly, shall be taken by a majority of the members present and voting.

8. Decisions on questions of substance shall be taken by a two-thirds majority of the members present and voting, provided that such majority includes a majority of the members participating in the session. When the issue arises as to whether a question is one of substance or not, that question shall be treated as one of substance unless otherwise decided by the Assembly by the majority required for decisions on questions of substance.

9. When a question of substance comes up for voting for the first time, the President may, and shall, if requested by at least one fifth of the members of the Assembly, defer the issue of taking a vote on that question for a period not exceeding five calendar days. This rule may be applied only once to any question, and shall not be applied so as to defer the question beyond the end of the session.

10. Upon a written request addressed to the President and sponsored by at least one fourth of the members of the Authority for an advisory opinion on the conformity with this Convention of a proposal before the Assembly on any matter, the Assembly shall request the Seabed Disputes Chamber of the International Tribunal for the Law of the Sea to give an advisory opinion thereon and shall defer voting on that proposal pending receipt of the advisory opinion by the Chamber. If the advisory opinion is not received before the final week of the session in which it is requested, the Assembly shall decide when it will meet to vote upon the deferred proposal.

Article 160   Powers and functions

1. The Assembly, as the sole organ of the Authority consisting of all the members, shall be considered the supreme organ of the Authority to which the other principal organs shall be accountable as specifically provided for in this Convention. The Assembly shall have the power to establish general policies in conformity with the relevant provisions of this Convention on any question or matter within the competence of the Authority.

2. In addition, the powers and functions of the Assembly shall be:

(a) to elect the members of the Council in accordance with article 161;

(b) to elect the Secretary-General from among the candidates proposed by the Council;

(c) to elect, upon the recommendation of the Council, the members of the Governing Board of the Enterprise and the Director-General of the Enterprise;

(d) to establish such subsidiary organs as it finds necessary for the exercise of its functions in accordance with this Part. In the composition of these subsidiary organs due account shall be taken of the principle of equitable geographical distribution and of special interests and the need for members qualified and competent in the relevant technical questions dealt with by such organs;

(e) to assess the contributions of members to the administrative budget of the Authority in accordance with an agreed scale of assessment based upon the scale used for the regular budget of the United Nations until the Authority shall have sufficient income from other sources to meet its administrative expenses;

(f) (i) to consider and approve, upon the recommendation of the Council, the rules, regulations and procedures on the equitable sharing of financial and other economic benefits derived from activities in the Area and the payments and contributions made pursuant to article 82, taking into particular consideration the interests and needs of developing States and peoples who have not attained full independence or other self-governing status. If the Assembly does not approve the recommendations of the Council, the Assembly shall return them to the Council for reconsideration in the light of the views expressed by the Assembly;

(ii) to consider and approve the rules, regulations and procedures of the Authority, and any amendments thereto, provisionally adopted by the Council pursuant to article 162, paragraph 2 (o)(ii). These rules, regulations and procedures shall relate to prospecting, exploration and exploitation in the Area, the financial management and internal administration of the Authority, and, upon the recommendation of the Governing Board of the Enterprise, to the transfer of funds from the Enterprise to the Authority;

(g) to decide upon the equitable sharing of financial and other economic benefits derived from activities in the Area, consistent with this Convention and the rules, regulations and procedures of the Authority;

(h) to consider and approve the proposed annual budget of the Authority submitted by the Council;

(i) to examine periodic reports from the Council and from the Enterprise and special reports requested from the Council or any other organ of the Authority;

(j) to initiate studies and make recommendations for the purpose of promoting international cooperation concerning activities in the Area and encouraging the progressive development of international law relating thereto and its codification;

(k) to consider problems of a general nature in connection with activities in the Area arising in particular for developing States, as well as those problems for States in connection with activities in the Area that are due to their geographical location, particularly for land-locked and geographically disadvantaged States;

(l) to establish, upon the recommendation of the Council, on the basis of advice from the Economic Planning Commission, a system of compensation or other measures of economic adjustment assistance as provided in article 151, paragraph 10;

(m) to suspend the exercise of rights and privileges of membership pursuant to article 185;

(n) to discuss any question or matter within the competence of the Authority and to decide as to which organ of the Authority shall deal with any such question or matter not specifically entrusted to a particular organ, consistent with the distribution of powers and functions among the organs of the Authority.

Subsection C   The Council

Article 161   Composition, procedure and voting

1. The Council shall consist of 36 members of the Authority elected by the Assembly in the following order:

(a) four members from among those States Parties which, during the last five years for which statistics are available, have either consumed more than 2 per cent of total world consumption or have had net imports of more than 2 per cent of total world imports of the commodities produced from the categories of minerals to be derived from the Area, and in any case one State from the Eastern European (Socialist) region, as well as the largest consumer;

(b) four members from among the eight States Parties which have the largest investments in preparation for and in the conduct of activities in the Area, either directly or through their nationals, including at least one State from the Eastern European (Socialist) region;

(c) four members from among States Parties which on the basis of production in areas under their jurisdiction are major net exporters of the categories of minerals to be derived from the Area, including at least two developing States whose exports of such minerals have a substantial bearing upon their economies;

(d) six members from among developing States Parties, representing special interests. The special interests to be represented shall include those of States with large populations, States which are land-locked or geographically disadvantaged, States which are major importers of the categories of minerals to be derived from the Area, States which are potential producers of such minerals, and least developed States;

(e) eighteen members elected according to the principle of ensuring an equitable geographical distribution of seats in the Council as a whole, provided that each geographical region shall have at least one member elected under this subparagraph. For this purpose, the geographical regions shall be Africa, Asia, Eastern European (Socialist), Latin America and Western European and Others.

2. In electing the members of the Council in accordance with paragraph 1, the Assembly shall ensure that:

(a) land-locked and geographically disadvantaged States are represented to a degree which is reasonably proportionate to their representation in the Assembly;

(b) coastal States, especially developing States, which do not qualify under paragraph 1(a), (b), (c) or (d) are represented to a degree which is reasonably proportionate to their representation in the Assembly;

(c) each group of States Parties to be represented on the Council is represented by those members, if any, which are nominated by that group.

3. Elections shall take place at regular sessions of the Assembly. Each member of the Council shall be elected for four years. At the first election, however, the term of one half of the members of each group referred to in paragraph 1 shall be two years.

4. Members of the Council shall be eligible for re-election, but due regard should be paid to the desirability of rotation of membership.

5. The Council shall function at the seat of the Authority, and shall meet as often as the business of the Authority may require, but not less than three times a year.

6. A majority of the members of the Council shall constitute a quorum.

7. Each member of the Council shall have one vote.

8. (a) Decisions on questions of procedure shall be taken by a majority of the members present and voting.

(b) Decisions on questions of substance arising under the following provisions shall be taken by a two-thirds majority of the members present and voting, provided that such majority includes a majority of the members of the Council: article 162, paragraph 2, subparagraphs (f); (g); (h); (i); (n); (p); (v); article 191.

(c) Decisions on questions of substance arising under the following provisions shall be taken by a three-fourths majority of the members present and voting, provided that such majority includes a majority of the members of the Council: article 162, paragraph 1; article 162, paragraph 2, subparagraphs (a); (b); (c); (d); (e); (l); (q); (r); (s); (t); (u) in cases of non-compliance by a contractor or a sponsor; (w) provided that orders issued thereunder may be binding for not more than 30 days unless confirmed by a decision taken in accordance with subparagraph (d); article 162, paragraph 2, subparagraphs (x); (y); (z); article 163, paragraph 2; article 174, paragraph 3; Annex IV, article 11.

(d) Decisions on questions of substance arising under the following provisions shall be taken by consensus: article 162, paragraph 2(m) and (o); adoption of amendments to Part XI.

(e) For the purposes of subparagraphs (d), (f) and (g), "consensus" means the absence of any formal objection. Within 14 days of the submission of a proposal to the Council, the President of the Council shall determine whether there would be a formal objection to the adoption of the proposal. If the President determines that there would be such an objection, the President shall establish and convene, within three days following such determination, a conciliation committee consisting of not more than nine members of the Council, with the President as chairman, for the purpose of reconciling the differences and producing a proposal which can be adopted by consensus. The committee shall work expeditiously and report to the Council within 14 days following its establishment. If the committee is unable to recommend a proposal which can be adopted by consensus, it shall set out in its report the grounds on which the proposal is being opposed.

(f) Decisions on questions not listed above which the Council is authorized to take by the rules, regulations and procedures of the Authority or otherwise shall be taken pursuant to the subparagraphs of this paragraph specified in the rules, regulations and procedures or, if not specified therein, then pursuant to the subparagraph determined by the Council if possible in advance, by consensus.

(g) When the issue arises as to whether a question is within subparagraph (a), (b), (c) or (d), the question shall be treated as being within the subparagraph requiring the higher or highest majority or consensus as the case may be, unless otherwise decided by the Council by the said majority or by consensus.

9. The Council shall establish a procedure whereby a member of the Authority not represented on the Council may send a representative to attend a meeting of the Council when a request is made by such member, or a matter particularly affecting it is under consideration. Such a representative shall be entitled to participate in the deliberations but not to vote.

Article 162   Powers and functions

1. The Council is the executive organ of the Authority. The Council shall have the power to establish, in conformity with this Convention and the general policies established by the Assembly, the specific policies to be pursued by the Authority on any question or matter within the competence of the Authority.

2. In addition, the Council shall:

(a) supervise and coordinate the implementation of the provisions of this Part on all questions and matters within the competence of the Authority and invite the attention of the Assembly to cases of non-compliance;

(b) propose to the Assembly a list of candidates for the election of the Secretary-General;

(c) recommend to the Assembly candidates for the election of the members of the Governing Board of the Enterprise and the Director-General of the Enterprise;

(d) establish, as appropriate, and with due regard to economy and efficiency, such subsidiary organs as it finds necessary for the exercise of its functions in accordance with this Part. In the composition of subsidiary organs, emphasis shall be placed on the need for members qualified and competent in relevant technical matters dealt with by those organs provided that due account shall be taken of the principle of equitable geographical distribution and of special interests;

(e) adopt its rules of procedure including the method of selecting its president;

(f) enter into agreements with the United Nations or other international organizations on behalf of the Authority and within its competence, subject to approval by the Assembly;

(g) consider the reports of the Enterprise and transmit them to the Assembly with its recommendations;

(h) present to the Assembly annual reports and such special reports as the Assembly may request;

(i) issue directives to the Enterprise in accordance with article 170;

(j) approve plans of work in accordance with Annex III, article 6. The Council shall act upon each plan of work within 60 days of its submission by the Legal and Technical Commission at a session of the Council in accordance with the following procedures:

(i) if the Commission recommends the approval of a plan of work, it shall be deemed to have been approved by the Council if no member of the Council submits in writing to the President within 14 days a specific objection alleging non-compliance with the requirements of Annex III, article 6. If there is an objection, the conciliation procedure set forth in article 161, paragraph 8(e), shall apply. If, at the end of the conciliation procedure, the objection is still maintained, the plan of work shall be deemed to have been approved by the Council unless the Council disapproves it by consensus among its members excluding any State or States making the application or sponsoring the applicant;

(ii) if the Commission recommends the disapproval of a plan of work or does not make a recommendation, the Council may approve the plan of work by a three-fourths majority of the members present and voting, provided that such majority includes a majority of the members participating in the session;

(k) approve plans of work submitted by the Enterprise in accordance with Annex IV, article 12, applying, *mutates mutandis*, the procedures set forth in subparagraph (j);

(l) exercise control over activities in the Area in accordance with article 153, paragraph 4, and the rules, regulations and procedures of the Authority;

(m) take, upon the recommendation of the Economic Planning Commission, necessary and appropriate measures in accordance with article 150, subparagraph (h), to provide protection from the adverse economic effects specified therein;

(n) make recommendations to the Assembly, on the basis of advice from the Economic Planning Commission, for a system of compensation or other measures of economic adjustment assistance as provided in article 151, paragraph 10;

(o) (i) recommend to the Assembly rules, regulations and procedures on the equitable sharing of financial and other economic benefits derived from activities in the Area and the payments and contributions made pursuant to article 82, taking into particular consideration the interests and needs of the developing States and peoples who have not attained full independence or other self-governing status;

(ii) adopt and apply provisionally, pending approval by the Assembly, the rules, regulations and procedures of the Authority, and any amendments thereto, taking into account the recommendations of the Legal and Technical Commission or other subordinate organ concerned. These rules, regulations and procedures shall relate to prospecting, exploration and exploitation in the Area and the financial management and internal administration of the Authority. Priority shall be given to the adoption of rules, regulations and procedures for the exploration for and exploitation of polymetallic nodules. Rules, regulations and procedures for the exploration for and exploitation of any resource other than polymetallic nodules shall be adopted within three years from the date of a request to the Authority by any of its members to adopt such rules, regulations and procedures in respect of such resource. All rules, regulations and procedures shall remain in effect on a provisional basis until approved by the Assembly or until amended by the Council in the light of any views expressed by the Assembly;

(p) review the collection of all payments to be made by or to the Authority in connection with operations pursuant to this Part;

(q) make the selection from among applicants for production authorizations pursuant to Annex III, article 7, where such selection is required by that provision;

(r) submit the proposed annual budget of the Authority to the Assembly for its approval;

(s) make recommendations to the Assembly concerning policies on any question or matter within the competence of the Authority;

(t) make recommendations to the Assembly concerning suspension of the exercise of the rights and privileges of membership pursuant to article 185;

(u) institute proceedings on behalf of the Authority before the Seabed Disputes Chamber in cases of non-compliance;

(v) notify the Assembly upon a decision by the Seabed Disputes Chamber in proceedings instituted under subparagraph (u), and make any recommendations which it may find appropriate with respect to measures to be taken;

(w) issue emergency orders, which may include orders for the suspension or adjustment of operations, to prevent serious harm to the marine environment arising out of activities in the Area;

(x) disapprove areas for exploitation by contractors or the Enterprise in cases where substantial evidence indicates the risk of serious harm to the marine environment;

(y) establish a subsidiary organ for the elaboration of draft financial rules, regulations and procedures relating to:

(i) financial management in accordance with articles 171 to 175; and

(ii) financial arrangements in accordance with Annex III, article 13 and article 17, paragraph 1(c);

(z) establish appropriate mechanisms for directing and supervising a staff of inspectors who shall inspect activities in the Area to determine whether this Part, the rules, regulations and procedures of the Authority, and the terms and conditions of any contract with the Authority are being complied with.

Article 163   Organs of the Council

1. There are hereby established the following organs of the Council:

(a) an Economic Planning Commission;

(b) a Legal and Technical Commission.

2. Each Commission shall be composed of 15 members, elected by the Council from among the candidates nominated by the States Parties. However, if necessary, the Council may decide to increase the size of either Commission having due regard to economy and efficiency.

3. Members of a Commission shall have appropriate qualifications in the area of competence of that Commission. States Parties shall nominate candidates of the highest standards of competence and integrity with qualifications in relevant fields so as to ensure the effective exercise of the functions of the Commissions.

4. In the election of members of the Commissions, due account shall be taken of the need for equitable geographical distribution and the representation of special interests.

5. No State Party may nominate more than one candidate for the same Commission. No person shall be elected to serve on more than one Commission.

6. Members of the Commissions shall hold office for a term of five years. They shall be eligible for re-election for a further term.

7. In the event of the death, incapacity or resignation of a member of a Commission prior to the expiration of the term of office, the Council shall elect for the remainder of the term, a member from the same geographical region or area of interest.

8. Members of Commissions shall have no financial interest in any activity relating to exploration and exploitation in the Area. Subject to their responsibilities to the Commissions upon which they serve, they shall not disclose, even after the termination of their functions, any industrial secret, proprietary data which are transferred to the Authority in accordance with Annex III, article 14, or any other confidential information coming to their knowledge by reason of their duties for the Authority.

9. Each Commission shall exercise its functions in accordance with such guidelines and directives as the Council may adopt.

10. Each Commission shall formulate and submit to the Council for approval such rules and regulations as may be necessary for the efficient conduct of the Commission's functions.

11. The decision-making procedures of the Commissions shall be established by the rules, regulations and procedures of the Authority. Recommendations to the Council shall, where necessary, be accompanied by a summary on the divergencies of opinion in the Commission.

12. Each Commission shall normally function at the seat of the Authority and shall meet as often as is required for the efficient exercise of its functions.

13. In the exercise of its functions, each Commission may, where appropriate, consult another commission, any competent organ of the United Nations or of its specialized agencies or any international organizations with competence in the subject-matter of such consultation.

Article 164   The Economic Planning Commission

1. Members of the Economic Planning Commission shall have appropriate qualifications such as those relevant to mining, management of mineral resource activities, international trade or international economics. The Council shall endeavour to ensure that the membership of the Commission reflects all appropriate qualifications. The Commission shall include at least two members from developing States whose exports of the categories of minerals to be derived from the Area have a substantial bearing upon their economies.

2. The Commission shall:

(a) propose, upon the request of the Council, measures to implement decisions relating to activities in the Area taken in accordance with this Convention;

(b) review the trends of and the factors affecting supply, demand and prices of minerals which may be derived from the Area, bearing in mind the interests of both importing and exporting countries, and in particular of the developing States among them;
(c) examine any situation likely to lead to the adverse effects referred to in article 150, subparagraph (h), brought to its attention by the State Party or States Parties concerned, and make appropriate recommendations to the Council;

(d) propose to the Council for submission to the Assembly, as provided in article 151, paragraph 10, a system of compensation or other measures of economic adjustment assistance for developing States which suffer adverse effects caused by activities in the Area. The Commission shall make the recommendations to the Council that are necessary for the application of the system or other measures adopted by the Assembly in specific cases.

Article 165   The Legal and Technical Commission

1. Members of the Legal and Technical Commission shall have appropriate qualifications such as those relevant to exploration for and exploitation and processing of mineral resources, oceanology, protection of the marine environment, or economic or legal matters relating to ocean mining and related fields of expertise. The Council shall endeavour to ensure that the membership of the Commission reflects all appropriate qualifications.

2. The Commission shall:

(a) make recommendations with regard to the exercise of the Authority's functions upon the request of the Council;

(b) review formal written plans of work for activities in the Area in accordance with article 153, paragraph 3, and submit appropriate recommendations to the Council. The Commission shall base its recommendations solely on the grounds stated in Annex III and shall report fully thereon to the Council;

(c) supervise, upon the request of the Council, activities in the Area, where appropriate, in consultation and collaboration with any entity carrying out such activities or State or States concerned and report to the Council;

(d) prepare assessments of the environmental implications of activities in the Area;

(e) make recommendations to the Council on the protection of the marine environment, taking into account the views of recognized experts in that field;

(f) formulate and submit to the Council the rules, regulations and procedures referred to in article 162, paragraph 2(o), taking into account all relevant factors including assessments of the environmental implications of activities in the Area;

(g) keep such rules, regulations and procedures under review and recommend to the Council from time to time such amendments thereto as it may deem necessary or desirable;

(h) make recommendations to the Council regarding the establishment of a monitoring programme to observe, measure, evaluate and analyse, by recognized scientific methods, on a regular basis, the risks or effects of pollution of the marine environment resulting from activities in the Area, ensure that existing regulations are adequate and are complied with and coordinate the implementation of the monitoring programme approved by the Council;

(i) recommend to the Council that proceedings be instituted on behalf of the Authority before the Seabed Disputes Chamber, in accordance with this Part and the relevant Annexes taking into account particularly article 187;

(j) make recommendations to the Council with respect to measures to be taken, upon a decision by the Seabed Disputes Chamber in proceedings instituted in accordance with subparagraph (i);

(k) make recommendations to the Council to issue emergency orders, which may include orders for the suspension or adjustment of operations, to prevent serious harm to the marine environment arising out of activities in the Area. Such recommendations shall be taken up by the Council on a priority basis;

(l) make recommendations to the Council to disapprove areas for exploitation by contractors or the Enterprise in cases where substantial evidence indicates the risk of serious harm to the marine environment;

(m) make recommendations to the Council regarding the direction and supervision of a staff of inspectors who shall inspect activities in the Area to determine whether the provisions of this Part, the rules, regulations and procedures of the Authority, and the terms and conditions of any contract with the Authority are being complied with;

(n) calculate the production ceiling and issue production authorizations on behalf of the Authority pursuant to article 151, paragraphs 2 to 7, following any necessary selection among applicants for production authorizations by the Council in accordance with Annex III, article 7.

3. The members of the Commission shall, upon request by any State Party or other party concerned, be accompanied by a representative of such State or other party concerned when carrying out their function of supervision and inspection.

Subsection D   The Secretariat

Article 166   The Secretariat

1. The Secretariat of the Authority shall comprise a Secretary-General and such staff as the Authority may require.

2. The Secretary-General shall be elected for four years by the Assembly from among the candidates proposed by the Council and may be re-elected.

3. The Secretary-General shall be the chief administrative officer of the Authority, and shall act in that capacity in all meetings of the Assembly, of the Council and of any subsidiary organ, and shall perform such other administrative functions as are entrusted to the Secretary-General by these organs.

4. The Secretary-General shall make an annual report to the Assembly on the work of the Authority.

Article 167   The staff of the Authority

1. The staff of the Authority shall consist of such qualified scientific and technical and other personnel as may be required to fulfil the administrative functions of the Authority.

2. The paramount consideration in the recruitment and employment of the staff and in the determination of their conditions of service shall be the necessity of securing the highest standards of efficiency, competence and integrity. Subject to this consideration, due regard shall be paid to the importance of recruiting the staff on as wide a geographical basis as possible.

3. The staff shall be appointed by the Secretary-General. The terms and conditions on which they shall be appointed, remunerated and dismissed shall be in accordance with the rules, regulations and procedures of the Authority.

Article 168   International character of the Secretariat

1. In the performance of their duties the Secretary-General and the staff shall not seek or receive instructions from any government or from any other source external to the Authority. They shall refrain from any action which might reflect on their position as international officials responsible only to the Authority. Each State Party undertakes to respect the exclusively international character of the responsibilities of the Secretary-General and the staff and not to seek to influence them in the discharge of their responsibilities. Any violation of responsibilities by a staff member shall be submitted to the appropriate administrative tribunal as provided in the rules, regulations and procedures of the Authority.

2. The Secretary-General and the staff shall have no financial interest in any activity relating to exploration and exploitation in the Area. Subject to their responsibilities to the Authority, they shall not disclose, even after the termination of their functions, any industrial secret, proprietary data which are transferred to the Authority in accordance with Annex III, article 14, or any other confidential information coming to their knowledge by reason of their employment with the Authority.

3. Violations of the obligations of a staff member of the Authority set forth in paragraph 2 shall, on the request of a State Party affected by such violation, or a natural or juridical person, sponsored by a State Party as provided in article 153, paragraph 2(b), and affected by such violation, be submitted by the Authority against the staff member concerned to a

tribunal designated by the rules, regulations and procedures of the Authority. The Party affected shall have the right to take part in the proceedings. If the tribunal so recommends, the Secretary-General shall dismiss the staff member concerned.

4. The rules, regulations and procedures of the Authority shall contain such provisions as are necessary to implement this article.

Article 169   Consultation and cooperation with international and non-governmental organizations

1. The Secretary-General shall, on matters within the competence of the Authority, make suitable arrangements, with the approval of the Council, for consultation and cooperation with international and non-governmental organizations recognized by the Economic and Social Council of the United Nations.

2. Any organization with which the Secretary-General has entered into an arrangement under paragraph 1 may designate representatives to attend meetings of the organs of the Authority as observers in accordance with the rules of procedure of these organs. Procedures shall be established for obtaining the views of such organizations in appropriate cases.

3. The Secretary-General may distribute to States Parties written reports submitted by the non-governmental organizations referred to in paragraph 1 on subjects in which they have special competence and which are related to the work of the Authority.

Subsection E   The Enterprise

Article 170   The Enterprise

1. The Enterprise shall be the organ of the Authority which shall carry out activities in the Area directly, pursuant to article 153, paragraph 2(a), as well as the transporting, processing and marketing of minerals recovered from the Area.

2. The Enterprise shall, within the framework of the international legal personality of the Authority, have such legal capacity as is provided for in the Statute set forth in Annex IV. The Enterprise shall act in accordance with this Convention and the rules, regulations and procedures of the Authority, as well as the general policies established

by the Assembly, and shall be subject to the directives and control of the Council.

3. The Enterprise shall have its principal place of business at the seat of the Authority.

4. The Enterprise shall, in accordance with article 173, paragraph 2, and Annex IV, article 11, be provided with such funds as it may require to carry out its functions, and shall receive technology as provided in article 144 and other relevant provisions of this Convention.

Subsection F   Financial arrangements of the authority

Article 171   Funds of the Authority

The funds of the Authority shall include:

(a) assessed contributions made by members of the Authority in accordance with article 160, paragraph 2(e);

(b) funds received by the Authority pursuant to Annex III, article 13, in connection with activities in the Area;

(c) funds transferred from the Enterprise in accordance with Annex IV, article 10;

(d) funds borrowed pursuant to article 174;

(e) voluntary contributions made by members or other entities; and

(f) payments to a compensation fund, in accordance with article 151, paragraph 10, whose sources are to be recommended by the Economic Planning Commission.

Article 172   Annual budget of the Authority

The Secretary-General shall draft the proposed annual budget of the Authority and submit it to the Council. The Council shall consider the proposed annual budget and submit it to the Assembly, together with any recommendations thereon. The Assembly shall consider and approve the proposed annual budget in accordance with article 160, paragraph 2(h).

Article 173   Expenses of the Authority

1. The contributions referred to in article 171, subparagraph (a), shall be paid into a special account to meet the administrative expenses of the Authority until the Authority has sufficient funds from other sources to meet those expenses.

2. The administrative expenses of the Authority shall be a first call upon the funds of the Authority. Except for the assessed contributions referred to in article 171, subparagraph (a), the funds which remain after payment of administrative expenses may, *inter alia*:

(a) be shared in accordance with article 140 and article 160, paragraph 2(g);

(b) be used to provide the Enterprise with funds in accordance with article 170, paragraph 4;

(c) be used to compensate developing States in accordance with article 151, paragraph 10, and article 160, paragraph 2(l).

Article 174   Borrowing power of the Authority

1. The Authority shall have the power to borrow funds.

2. The Assembly shall prescribe the limits on the borrowing power of the Authority in the financial regulations adopted pursuant to article 160, paragraph 2(f).

3. The Council shall exercise the borrowing power of the Authority.

4. States Parties shall not be liable for the debts of the Authority.

Article 175   Annual audit

The records, books and accounts of the Authority, including its annual financial statements, shall be audited annually by an independent auditor appointed by the Assembly.

Subsection G   Legal status, privileges and immunities

Article 176   Legal status

The Authority shall have international legal personality and such legal capacity as may be necessary for the exercise of its functions and the fulfilment of its purposes.

Article 177   Privileges and immunities

To enable the Authority to exercise its functions, it shall enjoy in the territory of each State Party the privileges and immunities set forth in this subsection. The privileges and immunities relating to the Enterprise shall be those set forth in Annex IV, article 13.

Article 178   Immunity from legal process

The Authority, its property and assets, shall enjoy immunity from legal process except to the extent that the Authority expressly waives this immunity in a particular case.

Article 179   Immunity from search and any form of seizure

The property and assets of the Authority, wherever located and by whomsoever held, shall be immune from search, requisition, confiscation, expropriation or any other form of seizure by executive or legislative action.

Article 180   Exemption from restrictions, regulations, controls and moratoria

The property and assets of the Authority shall be exempt from restrictions, regulations, controls and moratoria of any nature.

Article 181   Archives and official communications of the Authority

1. The archives of the Authority, wherever located, shall be inviolable.

2. Proprietary data, industrial secrets or similar information and personnel records shall not be placed in archives which are open to public inspection.

3. With regard to its official communications, the Authority shall be accorded by each State Party treatment no less favourable than that accorded by that State to other international organizations.

Article 182   Privileges and immunities of certain persons connected with the Authority

Representatives of States Parties attending meetings of the Assembly, the Council or organs of the Assembly or the Council, and the Secretary-General and staff of the Authority, shall enjoy in the territory of each State Party:

(a) immunity from legal process with respect to acts performed by them in the exercise of their functions, except to the extent that the State which they represent or the Authority, as appropriate, expressly waives this immunity in a particular case;

(b) if they are not nationals of that State Party, the same exemptions from immigration restrictions, alien registration requirements and national service obligations, the same facilities as regards exchange restrictions and the same treatment in respect of travelling facilities as are accorded by that State to the representatives, officials and employees of comparable rank of other States Parties.

Article 183   Exemption from taxes and customs duties

1. Within the scope of its official activities, the Authority, its assets and property, its income, and its operations and transactions, authorized by this Convention, shall be exempt from all direct taxation and goods imported or exported for its official use shall be exempt from all customs duties. The Authority shall not claim exemption from taxes which are no more than charges for services rendered.

2. When purchases of goods or services of substantial value necessary for the official activities of the Authority are made by or on behalf of the Authority, and when the price of such goods or services includes taxes or duties, appropriate measures shall, to the extent practicable, be taken by States Parties to grant exemption from such taxes or duties or provide for their reimbursement. Goods imported or purchased under an exemption provided for in this article shall not be sold or otherwise disposed of in the territory of the State Party which granted the exemption, except under conditions agreed with that State Party.

3. No tax shall be levied by States Parties on or in respect of salaries and emoluments paid or any other form of payment made by the Authority to the Secretary-General and staff of the Authority, as well as experts performing missions for the Authority, who are not their nationals.

Subsection H   Suspension of the exercise of rights and privileges of members

Article 184   Suspension of the exercise of voting rights

A State Party which is in arrears in the payment of its financial contributions to the Authority shall have no vote if the amount of its arrears equals or exceeds the amount of the contributions due from it for the preceding two full years. The Assembly may, nevertheless, permit such a member to vote if it is satisfied that the failure to pay is due to conditions beyond the control of the member.

Article 185   Suspension of exercise of rights and privileges of membership

1. A State Party which has grossly and persistently violated the provisions of this Part may be suspended from the exercise of the rights and privileges of membership by the Assembly upon the recommendation of the Council.

2. No action may be taken under paragraph 1 until the Seabed Disputes Chamber has found that a State Party has grossly and persistently violated the provisions of this Part.

SECTION 5   SETTLEMENT OF DISPUTES AND ADVISORY OPINIONS

Article 186   Seabed Disputes Chamber of the International Tribunal for the Law of the Sea

The establishment of the Seabed Disputes Chamber and the manner in which it shall exercise its jurisdiction shall be governed by the provisions of this section, of Part XV and of Annex VI.

Article 187   **Jurisdiction of the Seabed Disputes Chamber**

The Seabed Disputes Chamber shall have jurisdiction under this Part and the Annexes relating thereto in disputes with respect to activities in the Area falling within the following categories:

(a) disputes between States Parties concerning the interpretation or application of this Part and the Annexes relating thereto;

(b) disputes between a State Party and the Authority concerning:

(i) acts or omissions of the Authority or of a State Party alleged to be in violation of this Part or the Annexes relating thereto or of rules, regulations and procedures of the Authority adopted in accordance therewith; or

(ii) acts of the Authority alleged to be in excess of jurisdiction or a misuse of power;

(c) disputes between parties to a contract, being States Parties, the Authority or the Enterprise, state enterprises and natural or juridical persons referred to in article 153, paragraph 2(b), concerning:

(i) the interpretation or application of a relevant contract or a plan of work; or

(ii) acts or omissions of a party to the contract relating to activities in the Area and directed to the other party or directly affecting its legitimate interests;

(d) disputes between the Authority and a prospective contractor who has been sponsored by a State as provided in article 153, paragraph 2(b), and has duly fulfilled the conditions referred to in Annex III, article 4, paragraph 6, and article 13, paragraph 2, concerning the refusal of a contract or a legal issue arising in the negotiation of the contract;

(e) disputes between the Authority and a State Party, a state enterprise or a natural or juridical person sponsored by a State Party as provided for in article 153, paragraph 2(b), where it is alleged that the Authority has incurred liability as provided in Annex III, article 22;

(f) any other disputes for which the jurisdiction of the Chamber is specifically provided in this Convention.

**Article 188   Submission of disputes to a special chamber of the
International Tribunal for the Law of the Sea or an
ad hoc chamber of the Seabed Disputes Chamber or to
binding commercial arbitration**

1. Disputes between States Parties referred to in article 187,
subparagraph (a), may be submitted:

(a) at the request of the parties to the dispute, to a special chamber of
the International Tribunal for the Law of the Sea to be formed in
accordance with Annex VI, articles 15 and 17; or

(b) at the request of any party to the dispute, to an ad hoc chamber of
the Seabed Disputes Chamber to be formed in accordance with Annex
VI, article 36.

2. (a) Disputes concerning the interpretation or application of a contract
referred to in article 187, subparagraph (c)(i), shall be submitted, at the
request of any party to the dispute, to binding commercial arbitration,
unless the parties otherwise agree. A commercial arbitral tribunal to
which the dispute is submitted shall have no jurisdiction to decide any
question of interpretation of this Convention. When the dispute also
involves a question of the interpretation of Part XI and the Annexes
relating thereto, with respect to activities in the Area, that question
shall be referred to the Seabed Disputes Chamber for a ruling.

(b) If, at the commencement of or in the course of such arbitration, the
arbitral tribunal determines, either at the request of any party to the
dispute or *proprio motu,* that its decision depends upon a ruling of the
Seabed Disputes Chamber, the arbitral tribunal shall refer such
question to the Seabed Disputes Chamber for such ruling. The arbitral
tribunal shall then proceed to render its award in conformity with the
ruling of the Seabed Disputes Chamber.

(c) In the absence of a provision in the contract on the arbitration
procedure to be applied in the dispute, the arbitration shall be
conducted in accordance with the UNCITRAL Arbitration Rules or
such other arbitration rules as may be prescribed in the rules,
regulations and procedures of the Authority, unless the parties to the
dispute otherwise agree.

Article 189   Limitation on jurisdiction with regard to decisions of the Authority

The Seabed Disputes Chamber shall have no jurisdiction with regard to the exercise by the Authority of its discretionary powers in accordance with this Part; in no case shall it substitute its discretion for that of the Authority. Without prejudice to article 191, in exercising its jurisdiction pursuant to article 187, the Seabed Disputes Chamber shall not pronounce itself on the question of whether any rules, regulations and procedures of the Authority are in conformity with this Convention, nor declare invalid any such rules, regulations and procedures. Its jurisdiction in this regard shall be confined to deciding claims that the application of any rules, regulations and procedures of the Authority in individual cases would be in conflict with the contractual obligations of the parties to the dispute or their obligations under this Convention, claims concerning excess of jurisdiction or misuse of power, and to claims for damages to be paid or other remedy to be given to the party concerned for the failure of the other party to comply with its contractual obligations or its obligations under this Convention.

Article 190   Participation and appearance of sponsoring States Parties in proceedings

1. If a natural or juridical person is a party to a dispute referred to in article 187, the sponsoring State shall be given notice thereof and shall have the right to participate in the proceedings by submitting written or oral statements.

2. If an action is brought against a State Party by a natural or juridical person sponsored by another State Party in a dispute referred to in article 187, subparagraph (c), the respondent State may request the State sponsoring that person to appear in the proceedings on behalf of that person. Failing such appearance, the respondent State may arrange to be represented by a juridical person of its nationality.

Article 191   Advisory opinions

The Seabed Disputes Chamber shall give advisory opinions at the request of the Assembly or the Council on legal questions arising within the scope of their activities. Such opinions shall be given as a matter of urgency.

PART XII   PROTECTION AND PRESERVATION OF THE MARINE ENVIRONMENT

SECTION 1   GENERAL PROVISIONS

Article 192   General obligation

States have the obligation to protect and preserve the marine environment.

Article 193   Sovereign right of States to exploit their natural resources

States have the sovereign right to exploit their natural resources pursuant to their environmental policies and in accordance with their duty to protect and preserve the marine environment.

Article 194   Measures to prevent, reduce and control pollution of the marine environment

1. States shall take, individually or jointly as appropriate, all measures consistent with this Convention that are necessary to prevent, reduce and control pollution of the marine environment from any source, using for this purpose the best practicable means at their disposal and in accordance with their capabilities, and they shall endeavour to harmonize their policies in this connection.

2. States shall take all measures necessary to ensure that activities under their jurisdiction or control are so conducted as not to cause damage by pollution to other States and their environment, and that pollution arising from incidents or activities under their jurisdiction or control does not spread beyond the areas where they exercise sovereign rights in accordance with this Convention.

3. The measures taken pursuant to this Part shall deal with all sources of pollution of the marine environment. These measures shall include, *inter alia*, those designed to minimize to the fullest possible extent:

(a) the release of toxic, harmful or noxious substances, especially those which are persistent, from land-based sources, from or through the atmosphere or by dumping;

(b) pollution from vessels, in particular measures for preventing accidents and dealing with emergencies, ensuring the safety of operations at sea, preventing intentional and unintentional discharges, and regulating the design, construction, equipment, operation and manning of vessels;

(c) pollution from installations and devices used in exploration or exploitation of the natural resources of the seabed and subsoil, in particular measures for preventing accidents and dealing with emergencies, ensuring the safety of operations at sea, and regulating the design, construction, equipment, operation and manning of such installations or devices;

(d) pollution from other installations and devices operating in the marine environment, in particular measures for preventing accidents and dealing with emergencies, ensuring the safety of operations at sea, and regulating the design, construction, equipment, operation and manning of such installations or devices.

4. In taking measures to prevent, reduce or control pollution of the marine environment, States shall refrain from unjustifiable interference with activities carried out by other States in the exercise of their rights and in pursuance of their duties in conformity with this Convention.

5. The measures taken in accordance with this Part shall include those necessary to protect and preserve rare or fragile ecosystems as well as the habitat of depleted, threatened or endangered species and other forms of marine life.

Article 195   Duty not to transfer damage or hazards or transform one type of pollution into another

In taking measures to prevent, reduce and control pollution of the marine environment, States shall act so as not to transfer, directly or indirectly, damage or hazards from one area to another or transform one type of pollution into another.

Article 196   Use of technologies or introduction of alien or new species

1. States shall take all measures necessary to prevent, reduce and control pollution of the marine environment resulting from the use of technologies under their jurisdiction or control, or the intentional or accidental introduction of species, alien or new, to a particular part of the marine environment, which may cause significant and harmful changes thereto.

2. This article does not affect the application of this Convention regarding the prevention, reduction and control of pollution of the marine environment.

SECTION 2   GLOBAL AND REGIONAL COOPERATION

Article 197   Cooperation on a global or regional basis

States shall cooperate on a global basis and, as appropriate, on a regional basis, directly or through competent international organizations, in formulating and elaborating international rules, standards and recommended practices and procedures consistent with this Convention, for the protection and preservation of the marine environment, taking into account characteristic regional features.

Article 198   Notification of imminent or actual damage

When a State becomes aware of cases in which the marine environment is in imminent danger of being damaged or has been damaged by pollution, it shall immediately notify other States it deems likely to be affected by such damage, as well as the competent international organizations.

Article 199   Contingency plans against pollution

In the cases referred to in article 198, States in the area affected, in accordance with their capabilities, and the competent international organizations shall cooperate, to the extent possible, in eliminating the effects of pollution and preventing or minimizing the damage. To this end, States shall jointly develop and promote contingency plans for responding to pollution incidents in the marine environment.

Article 200 **Studies, research programmes and exchange of information and data**

States shall cooperate, directly or through competent international organizations, for the purpose of promoting studies, undertaking programmes of scientific research and encouraging the exchange of information and data acquired about pollution of the marine environment. They shall endeavour to participate actively in regional and global programmes to acquire knowledge for the assessment of the nature and extent of pollution, exposure to it, and its pathways, risks and remedies.

Article 201 **Scientific criteria for regulations**

In the light of the information and data acquired pursuant to article 200, States shall cooperate, directly or through competent international organizations, in establishing appropriate scientific criteria for the formulation and elaboration of rules, standards and recommended practices and procedures for the prevention, reduction and control of pollution of the marine environment.

SECTION 3 **TECHNICAL ASSISTANCE**

Article 202 **Scientific and technical assistance to developing States**

States shall, directly or through competent international organizations:

(a) promote programmes of scientific, educational, technical and other assistance to developing States for the protection and preservation of the marine environment and the prevention, reduction and control of marine pollution. Such assistance shall include, *inter alia*:

(i) training of their scientific and technical personnel;

(ii) facilitating their participation in relevant international programmes;

(iii) supplying them with necessary equipment and facilities;

(iv) enhancing their capacity to manufacture such equipment;

(v) advice on and developing facilities for research, monitoring, educational and other programmes;

(b) provide appropriate assistance, especially to developing States, for the minimization of the effects of major incidents which may cause serious pollution of the marine environment;

(c) provide appropriate assistance, especially to developing States, concerning the preparation of environmental assessments.

Article 203   Preferential treatment for developing States

Developing States shall, for the purposes of prevention, reduction and control of pollution of the marine environment or minimization of its effects, be granted preference by international organizations in:

(a) the allocation of appropriate funds and technical assistance; and

(b) the utilization of their specialized services.

SECTION 4   MONITORING AND ENVIRONMENTAL ASSESSMENT

Article 204   Monitoring of the risks or effects of pollution

1. States shall, consistent with the rights of other States, endeavour, as far as practicable, directly or through the competent international organizations, to observe, measure, evaluate and analyse, by recognized scientific methods, the risks or effects of pollution of the marine environment.

2. In particular, States shall keep under surveillance the effects of any activities which they permit or in which they engage in order to determine whether these activities are likely to pollute the marine environment.

Article 205   Publication of reports

States shall publish reports of the results obtained pursuant to article 204 or provide such reports at appropriate intervals to the competent international organizations, which should make them available to all States.

Article 206   Assessment of potential effects of activities

When States have reasonable grounds for believing that planned activities under their jurisdiction or control may cause substantial pollution of or significant and harmful changes to the marine environment, they shall, as far as practicable, assess the potential effects of such activities on the marine environment and shall communicate reports of the results of such assessments in the manner provided in article 205.

SECTION 5   INTERNATIONAL RULES AND NATIONAL LEGISLATION TO PREVENT, REDUCE AND CONTROL POLLUTION OF THE MARINE ENVIRONMENT

Article 207   Pollution from land-based sources

1. States shall adopt laws and regulations to prevent, reduce and control pollution of the marine environment from land-based sources, including rivers, estuaries, pipelines and outfall structures, taking into account internationally agreed rules, standards and recommended practices and procedures.

2. States shall take other measures as may be necessary to prevent, reduce and control such pollution.

3. States shall endeavour to harmonize their policies in this connection at the appropriate regional level.

4. States, acting especially through competent international organizations or diplomatic conference, shall endeavour to establish global and regional rules, standards and recommended practices and procedures to prevent, reduce and control pollution of the marine environment from land-based sources, taking into account characteristic regional features, the economic capacity of developing States and their need for economic development. Such rules, standards and recommended practices and procedures shall be re-examined from time to time as necessary.

5. Laws, regulations, measures, rules, standards and recommended practices and procedures referred to in paragraphs 1, 2 and 4 shall include those designed to minimize, to the fullest extent possible, the release of toxic, harmful or noxious substances, especially those which are persistent, into the marine environment.

Article 208   Pollution from seabed activities subject to national jurisdiction

1 Coastal States shall adopt laws and regulations to prevent, reduce and control pollution of the marine environment arising from or in connection with seabed activities subject to their jurisdiction and from artificial islands, installations and structures under their jurisdiction, pursuant to articles 60 and 80.

2. States shall take other measures as may be necessary to prevent, reduce and control such pollution.

3. Such laws, regulations and measures shall be no less effective than international rules, standards and recommended practices and procedures.

4. States shall endeavour to harmonize their policies in this connection at the appropriate regional level.

5. States, acting especially through competent international organizations or diplomatic conference, shall establish global and regional rules, standards and recommended practices and procedures to prevent, reduce and control pollution of the marine environment referred to in paragraph 1. Such rules, standards and recommended practices and procedures shall be re-examined from time to time as necessary.

Article 209   Pollution from activities in the Area

1. International rules, regulations and procedures shall be established in accordance with Part XI to prevent, reduce and control pollution of the marine environment from activities in the Area. Such rules, regulations and procedures shall be re-examined from time to time as necessary.

2. Subject to the relevant provisions of this section, States shall adopt laws and regulations to prevent, reduce and control pollution of the marine environment from activities in the Area undertaken by vessels, installations, structures and other devices flying their flag or of their registry or operating under their authority, as the case may be. The requirements of such laws and regulations shall be no less effective than the international rules, regulations and procedures referred to in paragraph 1.

Article 210   Pollution from dumping

1. States shall adopt laws and regulations to prevent, reduce and control pollution of the marine environment by dumping.

2. States shall take other measures as may be necessary to prevent, reduce and control such pollution.

3. Such laws, regulations and measures shall ensure that dumping is not carried out without the permission of the competent authorities of States.

4. States, acting especially through competent international organizations or diplomatic conference, shall endeavour to establish global and regional rules, standards and recommended practices and procedures to prevent, reduce and control such pollution. Such rules, standards and recommended practices and procedures shall be re-examined from time to time as necessary.

5. Dumping within the territorial sea and the exclusive economic zone or onto the continental shelf shall not be carried out without the express prior approval of the coastal State, which has the right to permit, regulate and control such dumping after due consideration of the matter with other States which by reason of their geographical situation may be adversely affected thereby.

6. National laws, regulations and measures shall be no less effective in preventing, reducing and controlling such pollution than the global rules and standards.

Article 211   Pollution from vessels

1. States, acting through the competent international organization or general diplomatic conference, shall establish international rules and standards to prevent, reduce and control pollution of the marine environment from vessels and promote the adoption, in the same manner, wherever appropriate, of routeing systems designed to minimize the threat of accidents which might cause pollution of the marine environment, including the coastline, and pollution damage to the related interests of coastal States. Such rules and standards shall, in the same manner, be re-examined from time to time as necessary.

2. States shall adopt laws and regulations for the prevention, reduction and control of pollution of the marine environment from vessels flying their flag or of their registry. Such laws and regulations shall at least have the same effect as that of generally accepted international rules and standards established through the competent international organization or general diplomatic conference.

3. States which establish particular requirements for the prevention, reduction and control of pollution of the marine environment as a condition for the entry of foreign vessels into their ports or internal waters or for a call at their off-shore terminals shall give due publicity to such requirements and shall communicate them to the competent international organization. Whenever such requirements are established in identical form by two or more coastal States in an endeavour to harmonize policy, the communication shall indicate which States are participating in such cooperative arrangements. Every State shall require the master of a vessel flying its flag or of its registry, when navigating within the territorial sea of a State participating in such cooperative arrangements, to furnish, upon the request of that State, information as to whether it is proceeding to a State of the same region participating in such cooperative arrangements and, if so, to indicate whether it complies with the port entry requirements of that State. This article is without prejudice to the continued exercise by a vessel of its right of innocent passage or to the application of article 25, paragraph 2.

4. Coastal States may, in the exercise of their sovereignty within their territorial sea, adopt laws and regulations for the prevention, reduction and control of marine pollution from foreign vessels, including vessels exercising the right of innocent passage. Such laws and regulations shall, in accordance with Part II, section 3, not hamper innocent passage of foreign vessels.

5. Coastal States, for the purpose of enforcement as provided for in section 6, may in respect of their exclusive economic zones adopt laws and regulations for the prevention, reduction and control of pollution from vessels conforming to and giving effect to generally accepted international rules and standards established through the competent international organization or general diplomatic conference.

6. (a) Where the international rules and standards referred to in paragraph 1 are inadequate to meet special circumstances and coastal States have reasonable grounds for believing that a particular, clearly defined area of their respective exclusive economic zones is an area where the adoption of special mandatory measures for the prevention

of pollution from vessels is required for recognized technical reasons in relation to its oceanographical and ecological conditions, as well as its utilization or the protection of its resources and the particular character of its traffic, the coastal States, after appropriate consultations through the competent international organization with any other States concerned, may, for that area, direct a communication to that organization, submitting scientific and technical evidence in support and information on necessary reception facilities. Within 12 months after receiving such a communication, the organization shall determine whether the conditions in that area correspond to the requirements set out above. If the organization so determines, the coastal States may, for that area, adopt laws and regulations for the prevention, reduction and control of pollution from vessels implementing such international rules and standards or navigational practices as are made applicable, through the organization, for special areas. These laws and regulations shall not become applicable to foreign vessels until 15 months after the submission of the communication to the organization.

(b) The coastal States shall publish the limits of any such particular, clearly defined area.

(c) If the coastal States intend to adopt additional laws and regulations for the same area for the prevention, reduction and control of pollution from vessels, they shall, when submitting the aforesaid communication, at the same time notify the organization thereof. Such additional laws and regulations may relate to discharges or navigational practices but shall not require foreign vessels to observe design, construction, manning or equipment standards other than generally accepted international rules and standards; they shall become applicable to foreign vessels 15 months after the submission of the communication to the organization, provided that the organization agrees within 12 months after the submission of the communication.

7. The international rules and standards referred to in this article should include *inter alia* those relating to prompt notification to coastal States, whose coastline or related interests may be affected by incidents, including maritime casualties, which involve discharges or probability of discharges.

Article 212   Pollution from or through the atmosphere

1. States shall adopt laws and regulations to prevent, reduce and control pollution of the marine environment from or through the atmosphere, applicable to the air space under their sovereignty and to vessels flying their flag or vessels or aircraft of their registry, taking into account internationally agreed rules, standards and recommended practices and procedures and the safety of air navigation.

2. States shall take other measures as may be necessary to prevent, reduce and control such pollution.

3. States, acting especially through competent international organizations or diplomatic conference, shall endeavour to establish global and regional rules, standards and recommended practices and procedures to prevent, reduce and control such pollution.

SECTION 6   ENFORCEMENT

Article 123   Enforcement with respect to pollution from land-based sources

States shall enforce their laws and regulations adopted in accordance with article 207 and shall adopt laws and regulations and take other measures necessary to implement applicable international rules and standards established through competent international organizations or diplomatic conference to prevent, reduce and control pollution of the marine environment from land-based sources.

Article 214   Enforcement with respect to pollution from seabed activities

States shall enforce their laws and regulations adopted in accordance with article 208 and shall adopt laws and regulations and take other measures necessary to implement applicable international rules and standards established through competent international organizations or diplomatic conference to prevent, reduce and control pollution of the marine environment arising from or in connection with seabed activities subject to their jurisdiction and from artificial islands, installations and structures under their jurisdiction, pursuant to articles 60 and 80.

Article 215   Enforcement with respect to pollution from activities in the Area

Enforcement of international rules, regulations and procedures established in accordance with Part XI to prevent, reduce and control pollution of the marine environment from activities in the Area shall be governed by that Part.

Article 216   Enforcement with respect to pollution by dumping

1. Laws and regulations adopted in accordance with this Convention and applicable international rules and standards established through competent international organizations or diplomatic conference for the prevention, reduction and control of pollution of the marine environment by dumping shall be enforced:

(a) by the coastal State with regard to dumping within its territorial sea or its exclusive economic zone or onto its continental shelf;

(b) by the flag State with regard to vessels flying its flag or vessels or aircraft of its registry;

(c) by any State with regard to acts of loading of wastes or other matter occurring within its territory or at its off-shore terminals.

2. No State shall be obliged by virtue of this article to institute proceedings when another State has already instituted proceedings in accordance with this article.

Article 217   Enforcement by flag States

1. States shall ensure compliance by vessels flying their flag or of their registry with applicable international rules and standards, established through the competent international organization or general diplomatic conference, and with their laws and regulations adopted in accordance with this Convention for the prevention, reduction and control of pollution of the marine environment from vessels and shall accordingly adopt laws and regulations and take other measures necessary for their implementation. Flag States shall provide for the effective enforcement of such rules, standards, laws and regulations, irrespective of where a violation occurs.

2. States shall, in particular, take appropriate measures in order to ensure that vessels flying their flag or of their registry are prohibited from sailing, until they can proceed to sea in compliance with the requirements of the international rules and standards referred to in paragraph 1, including requirements in respect of design, construction, equipment and manning of vessels.

3. States shall ensure that vessels flying their flag or of their registry carry on board certificates required by and issued pursuant to international rules and standards referred to in paragraph 1. States shall ensure that vessels flying their flag are periodically inspected in order to verify that such certificates are in conformity with the actual condition of the vessels. These certificates shall be accepted by other States as evidence of the condition of the vessels and shall be regarded as having the same force as certificates issued by them, unless there are clear grounds for believing that the condition of the vessel does not correspond substantially with the particulars of the certificates.

4. If a vessel commits a violation of rules and standards established through the competent international organization or general diplomatic conference, the flag State, without prejudice to articles 218, 220 and 228, shall provide for immediate investigation and where appropriate institute proceedings in respect of the alleged violation irrespective of where the violation occurred or where the pollution caused by such violation has occurred or has been spotted.

5. Flag States conducting an investigation of the violation may request the assistance of any other State whose cooperation could be useful in clarifying the circumstances of the case. States shall endeavour to meet appropriate requests of flag States.

6. States shall, at the written request of any State, investigate any violation alleged to have been committed by vessels flying their flag. If satisfied that sufficient evidence is available to enable proceedings to be brought in respect of the alleged violation, flag States shall without delay institute such proceedings in accordance with their laws.

7. Flag States shall promptly inform the requesting State and the competent international organization of the action taken and its outcome. Such information shall be available to all States.

8. Penalties provided for by the laws and regulations of States for vessels flying their flag shall be adequate in severity to discourage violations wherever they occur.

Article 218   Enforcement by port States

1. When a vessel is voluntarily within a port or at an off-shore terminal of a State, that State may undertake investigations and, where the evidence so warrants, institute proceedings in respect of any discharge from that vessel outside the internal waters, territorial sea or exclusive economic zone of that State in violation of applicable international rules and standards established through the competent international organization or general diplomatic conference.

2. No proceedings pursuant to paragraph 1 shall be instituted in respect of a discharge violation in the internal waters, territorial sea or exclusive economic zone of another State unless requested by that State, the flag State, or a State damaged or threatened by the discharge violation, or unless the violation has caused or is likely to cause pollution in the internal waters, territorial sea or exclusive economic zone of the State instituting the proceedings.

3. When a vessel is voluntarily within a port or at an off-shore terminal of a State, that State shall, as far as practicable, comply with requests from any State for investigation of a discharge violation referred to in paragraph 1, believed to have occurred in, caused, or threatened damage to the internal waters, territorial sea or exclusive economic zone of the requesting State. It shall likewise, as far as practicable, comply with requests from the flag State for investigation of such a violation, irrespective of where the violation occurred.

4. The records of the investigation carried out by a port State pursuant to this article shall be transmitted upon request to the flag State or to the coastal State. Any proceedings instituted by the port State on the basis of such an investigation may, subject to section 7, be suspended at the request of the coastal State when the violation has occurred within its internal waters, territorial sea or exclusive economic zone. The evidence and records of the case, together with any bond or other financial security posted with the authorities of the port State, shall in that event be transmitted to the coastal State. Such transmittal shall preclude the continuation of proceedings in the port State.

Article 219   Measures relating to seaworthiness of vessels to avoid pollution

Subject to section 7, States which, upon request or on their own initiative, have ascertained that a vessel within one of their ports or at one of their off-shore terminals is in violation of applicable international rules and standards relating to seaworthiness of vessels and thereby threatens damage to the marine environment shall, as far as practicable, take administrative measures to prevent the vessel from sailing. Such States may permit the vessel to proceed only to the nearest appropriate repair yard and, upon removal of the causes of the violation, shall permit the vessel to continue immediately.

Article 220   Enforcement by coastal States

1. When a vessel is voluntarily within a port or at an off-shore terminal of a State, that State may, subject to section 7, institute proceedings in respect of any violation of its laws and regulations adopted in accordance with this Convention or applicable international rules and standards for the prevention, reduction and control of pollution from vessels when the violation has occurred within the territorial sea or the exclusive economic zone of that State.

2. Where there are clear grounds for believing that a vessel navigating in the territorial sea of a State has, during its passage therein, violated laws and regulations of that State adopted in accordance with this Convention or applicable international rules and standards for the prevention, reduction and control of pollution from vessels, that State, without prejudice to the application of the relevant provisions of Part II, section 3, may undertake physical inspection of the vessel relating to the violation and may, where the evidence so warrants, institute proceedings, including detention of the vessel, in accordance with its laws, subject to the provisions of section 7.

3. Where there are clear grounds for believing that a vessel navigating in the exclusive economic zone or the territorial sea of a State has, in the exclusive economic zone, committed a violation of applicable international rules and standards for the prevention, reduction and control of pollution from vessels or laws and regulations of that State conforming and giving effect to such rules and standards, that State may require the vessel to give information regarding its identity and port of registry, its last and its next port of call and other relevant information required to establish whether a violation has occurred.

4. States shall adopt laws and regulations and take other measures so that vessels flying their flag comply with requests for information pursuant to paragraph 3.

5. Where there are clear grounds for believing that a vessel navigating in the exclusive economic zone or the territorial sea of a State has, in the exclusive economic zone, committed a violation referred to in paragraph 3 resulting in a substantial discharge causing or threatening significant pollution of the marine environment, that State may undertake physical inspection of the vessel for matters relating to the violation if the vessel has refused to give information or if the information supplied by the vessel is manifestly at variance with the evident factual situation and if the circumstances of the case justify such inspection.

6. Where there is clear objective evidence that a vessel navigating in the exclusive economic zone or the territorial sea of a State has, in the exclusive economic zone, committed a violation referred to in paragraph 3 resulting in a discharge causing major damage or threat of major damage to the coastline or related interests of the coastal State, or to any resources of its territorial sea or exclusive economic zone, that State may, subject to section 7, provided that the evidence so warrants, institute proceedings, including detention of the vessel, in accordance with its laws.

7. Notwithstanding the provisions of paragraph 6, whenever appropriate procedures have been established, either through the competent international organization or as otherwise agreed, whereby compliance with requirements for bonding or other appropriate financial security has been assured, the coastal State if bound by such procedures shall allow the vessel to proceed.

8. The provisions of paragraphs 3, 4, 5, 6and 7 also apply in respect of national laws and regulations adopted pursuant to article 211, paragraph 6.

Article 221   Measures to avoid pollution arising from maritime casualties

1. Nothing in this Part shall prejudice the right of States, pursuant to international law, both customary and conventional, to take and enforce measures beyond the territorial sea proportionate to the actual or threatened damage to protect their coastline or related interests, including fishing, from pollution or threat of pollution following upon a maritime casualty or acts relating to such a casualty, which may reasonably be expected to result in major harmful consequences.

2. For the purposes of this article, "maritime casualty" means a collision of vessels, stranding or other incident of navigation, or other occurrence on board a vessel or external to it resulting in material damage or imminent threat of material damage to a vessel or cargo.

Article 222   Enforcement with respect to pollution from or through the atmosphere

States shall enforce, within the air space under their sovereignty or with regard to vessels flying their flag or vessels or aircraft of their registry, their laws and regulations adopted in accordance with article 212, paragraph 1, and with other provisions of this Convention and shall adopt laws and regulations and take other measures necessary to implement applicable international rules and standards established through competent international organizations or diplomatic conference to prevent, reduce and control pollution of the marine environment from or through the atmosphere, in conformity with all relevant international rules and standards concerning the safety of air navigation.

SECTION 7   SAFEGUARDS

Article 223   Measures to facilitate proceedings

In proceedings instituted pursuant to this Part, States shall take measures to facilitate the hearing of witnesses and the admission of evidence submitted by authorities of another State, or by the competent international organization, and shall facilitate the attendance at such proceedings of official representatives of the competent international organization, the flag State and any State affected by pollution arising out of any violation. The official representatives attending such proceedings shall have such rights and duties as may be provided under national laws and regulations or international law.

Article 224   Exercise of powers of enforcement

The powers of enforcement against foreign vessels under this Part may only be exercised by officials or by warships, military aircraft, or other ships or aircraft clearly marked and identifiable as being on government service and authorized to that effect.

Article 225   Duty to avoid adverse consequences in the exercise of the powers of enforcement

In the exercise under this Convention of their powers of enforcement against foreign vessels, States shall not endanger the safety of navigation or otherwise create any hazard to a vessel, or bring it to an unsafe port or anchorage, or expose the marine environment to an unreasonable risk.

Article 226   Investigation of foreign vessels

1. (a) States shall not delay a foreign vessel longer than is essential for purposes of the investigations provided for in articles 216, 218 and 220. Any physical inspection of a foreign vessel shall be limited to an examination of such certificates, records or other documents as the vessel is required to carry by generally accepted international rules and standards or of any similar documents which it is carrying; further physical inspection of the vessel may be undertaken only after such an examination and only when:

   (i) there are clear grounds for believing that the condition of the vessel or its equipment does not correspond substantially with the particulars of those documents;

   (ii) the contents of such documents are not sufficient to confirm or verify a suspected violation; or

   (iii) the vessel is not carrying valid certificates and records.

   (b) If the investigation indicates a violation of applicable laws and regulations or international rules and standards for the protection and preservation of the marine environment, release shall be made promptly subject to reasonable procedures such as bonding or other appropriate financial security.

   (c) Without prejudice to applicable international rules and standards relating to the seaworthiness of vessels, the release of a vessel may, whenever it would present an unreasonable threat of damage to the marine environment, be refused or made conditional upon proceeding to the nearest appropriate repair yard. Where release has been refused or made conditional, the flag State of the vessel must be promptly notified, and may seek release of the vessel in accordance with Part XV.

2. States shall cooperate to develop procedures for the avoidance of unnecessary physical inspection of vessels at sea.

Article 227   Non-discrimination with respect to foreign vessels

In exercising their rights and performing their duties under this Part, States shall not discriminate in form or in fact against vessels of any other State.

Article 228   Suspension and restrictions on institution of proceedings

1. Proceedings to impose penalties in respect of any violation of applicable laws and regulations or international rules and standards relating to the prevention, reduction and control of pollution from vessels committed by a foreign vessel beyond the territorial sea of the State instituting proceedings shall be suspended upon the taking of proceedings to impose penalties in respect of corresponding charges by the flag State within six months of the date on which proceedings were first instituted, unless those proceedings relate to a case of major damage to the coastal State or the flag State in question has repeatedly disregarded its obligation to enforce effectively the applicable international rules and standards in respect of violations committed by its vessels. The flag State shall in due course make available to the State previously instituting proceedings a full dossier of the case and the records of the proceedings, whenever the flag State has requested the suspension of proceedings in accordance with this article. When proceedings instituted by the flag State have been brought to a conclusion, the suspended proceedings shall be terminated. Upon payment of costs incurred in respect of such proceedings, any bond posted or other financial security provided in connection with the suspended proceedings shall be released by the coastal State.

2. Proceedings to impose penalties on foreign vessels shall not be instituted after the expiry of three years from the date on which the violation was committed, and shall not be taken by any State in the event of proceedings having been instituted by another State subject to the provisions set out in paragraph 1.

3. The provisions of this article are without prejudice to the right of the flag State to take any measures, including proceedings to impose penalties, according to its laws irrespective of prior proceedings by another State.

Article 229   Institution of civil proceedings

Nothing in this Convention affects the institution of civil proceedings in respect of any claim for loss or damage resulting from pollution of the marine environment.

Article 230   Monetary penalties and the observance of recognized rights of the accused

1. Monetary penalties only may be imposed with respect to violations of national laws and regulations or applicable international rules and standards for the prevention, reduction and control of pollution of the marine environment, committed by foreign vessels beyond the territorial sea.

2. Monetary penalties only may be imposed with respect to violations of national laws and regulations or applicable international rules and standards for the prevention, reduction and control of pollution of the marine environment, committed by foreign vessels in the territorial sea, except in the case of a wilful and serious act of pollution in the territorial sea.

3. In the conduct of proceedings in respect of such violations committed by a foreign vessel which may result in the imposition of penalties, recognized rights of the accused shall be observed.

Article 231   Notification to the flag State and other States concerned

States shall promptly notify the flag State and any other State concerned of any measures taken pursuant to section 6 against foreign vessels, and shall submit to the flag State all official reports concerning such measures. However, with respect to violations committed in the territorial sea, the foregoing obligations of the coastal State apply only to such measures as are taken in proceedings. The diplomatic agents or consular officers and where possible the maritime authority of the flag State, shall be immediately informed of any such measures taken pursuant to section 6 against foreign vessels.

Article 232   Liability of States arising from enforcement measures

States shall be liable for damage or loss attributable to them arising from measures taken pursuant to section 6 when such measures are unlawful or exceed those reasonably required in the light of available information. States shall provide for recourse in their courts for actions in respect of such damage or loss.

Article 233   Safeguards with respect to straits used for international navigation

Nothing in sections 5, 6 and 7 affects the legal regime of straits used for international navigation. However, if a foreign ship other than those referred to in section 10 has committed a violation of the laws and regulations referred to in article 42, paragraph 1(a) and (b), causing or threatening major damage to the marine environment of the straits, the States bordering the straits may take appropriate enforcement measures and if so shall respect *mutatis mutandis* the provisions of this section.

SECTION 8   ICE-COVERED AREAS

Article 234   Ice-covered areas

Coastal States have the right to adopt and enforce non-discriminatory laws and regulations for the prevention, reduction and control of marine pollution from vessels in ice-covered areas within the limits of the exclusive economic zone, where particularly severe climatic conditions and the presence of ice covering such areas for most of the year create obstructions or exceptional hazards to navigation, and pollution of the marine environment could cause major harm to or irreversible disturbance of the ecological balance. Such laws and regulations shall have due regard to navigation and the protection and preservation of the marine environment based on the best available scientific evidence.

SECTION 9   RESPONSIBILITY AND LIABILITY

Article 235   Responsibility and liability

1. States are responsible for the fulfilment of their international obligations concerning the protection and preservation of the marine environment. They shall be liable in accordance with international law.

2. States shall ensure that recourse is available in accordance with their legal systems for prompt and adequate compensation or other relief in respect of damage caused by pollution of the marine environment by natural or juridical persons under their jurisdiction.

3. With the objective of assuring prompt and adequate compensation in respect of all damage caused by pollution of the marine environment, States shall cooperate in the implementation of existing international law and the further development of international law relating to responsibility and liability for the assessment of and compensation for damage and the settlement of related disputes, as well as, where appropriate, development of criteria and procedures for payment of adequate compensation, such as compulsory insurance or compensation funds.

SECTION 10   SOVEREIGN IMMUNITY

Article 236   Sovereign immunity

The provisions of this Convention regarding the protection and preservation of the marine environment do not apply to any warship, naval auxiliary, other vessels or aircraft owned or operated by a State and used, for the time being, only on government non-commercial service. However, each State shall ensure, by the adoption of appropriate measures not impairing operations or operational capabilities of such vessels or aircraft owned or operated by it, that such vessels or aircraft act in a manner consistent, so far as is reasonable and practicable, with this Convention.

SECTION 11   OBLIGATIONS UNDER OTHER CONVENTIONS ON THE PROTECTION AND PRESERVATION OF THE MARINE ENVIRONMENT

Article 237   Obligations under other conventions on the protection and preservation of the marine environment

1. The provisions of this Part are without prejudice to the specific obligations assumed by States under special conventions and agreements concluded previously which relate to the protection and preservation of the marine environment and to agreements which may be concluded in furtherance of the general principles set forth in this Convention.

2. Specific obligations assumed by States under special conventions, with respect to the protection and preservation of the marine environment, should be carried out in a manner consistent with the general principles and objectives of this Convention.

PART XIII   MARINE SCIENTIFIC RESEARCH

SECTION 1   GENERAL PROVISIONS

Article 238   Right to conduct marine scientific research

All States, irrespective of their geographical location, and competent international organizations have the right to conduct marine scientific research subject to the rights and duties of other States as provided for in this Convention.

Article 239   Promotion of marine scientific research

States and competent international organizations shall promote and facilitate the development and conduct of marine scientific research in accordance with this Convention.

Article 240   General principles for the conduct of marine scientific research

In the conduct of marine scientific research the following principles shall apply:

(a) marine scientific research shall be conducted exclusively for peaceful purposes;

(b) marine scientific research shall be conducted with appropriate scientific methods and means compatible with this Convention;

(c) marine scientific research shall not unjustifiably interfere with other legitimate uses of the sea compatible with this Convention and shall be duly respected in the course of such uses;

(d) marine scientific research shall be conducted in compliance with all relevant regulations adopted in conformity with this Convention including those for the protection and preservation of the marine environment.

Article 241   Non-recognition of marine scientific research activities as the legal basis for claims

Marine scientific research activities shall not constitute the legal basis for any claim to any part of the marine environment or its resources.

SECTION 2   INTERNATIONAL COOPERATION

Article 242   Promotion of international cooperation

1. States and competent international organizations shall, in accordance with the principle of respect for sovereignty and jurisdiction and on the basis of mutual benefit, promote international cooperation in marine scientific research for peaceful purposes.

2. In this context, without prejudice to the rights and duties of States under this Convention, a State, in the application of this Part, shall provide, as appropriate, other States with a reasonable opportunity to obtain from it, or with its cooperation, information necessary to prevent and control damage to the health and safety of persons and to the marine environment.

Article 243   Creation of favourable conditions

States and competent international organizations shall cooperate, through the conclusion of bilateral and multilateral agreements, to create favourable conditions for the conduct of marine scientific research in the marine environment and to integrate the efforts of scientists in studying the essence of phenomena and processes occurring in the marine environment and the interrelations between them.

Article 244   Publication and dissemination of information and knowledge

1. States and competent international organizations shall, in accordance with this Convention, make available by publication and dissemination through appropriate channels information on proposed major programmes and their objectives as well as knowledge resulting from marine scientific research.

2. For this purpose, States, both individually and in cooperation with other States and with competent international organizations, shall actively promote the flow of scientific data and information and the transfer of knowledge resulting from marine scientific research, especially to developing States, as well as the strengthening of the autonomous marine scientific research capabilities of developing States through, *inter alia*, programmes to provide adequate education and training of their technical and scientific personnel.

SECTION 3   CONDUCT AND PROMOTION OF MARINE SCIENTIFIC RESEARCH

Article 245   Marine scientific research in the territorial sea

Coastal States, in the exercise of their sovereignty, have the exclusive right to regulate, authorize and conduct marine scientific research in their territorial sea. Marine scientific research therein shall be conducted only with the express consent of and under the conditions set forth by the coastal State.

Article 246   Marine scientific research in the exclusive economic zone and on the continental shelf

1. Coastal States, in the exercise of their jurisdiction, have the right to regulate, authorize and conduct marine scientific research in their exclusive economic zone and on their continental shelf in accordance with the relevant provisions of this Convention.

2. Marine scientific research in the exclusive economic zone and on the continental shelf shall be conducted with the consent of the coastal State.

3. Coastal States shall, in normal circumstances, grant their consent for marine scientific research projects by other States or competent international organizations in their exclusive economic zone or on their continental shelf to be carried out in accordance with this Convention exclusively for peaceful purposes and in order to increase scientific knowledge of the marine environment for the benefit of all mankind. To this end, coastal States shall establish rules and procedures ensuring that such consent will not be delayed or denied unreasonably.

4. For the purposes of applying paragraph 3, normal circumstances may exist in spite of the absence of diplomatic relations between the coastal State and the researching State.

5. Coastal States may however in their discretion withhold their consent to the conduct of a marine scientific research project of another State or competent international organization in the exclusive economic zone or on the continental shelf of the coastal State if that project:

(a) is of direct significance for the exploration and exploitation of natural resources, whether living or non-living;

(b) involves drilling into the continental shelf, the use of explosives or the introduction of harmful substances into the marine environment;

(c) involves the construction, operation or use of artificial islands, installations and structures referred to in articles 60 and 80;

(d) contains information communicated pursuant to article 248 regarding the nature and objectives of the project which is inaccurate or if the researching State or competent international organization has outstanding obligations to the coastal State from a prior research project.

6. Notwithstanding the provisions of paragraph 5, coastal States may not exercise their discretion to withhold consent under subparagraph (a) of that paragraph in respect of marine scientific research projects to be undertaken in accordance with the provisions of this Part on the continental shelf, beyond 200 nautical miles from the baselines from which the breadth of the territorial sea is measured, outside those specific areas which coastal States may at any time publicly designate as areas in which exploitation or detailed exploratory operations focused on those areas are occurring or will occur within a reasonable period of time. Coastal States shall give reasonable notice of the designation of such areas, as well as any modifications thereto, but shall not be obliged to give details of the operations therein.

7. The provisions of paragraph 6 are without prejudice to the rights of coastal States over the continental shelf as established in article 77.

8. Marine scientific research activities referred to in this article shall not unjustifiably interfere with activities undertaken by coastal States in the exercise of their sovereign rights and jurisdiction provided for in this Convention.

Article 247   Marine scientific research projects undertaken by or under the auspices of international organizations

A coastal State which is a member of or has a bilateral agreement with an international organization, and in whose exclusive economic zone or on whose continental shelf that organization wants to carry out a marine scientific research project, directly or under its auspices, shall be deemed to have authorized the project to be carried out in conformity with the agreed specifications if that State approved the detailed project when the decision was made by the organization for the undertaking of the project, or is willing to participate in it, and has not expressed any objection within four months of notification of the project by the organization to the coastal State.

Article 248   Duty to provide information to the coastal State

States and competent international organizations which intend to undertake marine scientific research in the exclusive economic zone or on the continental shelf of a coastal State shall, not less than six months in advance of the expected starting date of the marine scientific research project, provide that State with a full description of:

(a) the nature and objectives of the project;

(b) the method and means to be used, including name, tonnage, type and class of vessels and a description of scientific equipment;

(c) the precise geographical areas in which the project is to be conducted;

(d) the expected date of first appearance and final departure of the research vessels, or deployment of the equipment and its removal, as appropriate;

(e) the name of the sponsoring institution, its director, and the person in charge of the project; and

(f) the extent to which it is considered that the coastal State should be able to participate or to be represented in the project.

Article 249   Duty to comply with certain conditions

1. States and competent international organizations when undertaking marine scientific research in the exclusive economic zone or on the continental shelf of a coastal State shall comply with the following conditions:

(a) ensure the right of the coastal State, if it so desires, to participate or be represented in the marine scientific research project, especially on board research vessels and other craft or scientific research installations, when practicable, without payment of any remuneration to the scientists of the coastal State and without obligation to contribute towards the costs of the project;

(b) provide the coastal State, at its request, with preliminary reports, as soon as practicable, and with the final results and conclusions after the completion of the research;

(c) undertake to provide access for the coastal State, at its request, to all data and samples derived from the marine scientific research project and likewise to furnish it with data which may be copied and samples which may be divided without detriment to their scientific value;

(d) if requested, provide the coastal State with an assessment of such data, samples and research results or provide assistance in their assessment or interpretation;

(e) ensure, subject to paragraph 2, that the research results are made internationally available through appropriate national or international channels, as soon as practicable;

(f) inform the coastal State immediately of any major change in the research programme;

(g) unless otherwise agreed, remove the scientific research installations or equipment once the research is completed.

2. This article is without prejudice to the conditions established by the laws and regulations of the coastal State for the exercise of its discretion to grant or withhold consent pursuant to article 246, paragraph 5, including requiring prior agreement for making internationally available the research results of a project of direct significance for the exploration and exploitation of natural resources.

Article 250   Communications concerning marine scientific research projects

Communications concerning the marine scientific research projects shall be made through appropriate official channels, unless otherwise agreed.

Article 251   General criteria and guidelines

States shall seek to promote through competent international organizations the establishment of general criteria and guidelines to assist States in ascertaining the nature and implications of marine scientific research.

Article 252   Implied consent

States or competent international organizations may proceed with a marine scientific research project six months after the date upon which the information required pursuant to article 248 was provided to the coastal State unless within four months of the receipt of the communication containing such information the coastal State has informed the State or organization conducting the research that:

(a) it has withheld its consent under the provisions of article 246; or

(b) the information given by that State or competent international organization regarding the nature or objectives of the project does not conform to the manifestly evident facts; or

(c) it requires supplementary information relevant to conditions and the information provided for under articles 248 and 249; or

(d) outstanding obligations exist with respect to a previous marine scientific research project carried out by that State or organization, with regard to conditions established in article 249.

Article 253   Suspension or cessation of marine scientific research activities

1. A coastal State shall have the right to require the suspension of any marine scientific research activities in progress within its exclusive economic zone or on its continental shelf if:

(a) the research activities are not being conducted in accordance with the information communicated as provided under article 248 upon which the consent of the coastal State was based; or

(b) the State or competent international organization conducting the research activities fails to comply with the provisions of article 249 concerning the rights of the coastal State with respect to the marine scientific research project.

2. A coastal State shall have the right to require the cessation of any marine scientific research activities in case of any non-compliance with the provisions of article 248 which amounts to a major change in the research project or the research activities.

3. A coastal State may also require cessation of marine scientific research activities if any of the situations contemplated in paragraph 1 are not rectified within a reasonable period of time.

4. Following notification by the coastal State of its decision to order suspension or cessation, States or competent international organizations authorized to conduct marine scientific research activities shall terminate the research activities that are the subject of such a notification.

5. An order of suspension under paragraph 1 shall be lifted by the coastal State and the marine scientific research activities allowed to continue once the researching State or competent international organization has complied with the conditions required under articles 248 and 249.

Article 254   Rights of neighbouring land-locked and geographically disadvantaged States

1. States and competent international organizations which have submitted to a coastal State a project to undertake marine scientific research referred to in article 246, paragraph 3, shall give notice to the neighbouring land-locked and geographically disadvantaged States of the proposed research project, and shall notify the coastal State thereof.

2. After the consent has been given for the proposed marine scientific research project by the coastal State concerned, in accordance with article 246 and other relevant provisions of this Convention, States and competent international organizations undertaking such a project shall provide to the neighbouring land-locked and geographically disadvantaged States, at their request and when appropriate, relevant information as specified in article 248 and article 249, paragraph 1(f).

3. The neighbouring land-locked and geographically disadvantaged States referred to above shall, at their request, be given the opportunity to participate, whenever feasible, in the proposed marine scientific research project through qualified experts appointed by them and not objected to by the coastal State, in accordance with the conditions agreed for the project, in conformity with the provisions of this Convention, between the coastal State concerned and the State or competent international organizations conducting the marine scientific research.

4. States and competent international organizations referred to in paragraph 1 shall provide to the above-mentioned land-locked and geographically disadvantaged States, at their request, the information and assistance specified in article 249, paragraph 1(d), subject to the provisions of article 249, paragraph 2.

Article 255   Measures to facilitate marine scientific research and assist research vessels

States shall endeavour to adopt reasonable rules, regulations and procedures to promote and facilitate marine scientific research conducted in accordance with this Convention beyond their territorial sea and, as appropriate, to facilitate, subject to the provisions of their laws and regulations, access to their harbours and promote assistance for marine scientific research vessels which comply with the relevant provisions of this Part.

Article 256   Marine scientific research in the Area

All States, irrespective of their geographical location, and competent international organizations have the right, in conformity with the provisions of Part XI, to conduct marine scientific research in the Area.

Article 257   Marine scientific research in the water column beyond the exclusive economic zone

All States, irrespective of their geographical location, and competent international organizations have the right, in conformity with this Convention, to conduct marine scientific research in the water column beyond the limits of the exclusive economic zone.

SECTION 4   SCIENTIFIC RESEARCH INSTALLATIONS OR EQUIPMENT IN THE MARINE ENVIRONMENT

Article 258   Deployment and use

The deployment and use of any type of scientific research installations or equipment in any area of the marine environment shall be subject to the same conditions as are prescribed in this Convention for the conduct of marine scientific research in any such area.

Article 259   Legal status

The installations or equipment referred to in this section do not possess the status of islands. They have no territorial sea of their own, and their presence does not affect the delimitation of the territorial sea, the exclusive economic zone or the continental shelf.

Article 260   Safety zones

Safety zones of a reasonable breadth not exceeding a distance of 500 metres may be created around scientific research installations in accordance with the relevant provisions of this Convention. All States shall ensure that such safety zones are respected by their vessels.

Article 261   Non-interference with shipping routes

The deployment and use of any type of scientific research installations or equipment shall not constitute an obstacle to established international shipping routes.

Article 262   Identification markings and warning signals

Installations or equipment referred to in this section shall bear identification markings indicating the State of registry or the international organization to which they belong and shall have adequate internationally agreed warning signals to ensure safety at sea and the safety of air navigation, taking into account rules and standards established by competent international organizations.

SECTION 5   RESPONSIBILITY AND LIABILITY

Article 263   Responsibility and liability

1. States and competent international organizations shall be responsible for ensuring that marine scientific research, whether undertaken by them or on their behalf, is conducted in accordance with this Convention.

2. States and competent international organizations shall be responsible and liable for the measures they take in contravention of this Convention in respect of marine scientific research conducted by other States, their natural or juridical persons or by competent international organizations, and shall provide compensation for damage resulting from such measures.

3. States and competent international organizations shall be responsible and liable pursuant to article 235 for damage caused by pollution of the marine environment arising out of marine scientific research undertaken by them or on their behalf.

SECTION 6   SETTLEMENT OF DISPUTES AND INTERIM MEASURES

Article 264   Settlement of disputes

Disputes concerning the interpretation or application of the provisions of this Convention with regard to marine scientific research shall be settled in accordance with Part XV, sections 2 and 3.

Article 265   Interim measures

Pending settlement of a dispute in accordance with Part XV, sections 2 and 3, the State or competent international organization authorized to conduct a marine scientific research project shall not allow research activities to commence or continue without the express consent of the coastal State concerned.

PART XIV   DEVELOPMENT AND TRANSFER OF MARINE
                  TECHNOLOGY

SECTION 1   GENERAL PROVISIONS

Article 266   Promotion of the development and transfer of
                  marine technology

1. States, directly or through competent international organizations,
shall cooperate in accordance with their capabilities to promote actively
the development and transfer of marine science and marine technology
on fair and reasonable terms and conditions.

2. States shall promote the development of the marine scientific and
technological capacity of States which may need and request technical
assistance in this field, particularly developing States, including land-
locked and geographically disadvantaged States, with regard to the
exploration, exploitation, conservation and management of marine
resources, the protection and preservation of the marine environment,
marine scientific research and other activities in the marine environment
compatible with this Convention, with a view to accelerating the social
and economic development of the developing States.

3. States shall endeavour to foster favourable economic and legal
conditions for the transfer of marine technology for the benefit of all
parties concerned on an equitable basis.

Article 267   Protection of legitimate interests

States, in promoting cooperation pursuant to article 266, shall have due
regard for all legitimate interests including, *inter alia*, the rights and
duties of holders, suppliers and recipients of marine technology.

Article 268   Basic objectives

States, directly or through competent international organizations, shall
promote:

(a) the acquisition, evaluation and dissemination of marine
technological knowledge and facilitate access to such information and
data;

(b) the development of appropriate marine technology;

(c) the development of the necessary technological infrastructure to facilitate the transfer of marine technology;

(d) the development of human resources through training and education of nationals of developing States and countries and especially the nationals of the least developed among them;

(e) international cooperation at all levels, particularly at the regional, subregional and bilateral levels.

Article 269   Measures to achieve the basic objectives

In order to achieve the objectives referred to in article 268, States, directly or through competent international organizations, shall endeavour, *inter alia*, to:

(a) establish programmes of technical cooperation for the effective transfer of all kinds of marine technology to States which may need and request technical assistance in this field, particularly the developing land-locked and geographically disadvantaged States, as well as other developing States which have not been able either to establish or develop their own technological capacity in marine science and in the exploration and exploitation of marine resources or to develop the infrastructure of such technology;

(b) promote favourable conditions for the conclusion of agreements, contracts and other similar arrangements, under equitable and reasonable conditions;

(c) hold conferences, seminars and symposia on scientific and technological subjects, in particular on policies and methods for the transfer of marine technology;

(d) promote the exchange of scientists and of technological and other experts;

(e) undertake projects and promote joint ventures and other forms of bilateral and multilateral cooperation.

SECTION 2   INTERNATIONAL COOPERATION

Article 270   Ways and means of international cooperation

International cooperation for the development and transfer of marine technology shall be carried out, where feasible and appropriate, through existing bilateral, regional or multilateral programmes, and also through expanded and new programmes in order to facilitate marine scientific research, the transfer of marine technology, particularly in new fields, and appropriate international funding for ocean research and development.

Article 271   Guidelines, criteria and standards

States, directly or through competent international organizations, shall promote the establishment of generally accepted guidelines, criteria and standards for the transfer of marine technology on a bilateral basis or within the framework of international organizations and other fora, taking into account, in particular, the interests and needs of developing States.

Article 272   Coordination of international programmes

In the field of transfer of marine technology, States shall endeavour to ensure that competent international organizations coordinate their activities, including any regional or global programmes, taking into account the interests and needs of developing States, particularly land-locked and geographically disadvantaged States.

Article 273   Cooperation with international organizations and
                the Authority

States shall cooperate actively with competent international organizations and the Authority to encourage and facilitate the transfer to developing States, their nationals and the Enterprise of skills and marine technology with regard to activities in the Area.

Article 274   Objectives of the Authority

Subject to all legitimate interests including, *inter alia*, the rights and duties of holders, suppliers and recipients of technology, the Authority, with regard to activities in the Area, shall ensure that:

(a) on the basis of the principle of equitable geographical distribution, nationals of developing States, whether coastal, land-locked or geographically disadvantaged, shall be taken on for the purposes of training as members of the managerial, research and technical staff constituted for its undertakings;

(b) the technical documentation on the relevant equipment, machinery, devices and processes is made available to all States, in particular developing States which may need and request technical assistance in this field;

(c) adequate provision is made by the Authority to facilitate the acquisition of technical assistance in the field of marine technology by States which may need and request it, in particular developing States, and the acquisition by their nationals of the necessary skills and know-how, including professional training;

(d) States which may need and request technical assistance in this field, in particular developing States, are assisted in the acquisition of necessary equipment, processes, plant and other technical know-how through any financial arrangements provided for in this Convention.

SECTION 3   NATIONAL AND REGIONAL MARINE SCIENTIFIC AND TECHNOLOGICAL CENTRES

Article 275   Establishment of national centres

1. States, directly or through competent international organizations and the Authority, shall promote the establishment, particularly in developing coastal States, of national marine scientific and technological research centers and the strengthening of existing national centres, in order to stimulate and advance the conduct of marine scientific research by developing coastal States and to enhance their national capabilities to utilize and preserve their marine resources for their economic benefit.

2. States, through competent international organizations and the Authority, shall give adequate support to facilitate the establishment and strengthening of such national centres so as to provide for advanced training facilities and necessary equipment, skills and know-how as well as technical experts to such States which may need and request such assistance.

Article 276   Establishment of regional centres

1. States, in coordination with the competent international organizations, the Authority and national marine scientific and technological research institutions, shall promote the establishment of regional marine scientific and technological research centres, particularly in developing States, in order to stimulate and advance the conduct of marine scientific research by developing States and foster the transfer of marine technology.

2. All States of a region shall cooperate with the regional centers therein to ensure the more effective achievement of their objectives.

Article 277   Functions of regional centres

The functions of such regional centres shall include, *inter alia*:

(a) training and educational programmes at all levels on various aspects of marine scientific and technological research, particularly marine biology, including conservation and management of living resources, oceanography, hydrography, engineering, geological exploration of the seabed, mining and desalination technologies;

(b) management studies;

(c) study programmes related to the protection and preservation of the marine environment and the prevention, reduction and control of pollution;

(d) organization of regional conferences, seminars and symposia;

(e) acquisition and processing of marine scientific and technological data and information;

(f) prompt dissemination of results of marine scientific and technological research in readily available publications;

(g) publicizing national policies with regard to the transfer of marine technology and systematic comparative study of those policies;

(h) compilation and systematization of information on the marketing of technology and on contracts and other arrangements concerning patents;

(i) technical cooperation with other States of the region.

SECTION 4   COOPERATION AMONG INTERNATIONAL ORGANIZATIONS

Article 278   Cooperation among international organizations

The competent international organizations referred to in this Part and in Part XIII shall take all appropriate measures to ensure, either directly or in close cooperation among themselves, the effective discharge of their functions and responsibilities under this Part.

PART XV   SETTLEMENT OF DISPUTES

SECTION 1   GENERAL PROVISIONS

Article 279   Obligation to settle disputes by peaceful means

States Parties shall settle any dispute between them concerning the interpretation or application of this Convention by peaceful means in accordance with Article 2, paragraph 3, of the Charter of the United Nations and, to this end, shall seek a solution by the means indicated in Article 33, paragraph 1, of the Charter.

Article 280   Settlement of disputes by any peaceful means chosen by the parties

Nothing in this Part impairs the right of any States Parties to agree at any time to settle a dispute between them concerning the interpretation or application of this Convention by any peaceful means of their own choice.

Article 281   Procedure where no settlement has been reached by the parties

1. If the States Parties which are parties to a dispute concerning the interpretation or application of this Convention have agreed to seek settlement of the dispute by a peaceful means of their own choice, the procedures provided for in this Part apply only where no settlement has been reached by recourse to such means and the agreement between the parties does not exclude any further procedure.

2. If the parties have also agreed on a time-limit, paragraph 1 applies only upon the expiration of that time-limit.

Article 282   Obligations under general, regional or bilateral agreements

If the States Parties which are parties to a dispute concerning the interpretation or application of this Convention have agreed, through a general, regional or bilateral agreement or otherwise, that such dispute shall, at the request of any party to the dispute, be submitted to a procedure that entails a binding decision, that procedure shall apply in lieu of the procedures provided for in this Part, unless the parties to the dispute otherwise agree.

Article 283   Obligation to exchange views

1. When a dispute arises between States Parties concerning the interpretation or application of this Convention, the parties to the dispute shall proceed expeditiously to an exchange of views regarding its settlement by negotiation or other peaceful means.

2. The parties shall also proceed expeditiously to an exchange of views where a procedure for the settlement of such a dispute has been terminated without a settlement or where a settlement has been reached and the circumstances require consultation regarding the manner of implementing the settlement.

Article 284   Conciliation

1. A State Party which is a party to a dispute concerning the interpretation or application of this Convention may invite the other party or parties to submit the dispute to conciliation in accordance with the procedure under Annex V, section 1, or another conciliation procedure.
2. If the invitation is accepted and if the parties agree upon the conciliation procedure to be applied, any party may submit the dispute to that procedure.

3. If the invitation is not accepted or the parties do not agree upon the procedure, the conciliation proceedings shall be deemed to be terminated.

4. Unless the parties otherwise agree, when a dispute has been submitted to conciliation, the proceedings may be terminated only in accordance with the agreed conciliation procedure.

Article 285   Application of this section to disputes submitted pursuant to Part XI

This section applies to any dispute which pursuant to Part XI, section 5, is to be settled in accordance with procedures provided for in this Part. If an entity other than a State Party is a party to such a dispute, this section applies *mutatis mutandis*.

SECTION 2   COMPULSORY PROCEDURES ENTAILING BINDING DECISIONS

Article 286   Application of measures under this section

Subject to section 3, any dispute concerning the interpretation or application of this Convention shall, where no settlement has been reached by recourse to section 1, be submitted at the request of any party to the dispute to the court or tribunal having jurisdiction under this section.

Article 287   Choice of procedure

1. When signing, ratifying or acceding to this Convention or at any time thereafter, a State shall be free to choose, by means of a written declaration, one or more of the following means for the settlement of disputes concerning the interpretation or application of this Convention:

(a) the International Tribunal for the Law of the Sea established in accordance with Annex VI;

(b) the International Court of Justice;

(c) an arbitral tribunal constituted in accordance with Annex VII;

(d) a special arbitral tribunal constituted in accordance with Annex VIII for one or more of the categories of disputes specified therein.

2. A declaration made under paragraph 1 shall not affect or be affected by the obligation of a State Party to accept the jurisdiction of the Seabed Disputes Chamber of the International Tribunal for the Law of the Sea to the extent and in the manner provided for in Part XI, section 5.

3. A State Party, which is a party to a dispute not covered by a declaration in force, shall be deemed to have accepted arbitration in accordance with Annex VII.

4. If the parties to a dispute have accepted the same procedure for the settlement of the dispute, it may be submitted only to that procedure, unless   the parties otherwise agree.

5. If the parties to a dispute have not accepted the same procedure for the settlement of the dispute, it may be submitted only to arbitration in accordance with Annex VII, unless the parties otherwise agree.

6. A declaration made under paragraph 1 shall remain in force until three months after notice of revocation has been deposited with the Secretary-General of the United Nations.

7. A new declaration, a notice of revocation or the expiry of a declaration does not in any way affect proceedings pending before a court or tribunal having jurisdiction under this article, unless the parties otherwise agree.

8. Declarations and notices referred to in this article shall be deposited with the Secretary-General of the United Nations, who shall transmit copies thereof to the States Parties.

Article 288   Jurisdiction

1. A court or tribunal referred to in article 287 shall have jurisdiction over any dispute concerning the interpretation or application of this Convention which is submitted to it in accordance with this Part.

2. A court or tribunal referred to in article 287 shall also have jurisdiction over any dispute concerning the interpretation or application of an international agreement related to the purposes of this Convention, which is submitted to it in accordance with the agreement.

3. The Seabed Disputes Chamber of the International Tribunal for the Law of the Sea established in accordance with Annex VI, and any other chamber or arbitral tribunal referred to in Part XI, section 5, shall have jurisdiction in any matter which is submitted to it in accordance therewith.

4. In the event of a dispute as to whether a court or tribunal has jurisdiction, the matter shall be settled by decision of that court or tribunal.

Article 289   Experts

In any dispute involving scientific or technical matters, a court or tribunal exercising jurisdiction under this section may, at the request of a party or *proprio motu*, select in consultation with the parties no fewer than two scientific or technical experts chosen preferably from the relevant list prepared in accordance with Annex VIII, article 2, to sit with the court or tribunal but without the right to vote.

Article 290   Provisional measures

1. If a dispute has been duly submitted to a court or tribunal which considers that *prima facie* it has jurisdiction under this Part or Part XI, section 5, the court or tribunal may prescribe any provisional measures which it considers appropriate under the circumstances to preserve the respective rights of the parties to the dispute or to prevent serious harm to the marine environment, pending the final decision.

2. Provisional measures may be modified or revoked as soon as the circumstances justifying them have changed or ceased to exist.

3. Provisional measures may be prescribed, modified or revoked under this article only at the request of a party to the dispute and after the parties have been given an opportunity to be heard.

4. The court or tribunal shall forthwith give notice to the parties to the dispute, and to such other States Parties as it considers appropriate, of the prescription, modification or revocation of provisional measures.

5. Pending the constitution of an arbitral tribunal to which a dispute is being submitted under this section, any court or tribunal agreed upon by the parties or, failing such agreement within two weeks from the date of the request for provisional measures, the International Tribunal for the Law of the Sea or, with respect to activities in the Area, the Seabed Disputes Chamber, may prescribe, modify or revoke provisional measures in accordance with this article if it considers that *prima facie* the tribunal which is to be constituted would have jurisdiction and that the urgency of the situation so requires. Once constituted, the tribunal to which the dispute has been submitted may modify, revoke or affirm those provisional measures, acting in conformity with paragraphs 1 to 4.

6. The parties to the dispute shall comply promptly with any provisional measures prescribed under this article.

Article 291   Access

1. All the dispute settlement procedures specified in this Part shall be open to States Parties.

2. The dispute settlement procedures specified in this Part shall be open to entities other than States Parties only as specifically provided for in this Convention.

Article 292   Prompt release of vessels and crews

1. Where the authorities of a State Party have detained a vessel flying the flag of another State Party and it is alleged that the detaining State has not complied with the provisions of this Convention for the prompt release of the vessel or its crew upon the posting of a reasonable bond or other financial security, the question of release from detention may be submitted to any court or tribunal agreed upon by the parties or, failing such agreement within 10 days from the time of detention, to a court or tribunal accepted by the detaining State under article 287 or to the International Tribunal for the Law of the Sea, unless the parties otherwise agree.

2. The application for release may be made only by or on behalf of the flag State of the vessel.

3. The court or tribunal shall deal without delay with the application for release and shall deal only with the question of release, without prejudice to the merits of any case before the appropriate domestic forum against the vessel, its owner or its crew. The authorities of the detaining State remain competent to release the vessel or its crew at any time.

4. Upon the posting of the bond or other financial security determined by the court or tribunal, the authorities of the detaining State shall comply promptly with the decision of the court or tribunal concerning the release of the vessel or its crew.

Article 293   Applicable law

1. A court or tribunal having jurisdiction under this section shall apply this Convention and other rules of international law not incompatible with this Convention.

2. Paragraph 1 does not prejudice the power of the court or tribunal having jurisdiction under this section to decide a case *ex aequo et bono*, if the parties so agree.

Article 294   Preliminary proceedings

1. A court or tribunal provided for in article 287 to which an application is made in respect of a dispute referred to in article 297 shall determine at the request of a party, or may determine *proprio motu*, whether the claim constitutes an abuse of legal process or whether *prima facie* it is well founded. If the court or tribunal determines that the claim constitutes an abuse of legal process or is *prima facie* unfounded, it shall take no further action in the case.

2. Upon receipt of the application, the court or tribunal shall immediately notify the other party or parties of the application, and shall fix a reasonable time-limit within which they may request it to make a determination in accordance with paragraph 1.

3. Nothing in this article affects the right of any party to a dispute to make preliminary objections in accordance with the applicable rules of procedure.

Article 295   Exhaustion of local remedies

Any dispute between States Parties concerning the interpretation or application of this Convention may be submitted to the procedures provided for in this section only after local remedies have been exhausted where this is required by international law.

Article 296   Finality and binding force of decisions

1. Any decision rendered by a court or tribunal having jurisdiction under this section shall be final and shall be complied with by all the parties to the dispute.

2. Any such decision shall have no binding force except between the parties and in respect of that particular dispute.

SECTION 3   LIMITATIONS AND EXCEPTIONS TO APPLICABILITY OF SECTION 2

Article 297   Limitations on applicability of section 2

1. Disputes concerning the interpretation or application of this Convention with regard to the exercise by a coastal State of its sovereign rights or jurisdiction provided for in this Convention shall be subject to the procedures provided for in section 2 in the following cases:

(a) when it is alleged that a coastal State has acted in contravention of the provisions of this Convention in regard to the freedoms and rights of navigation, overflight or the laying of submarine cables and pipelines, or in regard to other internationally lawful uses of the sea specified in article 58;

(b) when it is alleged that a State in exercising the aforementioned freedoms, rights or uses has acted in contravention of this Convention or of laws or regulations adopted by the coastal State in conformity with this Convention and other rules of international law not incompatible with this Convention; or

(c) when it is alleged that a coastal State has acted in contravention of specified international rules and standards for the protection and preservation of the marine environment which are applicable to the coastal State and which have been established by this Convention or through a competent international organization or diplomatic conference in accordance with this Convention.

2. (a) Disputes concerning the interpretation or application of the provisions of this Convention with regard to marine scientific research shall be settled in accordance with section 2, except that the coastal State shall not be obliged to accept the submission to such settlement of any dispute arising out of:

(i) the exercise by the coastal State of a right or discretion in accordance with article 246; or

(ii) a decision by the coastal State to order suspension or cessation of a research project in accordance with article 253.

(b) A dispute arising from an allegation by the researching State that with respect to a specific project the coastal State is not exercising its rights under articles 246 and 253 in a manner compatible with this

Convention shall be submitted, at the request of either party, to conciliation under Annex V, section 2, provided that the conciliation commission shall not call in question the exercise by the coastal State of its discretion to designate specific areas as referred to in article 246, paragraph 6, or of its discretion to withhold consent in accordance with article 246, paragraph 5.

3. (a) Disputes concerning the interpretation or application of the provisions of this Convention with regard to fisheries shall be settled in accordance with section 2, except that the coastal State shall not be obliged to accept the submission to such settlement of any dispute relating to its sovereign rights with respect to the living resources in the exclusive economic zone or their exercise, including its discretionary powers for determining the allowable catch, its harvesting capacity, the allocation of surpluses to other States and the terms and conditions established in its conservation and management laws and regulations.

(b) Where no settlement has been reached by recourse to section 1 of this Part, a dispute shall be submitted to conciliation under Annex V, section 2, at the request of any party to the dispute, when it is alleged that:

(i) a coastal State has manifestly failed to comply with its obligations to ensure through proper conservation and management measures that the maintenance of the living resources in the exclusive economic zone is not seriously endangered;

(ii) a coastal State has arbitrarily refused to determine, at the request of another State, the allowable catch and its capacity to harvest living resources with respect to stocks which that other State is interested in fishing; or

(iii) a coastal State has arbitrarily refused to allocate to any State, under articles 62, 69 and 70 and under the terms and conditions established by the coastal State consistent with this Convention, the whole or part of the surplus it has declared to exist.

(c) In no case shall the conciliation commission substitute its discretion for that of the coastal State.

(d) The report of the conciliation commission shall be communicated to the appropriate international organizations.

(e) In negotiating agreements pursuant to articles 69 and 70, States Parties, unless they otherwise agree, shall include a clause on measures which they shall take in order to minimize the possibility of a disagreement concerning the interpretation or application of the agreement, and on how they should proceed if a disagreement nevertheless arises.

Article 298   Optional exceptions to applicability of section 2

1. When signing, ratifying or acceding to this Convention or at any time thereafter, a State may, without prejudice to the obligations arising under section 1, declare in writing that it does not accept any one or more of the procedures provided for in section 2 with respect to one or more of the following categories of disputes:

(a) (i) disputes concerning the interpretation or application of articles 15, 74 and 83 relating to sea boundary delimitations, or those involving historic bays or titles, provided that a State having made such a declaration shall, when such a dispute arises subsequent to the entry into force of this Convention and where no agreement within a reasonable period of time is reached in negotiations between the parties, at the request of any party to the dispute, accept submission of the matter to conciliation under Annex V, section 2; and provided further that any dispute that necessarily involves the concurrent consideration of any unsettled dispute concerning sovereignty or other rights over continental or insular land territory shall be excluded from such submission;

(ii) after the conciliation commission has presented its report, which shall state the reasons on which it is based, the parties shall negotiate an agreement on the basis of that report; if these negotiations do not result in an agreement, the parties shall, by mutual consent, submit the question to one of the procedures provided for in section 2, unless the parties otherwise agree;

(iii) this subparagraph does not apply to any sea boundary dispute finally settled by an arrangement between the parties, or to any such dispute which is to be settled in accordance with a bilateral or multilateral agreement binding upon those parties;

(b) disputes concerning military activities, including military activities by government vessels and aircraft engaged in non-commercial service, and disputes concerning law enforcement activities in regard to the exercise of sovereign rights or jurisdiction excluded from the jurisdiction of a court or tribunal under article 297, paragraph 2 or 3;

(c) disputes in respect of which the Security Council of the United Nations is exercising the functions assigned to it by the Charter of the United Nations, unless the Security Council decides to remove the matter from its agenda or calls upon the parties to settle it by the means provided for in this Convention.

2. A State Party which has made a declaration under paragraph 1 may at any time withdraw it, or agree to submit a dispute excluded by such declaration to any procedure specified in this Convention.

3. A State Party which has made a declaration under paragraph 1 shall not be entitled to submit any dispute falling within the excepted category of disputes to any procedure in this Convention as against another State Party, without the consent of that party.

4. If one of the States Parties has made a declaration under paragraph 1(a), any other State Party may submit any dispute falling within an excepted category against the declarant party to the procedure specified in such declaration.

5. A new declaration, or the withdrawal of a declaration, does not in any way affect proceedings pending before a court or tribunal in accordance with this article, unless the parties otherwise agree.

6. Declarations and notices of withdrawal of declarations under this article shall be deposited with the Secretary-General of the United Nations, who shall transmit copies thereof to the States Parties.

Article 299   Right of the parties to agree upon a procedure

1. A dispute excluded under article 297 or excepted by a declaration made under article 298 from the dispute settlement procedures provided for in section 2 may be submitted to such procedures only by agreement of the parties to the dispute.

2. Nothing in this section impairs the right of the parties to the dispute to agree to some other procedure for the settlement of such dispute or to each an amicable settlement.

PART XVI   GENERAL PROVISIONS

Article 300   Good faith and abuse of rights

States Parties shall fulfil in good faith the obligations assumed under this Convention and shall exercise the rights, jurisdiction and freedoms recognized in this Convention in a manner which would not constitute an abuse of right.

Article 301   Peaceful use of the seas

In exercising their rights and performing their duties under this Convention, States Parties shall refrain from any threat or use of force against the territorial integrity or political independence of any State, or in any other manner inconsistent with the principles of international law embodied in the Charter of the United Nations.

Article 302   Disclosure of information

Without prejudice to the right of a State Party to resort to the procedures for the settlement of disputes provided for in this Convention, nothing in this Convention shall be deemed to require a State Party, in the fulfilment of its obligations under this Convention, to supply information the disclosure of which is contrary to the essential interests of its security.

Article 303   Archaeological and historical objects found at sea

1. States have the duty to protect objects of an archaeological and historical nature found at sea and shall cooperate for this purpose.

2. In order to control traffic in such objects, the coastal State may, in applying article 33, presume that their removal from the seabed in the zone referred to in that article without its approval would result in an infringement within its territory or territorial sea of the laws and regulations referred to in that article.

3. Nothing in this article affects the rights of identifiable owners, the law of salvage or other rules of admiralty, or laws and practices with respect to cultural exchanges.

4. This article is without prejudice to other international agreements and rules of international law regarding the protection of objects of an archaeological and historical nature.

Article 304   Responsibility and liability for damage

The provisions of this Convention regarding responsibility and liability for damage are without prejudice to the application of existing rules and the development of further rules regarding responsibility and liability under international law.

PART XVII   FINAL PROVISIONS

Article 305   Signature

1. This Convention shall be open for signature by:

(a) all States;

(b) Namibia, represented by the United Nations Council for Namibia;

(c) all self-governing associated States which have chosen that status in an act of self-determination supervised and approved by the United Nations in accordance with General Assembly resolution 1514 (XV) and which have competence over the matters governed by this Convention, including the competence to enter into treaties in respect of those matters;

(d) all self-governing associated States which, in accordance with their respective instruments of association, have competence over the matters governed by this Convention, including the competence to enter into treaties in respect of those matters;

(e) all territories which enjoy full internal self-government, recognized as such by the United Nations, but have not attained full independence in accordance with General Assembly resolution 1514 (XV) and which have competence over the matters governed by this Convention, including the competence to enter into treaties in respect of those matters;

(f) international organizations, in accordance with Annex IX.

2. This Convention shall remain open for signature until 9 December 1984 at the Ministry of Foreign Affairs of Jamaica and also, from 1 July 1983 until 9 December 1984, at United Nations Headquarters in New York.

Article 306   Ratification and formal confirmation

This Convention is subject to ratification by States and the other entities referred to in article 305, paragraph l(b), (c), (d) and (e), and to formal confirmation, in accordance with Annex IX, by the entities referred to in article 305, paragraph l(f). The instruments of ratification and of formal confirmation shall be deposited with the Secretary-General of the United Nations.

Article 307   Accession

This Convention shall remain open for accession by States and the other entities referred to in article 305. Accession by the entities referred to in article 305, paragraph l(f), shall be in accordance with Annex IX. The instruments of accession shall be deposited with the Secretary-General of the United Nations.

Article 308   Entry into force

1. This Convention shall enter into force 12 months after the date of deposit of the sixtieth instrument of ratification or accession.

2. For each State ratifying or acceding to this Convention after the deposit of the sixtieth instrument of ratification or accession, the Convention shall enter into force on the thirtieth day following the deposit of its instrument of ratification or accession, subject to paragraph 1.

3. The Assembly of the Authority shall meet on the date of entry into force of this Convention and shall elect the Council of the Authority. The first Council shall be constituted in a manner consistent with the purpose of article 161 if the provisions of that article cannot be strictly applied.

4. The rules, regulations and procedures drafted by the Preparatory Commission shall apply provisionally pending their formal adoption by the Authority in accordance with Part XI.

5. The Authority and its organs shall act in accordance with resolution II of the Third United Nations Conference on the Law of the Sea relating to preparatory investment and with decisions of the Preparatory Commission taken pursuant to that resolution.

Article 309   Reservations and exceptions

No reservations or exceptions may be made to this Convention unless expressly permitted by other articles of this Convention.

Article 310   Declarations and statements

Article 309 does not preclude a State, when signing, ratifying or acceding to this Convention, from making declarations or statements, however phrased or named, with a view, *inter alia*, to the harmonization of its laws and regulations with the provisions of this Convention, provided that such declarations or statements do not purport to exclude or to modify the legal effect of the provisions of this Convention in their application to that State.

Article 311   Relation to other conventions and international agreements

1. This Convention shall prevail, as between States Parties, over the Geneva Conventions on the Law of the Sea of 29 April 1958.

2. This Convention shall not alter the rights and obligations of States Parties which arise from other agreements compatible with this Convention and which do not affect the enjoyment by other States Parties of their rights or the performance of their obligations under this Convention.

3. Two or more States Parties may conclude agreements modifying or suspending the operation of provisions of this Convention, applicable solely to the relations between them, provided that such agreements do not relate to a provision derogation from which is incompatible with the effective execution of the object and purpose of this Convention, and provided further that such agreements shall not affect the application of the basic principles embodied herein, and that the provisions of such agreements do not affect the enjoyment by other States Parties of their rights or the performance of their obligations under this Convention.

4. States Parties intending to conclude an agreement referred to in paragraph 3 shall notify the other States Parties through the depositary of this Convention of their intention to conclude the agreement and of the modification or suspension for which it provides.

5. This article does not affect international agreements expressly permitted or preserved by other articles of this Convention.

6. States Parties agree that there shall be no amendments to the basic principle relating to the common heritage of mankind set forth in article 136 and that they shall not be party to any agreement in derogation thereof.

Article 312   Amendment

1. After the expiry of a period of 10 years from the date of entry into force of this Convention, a State Party may, by written communication addressed to the Secretary-General of the United Nations, propose specific amendments to this Convention, other than those relating to activities in the Area, and request the convening of a conference to consider such proposed amendments. The Secretary-General shall circulate such communication to all States Parties. If, within 12 months from the date of the circulation of the communication, not less than one half of the States Parties reply favourably to the request, the Secretary-General shall convene the conference.

2. The decision-making procedure applicable at the amendment conference shall be the same as that applicable at the Third United Nations Conference on the Law of the Sea unless otherwise decided by the conference. The conference should make every effort to reach agreement on any amendments by way of consensus and there should be no voting on them until all efforts at consensus have been exhausted.

Article 313   Amendment by simplified procedure

1. A State Party may, by written communication addressed to the Secretary-General of the United Nations, propose an amendment to this Convention, other than an amendment relating to activities in the Area, to be adopted by the simplified procedure set forth in this article without convening a conference. The Secretary-General shall circulate the communication to all States Parties.

2. If, within a period of 12 months from the date of the circulation of the communication, a State Party objects to the proposed amendment or to the proposal for its adoption by the simplified procedure, the amendment shall be considered rejected. The Secretary-General shall immediately notify all States Parties accordingly.

3. If, 12 months from the date of the circulation of the communication, no State Party has objected to the proposed amendment or to the proposal for its adoption by the simplified procedure, the proposed

amendment shall be considered adopted. The Secretary-General shall notify all States Parties that the proposed amendment has been adopted.

Article 314   Amendments to the provisions of this Convention relating exclusively to activities in the Area

1. A State Party may, by written communication addressed to the Secretary-General of the Authority, propose an amendment to the provisions of this Convention relating exclusively to activities in the Area, including Annex VI, section 4. The Secretary-General shall circulate such communication to all States Parties. The proposed amendment shall be subject to approval by the Assembly following its approval by the Council. Representatives of States Parties in those organs shall have full powers to consider and approve the proposed amendment. The proposed amendment as approved by the Council and the Assembly shall be considered adopted.

2. Before approving any amendment under paragraph 1, the Council and the Assembly shall ensure that it does not prejudice the system of exploration for and exploitation of the resources of the Area, pending the Review Conference in accordance with article 155.

Article 315   Signature, ratification of, accession to and authentic texts of amendments

1. Once adopted, amendments to this Convention shall be open for signature by States Parties for 12 months from the date of adoption, at United Nations Headquarters in New York, unless otherwise provided in the amendment itself.

2. Articles 306, 307 and 320 apply to all amendments to this Convention.

Article 316   Entry into force of amendments

1. Amendments to this Convention, other than those referred to in paragraph 5, shall enter into force for the States Parties ratifying or acceding to them on the thirtieth day following the deposit of instruments of ratification or accession by two thirds of the States Parties or by 60 States Parties, whichever is greater. Such amendments shall not affect the enjoyment by other States Parties of their rights or the performance of their obligations under this Convention.

2. An amendment may provide that a larger number of ratifications or accessions shall be required for its entry into force than are required by this article.

3. For each State Party ratifying or acceding to an amendment referred to in paragraph 1 after the deposit of the required number of instruments of ratification or accession, the amendment shall enter into force on the thirtieth day following the deposit of its instrument of ratification or accession.

4. A State which becomes a Party to this Convention after the entry into force of an amendment in accordance with paragraph 1 shall, failing an expression of a different intention by that State:

   (a) be considered as a Party to this Convention as so amended; and

   (b) be considered as a Party to the unamended Convention in relation to any State Party not bound by the amendment.

5. Any amendment relating exclusively to activities in the Area and any amendment to Annex VI shall enter into force for all States Parties one year following the deposit of instruments of ratification or accession by three fourths of the States Parties.

6. A State which becomes a Party to this Convention after the entry into force of amendments in accordance with paragraph 5 shall be considered as a Party to this Convention as so amended.

Article 317   Denunciation

1. A State Party may, by written notification addressed to the Secretary-General of the United Nations, denounce this Convention and may indicate its reasons. Failure to indicate reasons shall not affect the validity of the denunciation. The denunciation shall take effect one year after the date of receipt of the notification, unless the notification specifies a later date.

2. A State shall not be discharged by reason of the denunciation from the financial and contractual obligations which accrued while it was a Party to this Convention, nor shall the denunciation affect any right, obligation or legal situation of that State created through the execution of this Convention prior to its termination for that State.

3. The denunciation shall not in any way affect the duty of any State Party to fulfil any obligation embodied in this Convention to which it would be subject under international law independently of this Convention.

Article 318   Status of Annexes

The Annexes form an integral part of this Convention and, unless expressly provided otherwise, a reference to this Convention or to one of its Parts includes a reference to the Annexes relating thereto.

Article 319   Depositary

1. The Secretary-General of the United Nations shall be the depositary of this Convention and amendments thereto.

2. In addition to his functions as depositary, the Secretary-General shall:

(a) report to all States Parties, the Authority and competent international organizations on issues of a general nature that have arisen with respect to this Convention;

(b) notify the Authority of ratifications and formal confirmations of and accessions to this Convention and amendments thereto, as well as of denunciations of this Convention;

(c) notify States Parties of agreements in accordance with article 311, paragraph 4;

(d) circulate amendments adopted in accordance with this Convention to States Parties for ratification or accession;

(e) convene necessary meetings of States Parties in accordance with this Convention.

3. (a) The Secretary-General shall also transmit to the observers referred to in article 156:

(i) reports referred to in paragraph 2(a);

(ii) notifications referred to in paragraph 2(b) and (c); and

(iii) texts of amendments referred to in paragraph 2(d), for their information.

(b) The Secretary-General shall also invite those observers to participate as observers at meetings of States Parties referred to in paragraph 2(e).

Article 320   Authentic texts

The original of this Convention, of which the Arabic, Chinese, English, French, Russian and Spanish texts are equally authentic, shall, subject to article 305, paragraph 2, be deposited with the Secretary-General of the United Nations.

IN WITNESS WHEREOF, the undersigned Plenipotentiaries, being duly authorized thereto, have signed this Convention.

DONE AT MONTEGO BAY, this tenth day of December, one thousand nine hundred and eighty-two.

ANNEX I   HIGHLY MIGRATORY SPECIES

1. Albacore tuna: *Thunnus alalunga.*

2. Bluefin tuna: *Thunnus thynnus.*

3. Bigeye tuna: *Thunnus obesus.*

4. Skipjack tuna: *Katsuwonus pelamis.*

5. Yellowfin tuna: *Thunnus albacares.*

6. Blackfin tuna: *Thunnus atlanticus.*

7. Little tuna: *Euthynnus alletteratus; Euthynnus affinis.*

8. Southern bluefin tuna: *Thunnus maccoyii.*

9. Frigate mackerel: *Auxis thazard; Auxis rochei.*

10. Pomfrets: Family *Bramidae.*

11. Marlins: *Tetrapturus angustirostris; Tetrapturus belone; Tetrapturus pfluegeri; Tetrapturus albidus; Tetrapturus audax; Tetrapturus georgei; Makaira mazara; Makaira indica; Makaira nigricans.*

12. Sail-fishes: *Istiophorus platypterus; Istiophorus albicans.*

13. Swordfish: *Xiphias gladius.*

14. Sauries: *Scomberesox saurus; Cololabis saira; Cololabis adocetus; Scomberesox saurus scombroides.*

15. Dolphin: *Coryphaena hippurus; Coryphaena equiselis.*

16. Oceanic sharks: *Hexanchus griseus; Cetorhinus maximus;* Family *Alopiidae; Rhincodon typus;* Family *Carcharhinidae;* Family *Sphyrnidae;* Family *Isurida.*

17. Cetaceans: Family *Physeteridae;* Family *Balaenopteridae;* Family *Balaenidae;* Family *Eschrichtiidae;* Family *Monodontidae;* Family *Ziphiidae;* Family *Delphinidae.*

ANNEX II   COMMISSION ON THE LIMITS OF THE CONTINENTAL SHELF

Article 1

In accordance with the provisions of article 76, a Commission on the Limits of the Continental Shelf beyond 200 nautical miles shall be established in conformity with the following articles.

Article 2

1. The Commission shall consist of 21 members who shall be experts in the field of geology, geophysics or hydrography, elected by States Parties to this Convention from among their nationals, having due regard to the need to ensure equitable geographical representation, who shall serve in their personal capacities.

2. The initial election shall be held as soon as possible but in any case within 18 months after the date of entry into force of this Convention. At least three months before the date of each election, the Secretary-General of the United Nations shall address a letter to the States Parties, inviting the submission of nominations, after appropriate regional consultations, within three months. The Secretary-General shall prepare a list in alphabetical order of all persons thus nominated and shall submit it to all the States Parties.

3. Elections of the members of the Commission shall be held at a meeting of States Parties convened by the Secretary-General at United Nations Headquarters. At that meeting, for which two thirds of the States Parties shall constitute a quorum, the persons elected to the Commission shall be those nominees who obtain a two-thirds majority of the votes of the representatives of States Parties present and voting. Not less than three members shall be elected from each geographical region.

4. The members of the Commission shall be elected for a term of five years. They shall be eligible for re-election.

5. The State Party which submitted the nomination of a member of the Commission shall defray the expenses of that member while in performance of Commission duties. The coastal State concerned shall defray the expenses incurred in respect of the advice referred to in article 3, paragraph 1(b), of this Annex. The secretariat of the Commission shall be provided by the Secretary-General of the United Nations.

Article 3

1. The functions of the Commission shall be:

(a) to consider the data and other material submitted by coastal States concerning the outer limits of the continental shelf in areas where those limits extend beyond 200 nautical miles, and to make recommendations in accordance with article 76 and the Statement of Understanding adopted on 29 August 1980 by the Third United Nations Conference on the Law of the Sea;

(b) to provide scientific and technical advice, if requested by the coastal State concerned during the preparation of the data referred to in subparagraph (a).

2. The Commission may cooperate, to the extent considered necessary and useful, with the Intergovernmental Oceanographic Commission of UNESCO, the International Hydrographic Organization and other competent international organizations with a view to exchanging scientific and technical information which might be of assistance in discharging the Commission's responsibilities.

Article 4

Where a coastal State intends to establish, in accordance with article 76, the outer limits of its continental shelf beyond 200 nautical miles, it shall submit particulars of such limits to the Commission along with supporting scientific and technical data as soon as possible but in any case within 10 years of the entry into force of this Convention for that State. The coastal State shall at the same time give the names of any Commission members who have provided it with scientific and technical advice.

Article 5

Unless the Commission decides otherwise, the Commission shall function by way of sub-commissions composed of seven members, appointed in a balanced manner taking into account the specific elements of each submission by a coastal State. Nationals of the coastal State making the submission who are members of the Commission and any Commission member who has assisted a coastal State by providing scientific and technical advice with respect to the delineation shall not be a member of the sub-commission dealing with that submission but has the right to participate as a member in the proceedings of the

Commission concerning the said submission. The coastal State which has made a submission to the Commission may send its representatives to participate in the relevant proceedings without the right to vote.

Article 6

1. The sub-commission shall submit its recommendations to the Commission.

2. Approval by the Commission of the recommendations of the sub-commission shall be by a majority of two thirds of Commission members present and voting.

3. The recommendations of the Commission shall be submitted in writing to the coastal State which made the submission and to the Secretary-General of the United Nations.

Article 7

Coastal States shall establish the outer limits of the continental shelf in conformity with the provisions of article 76, paragraph 8, and in accordance with the appropriate national procedures.

Article 8

In the case of disagreement by the coastal State with the recommendations of the Commission, the coastal State shall, within a reasonable time, make a revised or new submission to the Commission.

Article 9

The actions of the Commission shall not prejudice matters relating to delimitation of boundaries between States with opposite or adjacent coasts.

**ANNEX III   BASIC CONDITIONS OF PROSPECTING,
                EXPLORATION AND EXPLOITATION**

Article 1   Title to minerals

Title to minerals shall pass upon recovery in accordance with this
Convention.

Article 2   Prospecting

1. (a) The Authority shall encourage prospecting in the Area.

(b) Prospecting shall be conducted only after the Authority has
received a satisfactory written undertaking that the proposed
prospector will comply with this Convention and the relevant rules,
regulations and procedures of the Authority concerning cooperation in
the training programmes referred to in articles 143 and 144 and the
protection of the marine environment, and will accept verification by
the Authority of compliance therewith. The proposed prospector shall,
at the same time, notify the Authority of the approximate area or areas
in which prospecting is to be conducted.

(c) Prospecting may be conducted simultaneously by more than one
prospector in the same area or areas.

2. Prospecting shall not confer on the prospector any rights with respect
to resources. A prospector may, however, recover a reasonable quantity
of minerals to be used for testing.

Article 3   Exploration and exploitation

1. The Enterprise, States Parties, and the other entities referred to in
article 153, paragraph 2(b), may apply to the Authority for approval of
plans of work for activities in the Area.

2. The Enterprise may apply with respect to any part of the Area, but
applications by others with respect to reserved areas are subject to the
additional requirements of article 9 of this Annex.

3. Exploration and exploitation shall be carried out only in areas
specified in plans of work referred to in article 153, paragraph 3, and
approved by the Authority in accordance with this Convention and the
relevant rules, regulations and procedures of the Authority.

4. Every approved plan of work shall:

(a) be in conformity with this Convention and the rules, regulations and procedures of the Authority;

(b) provide for control by the Authority of activities in the Area in accordance with article 153, paragraph 4;

(c) confer on the operator, in accordance with the rules, regulations and procedures of the Authority, the exclusive right to explore for and exploit the specified categories of resources in the area covered by the plan of work. If, however, the applicant presents for approval a plan of work covering only the stage of exploration or the stage of exploitation, the approved plan of work shall confer such exclusive right with respect to that stage only.

5. Upon its approval by the Authority, every plan of work, except those presented by the Enterprise, shall be in the form of a contract concluded between the Authority and the applicant or applicants.

Article 4   Qualifications of applicants

1. Applicants, other than the Enterprise, shall be qualified if they have the nationality or control and sponsorship required by article 153, paragraph 2(b), and if they follow the procedures and meet the qualification standards set forth in the rules, regulations and procedures of the Authority.

2. Except as provided in paragraph 6, such qualification standards shall relate to the financial and technical capabilities of the applicant and his performance under any previous contracts with the Authority.

3. Each applicant shall be sponsored by the State Party of which it is a national unless the applicant has more than one nationality, as in the case of a partnership or consortium of entities from several States, in which event all States Parties involved shall sponsor the application, or unless the applicant is effectively controlled by another State Party or its nationals, in which event both States Parties shall sponsor the application. The criteria and procedures for implementation of the sponsorship requirements shall be set forth in the rules, regulations and procedures of the Authority.

4. The sponsoring State or States shall, pursuant to article 139, have the responsibility to ensure, within their legal systems, that a contractor so sponsored shall carry out activities in the Area in conformity with the terms of its contract and its obligations under this Convention. A sponsoring State shall not, however, be liable for damage caused by any failure of a contractor sponsored by it to comply with its obligations if that State Party has adopted laws and regulations and taken administrative measures which are, within the framework of its legal system, reasonably appropriate for securing compliance by persons under its jurisdiction.

5. The procedures for assessing the qualifications of States Parties which are applicants shall take into account their character as States.

6. The qualification standards shall require that every applicant, without exception, shall as part of his application undertake:

(a) to accept as enforceable and comply with the applicable obligations created by the provisions of Part XI, the rules, regulations and procedures of the Authority, the decisions of the organs of the Authority and terms of his contracts with the Authority;

(b) to accept control by the Authority of activities in the Area, as authorized by this Convention;

(c) to provide the Authority with a written assurance that his obligations under the contract will be fulfilled in good faith;

(d) to comply with the provisions on the transfer of technology set forth in article 5 of this Annex.

Article 5   Transfer of technology

1. When submitting a plan of work, every applicant shall make available to the Authority a general description of the equipment and methods to be used in carrying out activities in the Area, and other relevant non-proprietary information about the characteristics of such technology and information as to where such technology is available.

2. Every operator shall inform the Authority of revisions in the description and information made available pursuant to paragraph 1 whenever a substantial technological change or innovation is introduced.

3. Every contract for carrying out activities in the Area shall contain the following undertakings by the contractor:

(a) to make available to the Enterprise on fair and reasonable commercial terms and conditions, whenever the Authority so requests, the technology which he uses in carrying out activities in the Area under the contract, which the contractor is legally entitled to transfer. This shall be done by means of licences or other appropriate arrangements which the contractor shall negotiate with the Enterprise and which shall be set forth in a specific agreement supplementary to the contract. This undertaking may be invoked only if the Enterprise finds that it is unable to obtain the same or equally efficient and useful technology on the open market on fair and reasonable commercial terms and conditions;

(b) to obtain a written assurance from the owner of any technology used in carrying out activities in the Area under the contract, which is not generally available on the open market and which is not covered by subparagraph (a), that the owner will, whenever the Authority so requests, make that technology available to the Enterprise under licence or other appropriate arrangements and on fair and reasonable commercial terms and conditions, to the same extent as made available to the contractor. If this assurance is not obtained, the technology in question shall not be used by the contractor in carrying out activities in the Area;

(c) to acquire from the owner by means of an enforceable contract, upon the request of the Enterprise and if it is possible to do so without substantial cost to the contractor, the legal right to transfer to the Enterprise any technology used by the contractor, in carrying out activities in the Area under the contract, which the contractor is otherwise not legally entitled to transfer and which is not generally available on the open market. In cases where there is a substantial corporate relationship between the contractor and the owner of the technology, the closeness of this relationship and the degree of control or influence shall be relevant to the determination whether all feasible measures have been taken to acquire such a right. In cases where the contractor exercises effective control over the owner, failure to acquire from the owner the legal right shall be considered relevant to the contractor's qualification for any subsequent application for approval of a plan of work;

(d) to facilitate, upon the request of the Enterprise, the acquisition by the Enterprise of any technology covered by subparagraph (b), under licence or other appropriate arrangements and on fair and reasonable commercial terms and conditions, if the Enterprise decides to negotiate directly with the owner of the technology;

(e) to take the same measures as are prescribed in subparagraphs (a), (b), (c) and (d) for the benefit of a developing State or group of developing States which has applied for a contract under article 9 of this Annex, provided that these measures shall be limited to the exploitation of the part of the area proposed by the contractor which has been reserved pursuant to article 8 of this Annex and provided that activities under the contract sought by the developing State or group of developing States would not involve transfer of technology to a third State or the nationals of a third State. The obligation under this provision shall only apply with respect to any given contractor where technology has not been requested by the Enterprise or transferred by that contractor to the Enterprise.

4. Disputes concerning undertakings required by paragraph 3, like other provisions of the contracts, shall be subject to compulsory settlement in accordance with Part XI and, in cases of violation of these undertakings, suspension or termination of the contract or monetary penalties may be ordered in accordance with article 18 of this Annex. Disputes as to whether offers made by the contractor are within the range of fair and reasonable commercial terms and conditions may be submitted by either party to binding commercial arbitration in accordance with the UNCITRAL Arbitration Rules or such other arbitration rules as may be prescribed in the rules, regulations and procedures of the Authority. If the finding is that the offer made by the contractor is not within the range of fair and reasonable commercial terms and conditions, the contractor shall be given 45 days to revise his offer to bring it within that range before the Authority takes any action in accordance with article 18 of this Annex.

5. If the Enterprise is unable to obtain on fair and reasonable commercial terms and conditions appropriate technology to enable it to commence in a timely manner the recovery and processing of minerals from the Area, either the Council or the Assembly may convene a group of States Parties composed of those which are engaged in activities in the Area, those which have sponsored entities which are engaged in activities in the Area and other States Parties having access to such technology. This group shall consult together and shall take effective measures to ensure that such technology is made available to the Enterprise on fair and reasonable commercial terms and conditions. Each such State Party shall take all feasible measures to this end within its own legal system.

6. In the case of joint ventures with the Enterprise, transfer of technology will be in accordance with the terms of the joint venture agreement.

7. The undertakings required by paragraph 3 shall be included in each contract for the carrying out of activities in the Area until 10 years after the commencement of commercial production by the Enterprise, and may be invoked during that period.

8. For the purposes of this article, "technology" means the specialized equipment and technical know-how, including manuals, designs, operating instructions, training and technical advice and assistance, necessary to assemble, maintain and operate a viable system and the legal right to use these items for that purpose on a non-exclusive basis.

Article 6   Approval of plans to work

1. Six months after the entry into force of this Convention, and thereafter each fourth month, the Authority shall take up for consideration proposed plans of work.

2. When considering an application for approval of a plan of work in the form of a contract, the Authority shall first ascertain whether:

(a) the applicant has complied with the procedures established for applications in accordance with article 4 of this Annex and has given the Authority the undertakings and assurances required by that article. In cases of non-compliance with these procedures or in the absence of any of these undertakings and assurances, the applicant shall be given 45 days to remedy these defects;

(b) the applicant possesses the requisite qualifications provided for in article 4 of this Annex.

3. All proposed plans of work shall be taken up in the order in which they are received. The proposed plans of work shall comply with and be governed by the relevant provisions of this Convention and the rules, regulations and procedures of the Authority, including those on operational requirements, financial contributions and the undertakings concerning the transfer of technology. If the proposed plans of work conform to these requirements, the Authority shall approve them provided that they are in accordance with the uniform and non-discriminatory requirements set forth in the rules, regulations and procedures of the Authority, unless:

(a) part or all of the area covered by the proposed plan of work is included in an approved plan of work or a previously submitted proposed plan of work which has not yet been finally acted on by the Authority;

(b) part or all of the area covered by the proposed plan of work is disapproved by the Authority pursuant to article 162, paragraph 2(x); or

(c) the proposed plan of work has been submitted or sponsored by a State Party which already holds:

(i) plans of work for exploration and exploitation of polymetallic nodules in non-reserved areas that, together with either part of the area covered by the application for a plan of work, exceed in size 30 per cent of a circular area of 400,000 square kilometres surrounding the centre of either part of the area covered by the proposed plan of work;

(ii) plans of work for the exploration and exploitation of polymetallic nodules in non-reserved areas which, taken together, constitute 2 per cent of the total seabed area which is not reserved or disapproved for exploitation pursuant to article 162, paragraph (2)(x).

4. For the purpose of the standard set forth in paragraph 3(c), a plan of work submitted by a partnership or consortium shall be counted on a *pro rata* basis among the sponsoring States Parties involved in accordance with article 4, paragraph 3, of this Annex. The Authority may approve plans of work covered by paragraph 3(c) if it determines that such approval would not permit a State Party or entities sponsored by it to monopolize the conduct of activities in the Area or to preclude other States Parties from activities in the Area.

5. Notwithstanding paragraph 3(a), after the end of the interim period specified in article 151, paragraph 3, the Authority may adopt by means of rules, regulations and procedures other procedures and criteria consistent with this Convention for deciding which applicants shall have plans of work approved in cases of selection among applicants for a proposed area. These procedures and criteria shall ensure approval of plans of work on an equitable and non-discriminatory basis.

Article 7   Selection among applicants for production authorizations

1. Six months after the entry into force of this Convention, and thereafter each fourth month, the Authority shall take up for consideration applications for production authorizations submitted during the immediately preceding period. The Authority shall issue the authorizations applied for if all such applications can be approved without exceeding the production limitation or contravening the obligations of the Authority under a commodity agreement or arrangement to which it has become a party, as provided in article 151.

2. When a selection must be made among applicants for production authorizations because of the production limitation set forth in article 151, paragraphs 2 to 7, or because of the obligations of the Authority under a commodity agreement or arrangement to which it has become a party, as provided for in article 151, paragraph 1, the Authority shall make the selection on the basis of objective and non-discriminatory standards set forth in its rules, regulations and procedures.

3. In the application of paragraph 2, the Authority shall give priority to those applicants which:

(a) give better assurance of performance, taking into account their financial and technical qualifications and their performance, if any, under previously approved plans of work;

(b) provide earlier prospective financial benefits to the Authority, taking into account when commercial production is scheduled to begin;

(c) have already invested the most resources and effort in prospecting or exploration.

4. Applicants which are not selected in any period shall have priority in subsequent periods until they receive a production authorization.

5. Selection shall be made taking into account the need to enhance opportunities for all States Parties, irrespective of their social and economic systems or geographical locations so as to avoid discrimination against any State or system, to participate in activities in the Area and to prevent monopolization of those activities.

6. Whenever fewer reserved areas than non-reserved areas are under exploitation, applications for production authorizations with respect to reserved areas shall have priority.

7. The decisions referred to in this article shall be taken as soon as possible after the close of each period.

Article 8   Reservation of areas

Each application, other than those submitted by the Enterprise or by any other entities for reserved areas, shall cover a total area, which need not be a single continuous area, sufficiently large and of sufficient estimated commercial value to allow two mining operations. The applicant shall indicate the coordinates dividing the area into two parts of equal estimated commercial value and submit all the data obtained by him with respect to both parts. Without prejudice to the powers of the Authority pursuant to article 17 of this Annex, the data to be submitted concerning polymetallic nodules shall relate to mapping, sampling, the abundance of nodules, and their metal content. Within 45 days of receiving such data, the Authority shall designate which part is to be reserved solely for the conduct of activities by the Authority through the Enterprise or in association with developing States.

This designation may be deferred for a further period of 45 days if the Authority requests an independent expert to assess whether all data required by this article has been submitted. The area designated shall become a reserved area as soon as the plan of work for the non-reserved area is approved and the contract is signed.

Article 9   Activities on reserved areas

1. The Enterprise shall be given an opportunity to decide whether it intends to carry out activities in each reserved area. This decision may be taken at any time, unless a notification pursuant to paragraph 4 is received by the Authority, in which event the Enterprise shall take its decision within a reasonable time. The Enterprise may decide to exploit such areas in joint ventures with the interested State or entity.

2. The Enterprise may conclude contracts for the execution of part of its activities in accordance with Annex IV, article 12. It may also enter into joint ventures for the conduct of such activities with any entities which are eligible to carry out activities in the Area pursuant to article 153, paragraph 2(b). When considering such joint ventures, the Enterprise shall offer to States Parties which are developing States and their nationals the opportunity of effective participation.

3. The Authority may prescribe, in its rules, regulations and procedures, substantive and procedural requirements and conditions with respect to such contracts and joint ventures.

4. Any State Party which is a developing State or any natural or juridical person sponsored by it and effectively controlled by it or by other developing State which is a qualified applicant, or any group of the foregoing, may notify the Authority that it wishes to submit a plan of work pursuant to article 6 of this Annex with respect to a reserved area. The plan of work shall be considered if the Enterprise decides, pursuant to paragraph 1, that it does not intend to carry out activities in that area.

Article 10   Preference and priority among applicants

An operator who has an approved plan of work for exploration only, as provided in article 3, paragraph 4(c), of this Annex shall have a preference and a priority among applicants for a plan of work covering exploitation of the same area and resources. However, such preference or priority may be withdrawn if the operator's performance has not been satisfactory.

Article 11   Joint arrangements

1. Contracts may provide for joint arrangements between the contractor and the Authority through the Enterprise, in the form of joint ventures or production sharing, as well as any other form of joint arrangement, which shall have the same protection against revision, suspension or termination as contracts with the Authority.

2. Contractors entering into such joint arrangements with the Enterprise may receive financial incentives as provided for in article 13 of this Annex.

3. Partners in joint ventures with the Enterprise shall be liable for the payments required by article 13 of this Annex to the extent of their share in the joint ventures, subject to financial incentives as provided for in that article.

Article 12   Activities carried out by the Enterprise

1. Activities in the Area carried out by the Enterprise pursuant to article 153, paragraph 2(a), shall be governed by Part XI, the rules, regulations and procedures of the Authority and its relevant decisions.

2. Any plan of work submitted by the Enterprise shall be accompanied by evidence supporting its financial and technical capabilities.

Article 13   Financial terms of contracts

1. In adopting rules, regulations and procedures concerning the financial terms of a contract between the Authority and the entities referred to in article 153, paragraph 2(b), and in negotiating those financial terms in accordance with Part XI and those rules, regulations and procedures, the Authority shall be guided by the following objectives:

(a) to ensure optimum revenues for the Authority from the proceeds of commercial production;

(b) to attract investments and technology to the exploration and exploitation of the Area;

(c) to ensure equality of financial treatment and comparable financial obligations for contractors;

(d) to provide incentives on a uniform and non-discriminatory basis for contractors to undertake joint arrangements with the Enterprise and developing States or their nationals, to stimulate the transfer of technology thereto, and to train the personnel of the Authority and of developing States;

(e) to enable the Enterprise to engage in seabed mining effectively at the same time as the entities referred to in article 153, paragraph 2(b); and

(f) to ensure that, as a result of the financial incentives provided to contractors under paragraph 14, under the terms of contracts reviewed in accordance with article 19 of this Annex or under the provisions of article 11 of this Annex with respect to joint ventures, contractors are not subsidized so as to be given an artificial competitive advantage with respect to land-based miners.

2. A fee shall be levied for the administrative cost of processing an application for approval of a plan of work in the form of a contract and shall be fixed at an amount of $US 500,000 per application. The amount of the fee shall be reviewed from time to time by the Council in order to ensure that it covers the administrative cost incurred. If such administrative cost incurred by the Authority in processing an application is less than the fixed amount, the Authority shall refund the difference to the applicant.

3. A contractor shall pay an annual fixed fee of $US 1 million from the date of entry into force of the contract. If the approved date of commencement of commercial production is postponed because of a delay in issuing the production authorization, in accordance with article 151, the annual fixed fee shall be waived for the period of postponement. From the date of commencement of commercial production, the contractor shall pay either the production charge or the annual fixed fee, whichever is greater.

4. Within a year of the date of commencement of commercial production, in conformity with paragraph 3, a contractor shall choose to make his financial contribution to the Authority by either:

   (a) paying a production charge only; or

   (b) paying a combination of a production charge and a share of net proceeds.

5. (a) If a contractor chooses to make his financial contribution to the Authority by paying a production charge only, it shall be fixed at a percentage of the market value of the processed metals produced from the polymetallic nodules recovered from the area covered by the contract. This percentage shall be fixed as follows:

   (i) years 1-10 of commercial production 5 per cent

   (ii) years 11 to the end of commercial production 12 per cent

(b) The said market value shall be the product of the quantity of the processed metals produced from the polymetallic nodules extracted from the area covered by the contract and the average price for those metals during the relevant accounting year, as defined in paragraphs 7 and 8.

6. If a contractor chooses to make his financial contribution to the Authority by paying a combination of a production charge and a share of net proceeds, such payments shall be determined as follows:

(a) The production charge shall be fixed at a percentage of the market value, determined in accordance with subparagraph (b), of the processed metals produced from the polymetallic nodules recovered from the area covered by the contract. This percentage shall be fixed as follows:

(i) first period of commercial production 2 per cent

(ii) second period of commercial production 4 per cent

If, in the second period of commercial production, as defined in subparagraph (d), the return on investment in any accounting year as defined in subparagraph (m) falls below 15 per cent as a result of the payment of the production charge at 4 per cent, the production charge shall be 2 per cent instead of 4 per cent in that accounting year.

(b) The said market value shall be the product of the quantity of the processed metals produced from the polymetallic nodules recovered from the area covered by the contract and the average price for those metals during the relevant accounting year as defined in paragraphs 7 and 8.

(c) (i) The Authority's share of net proceeds shall be taken out of that portion of the contractor's net proceeds which is attributable to the mining of the resources of the area covered by the contract, referred to hereinafter as attributable net proceeds.

(ii) The Authority's share of attributable net proceeds shall be determined in accordance with the following incremental schedule:

Portion of attributable net proceeds	Share of the Authority	
	First period of commercial production	Second period of commercial production
That portion representing a return on investment which is greater than 0 per cent, but less than 10 per cent	35 per cent	40 per cent
That portion representing a return on investment which is 10 per cent or greater, but less than 20 per cent	42.5 per cent	50 per cent
That portion representing a return on investment which is 20 per cent or greater	50 per cent	70 per cent

(d) (i) The first period of commercial production referred to in subparagraphs (a) and (c) shall commence in the first accounting year of commercial production and terminate in the accounting year in which the contractor's development costs with interest on the unrecovered portion thereof are fully recovered by his cash surplus, as follows:

In the first accounting year during which development costs are incurred, unrecovered development costs shall equal the development costs less cash surplus in that year.

In each subsequent accounting year, unrecovered development costs shall equal the unrecovered development costs at the end of the preceding accounting year, plus interest thereon at the rate of 10 per cent per annum, plus development costs incurred in the current accounting year and less contractor's cash surplus in the current accounting year. The accounting year in which unrecovered development costs become zero for the first time shall be the accounting year in which the contractor's development costs with interest on the unrecovered portion thereof are fully recovered by his cash surplus.

The contractor's cash surplus in any accounting year shall be his gross proceeds less his operating costs and less his payments to the Authority under subparagraph (c).

(ii) The second period of commercial production shall commence in the accounting year following the termination of the first period of commercial production and shall continue until the end of the contract.

(e) "Attributable net proceeds" means the product of the contractor's net proceeds and the ratio of the development costs in the mining sector to the contractor's development costs. If the contractor engages in mining, transporting polymetallic nodules and production primarily of three processed metals, namely, cobalt, copper and nickel, the amount of attributable net proceeds shall not be less than 25 per cent of the contractor's net proceeds. Subject to subparagraph (n), in all other cases, including those where the contractor engages in mining, transporting polymetallic nodules, and production primarily of four processed metals, namely, cobalt, copper, manganese and nickel, the Authority may, in its rules, regulations and procedures, prescribe appropriate floors which shall bear the same relationship to each case as the 25 per cent floor does to the three-metal case.

(f) "Contractor's net proceeds" means the contractor's gross proceeds less his operating costs and less the recovery of his development costs as set out in subparagraph (j).

(g) (i) If the contractor engages in mining, transporting polymetallic nodules and production of processed metals, "contractor's gross proceeds" means the gross revenues from the sale of the processed metals and any other monies deemed reasonably attributable to operations under the contract in accordance with the financial rules, regulations and procedures of the Authority.

(ii) In all cases other than those specified in subparagraphs (g)(i) and (n)(iii), "contractor's gross proceeds" means the gross revenues from the sale of the semi-processed metals from the polymetallic nodules recovered from the area covered by the contract, and any other monies deemed reasonably attributable to operations under the contract in accordance with the financial rules, regulations and procedures of the Authority.

(h) "Contractor's development costs" means:

(i) all expenditures incurred prior to the commencement of commercial production which are directly related to the development of the productive capacity of the area covered by the contract and the activities related thereto for operations under the contract in all cases other than that specified in subparagraph (n), in conformity with generally recognized accounting principles, including, *inter alia*, costs of machinery, equipment, ships, processing plant, construction, buildings, land, roads, prospecting and exploration of the area covered by the contract, research and development, interest, required leases, licences and fees; and

(ii) expenditures similar to those set forth in (i) above incurred subsequent to the commencement of commercial production and necessary to carry out the plan of work, except those chargeable to operating costs.

(i) The proceeds from the disposal of capital assets and the market value of those capital assets which are no longer required for operations under the contract and which are not sold shall be deducted from the contractor's development costs during the relevant accounting year. When these deductions exceed the contractor's development costs the excess shall be added to the contractor's gross proceeds.

(j) The contractor's development costs incurred prior to the commencement of commercial production referred to in subparagraphs (h)(i) and (n)(iv) shall be recovered in 10 equal annual instalments from the date of commencement of commercial production. The contractor's development costs incurred subsequent to the commencement of commercial production referred to in subparagraphs (h)(ii) and (n)(iv) shall be recovered in 10 or fewer equal annual instalments so as to ensure their complete recovery by the end of the contract.

(k) "Contractor's operating costs" means all expenditures incurred after the commencement of commercial production in the operation of the productive capacity of the area covered by the contract and the activities related thereto for operations under the contract, in conformity with generally recognized accounting principles, including, *inter alia*, the annual fixed fee or the production charge, whichever is greater, expenditures for wages, salaries, employee benefits, materials, services, transporting, processing and marketing costs, interest, utilities, preservation of the marine environment, overhead and administrative costs specifically related to operations under the contract, and any net operating losses carried forward or backward as specified herein. Net operating losses may be carried forward for two consecutive years except in the last two years of the contract in which case they may be carried backward to the two preceding years.

(l) If the contractor engages in mining, transporting of polymetallic nodules, and production of processed and semi-processed metals, "development costs of the mining sector" means the portion of the contractor's development costs which is directly related to the mining of the resources of the area covered by the contract, in conformity with generally recognized accounting principles, and the financial rules, regulations and procedures of the Authority, including, *inter alia*, application fee, annual fixed fee and, where applicable, costs of prospecting and exploration of the area covered by the contract, and a portion of research and development costs.

(m) "Return on investment" in any accounting year means the ratio of attributable net proceeds in that year to the development costs of the mining sector. For the purpose of computing this ratio the development costs of the mining sector shall include expenditures on new or replacement equipment in the mining sector less the original cost of the equipment replaced.

(n) If the contractor engages in mining only:

(i) "attributable net proceeds" means the whole of the contractor's net proceeds;

(ii) "contractor's net proceeds" shall be as defined in subparagraph (f);

(iii) "contractor's gross proceeds" means the gross revenues from the sale of the polymetallic nodules, and any other monies deemed reasonably attributable to operations under the contract in accordance with the financial rules, regulations and procedures of the Authority;

(iv) "contractor's development costs" means all expenditures incurred prior to the commencement of commercial production as set forth in subparagraph (h)(i), and all expenditures incurred subsequent to the commencement of commercial production as set forth in subparagraph (h)(ii), which are directly related to the mining of the resources of the area covered by the contract, in conformity with generally recognized accounting principles;

(v) "contractor's operating costs" means the contractor's operating costs as in subparagraph (k) which are directly related to the mining of the resources of the area covered by the contract in conformity with generally recognized accounting principles;

(vi) "return on investment" in any accounting year means the ratio of the contractor's net proceeds in that year to the contractor's development costs. For the purpose of computing this ratio, the contractor's development costs shall include expenditures on new or replacement equipment less the original cost of the equipment replaced.

(o) The costs referred to in subparagraphs (h), (k), (l) and (n) in respect of interest paid by the contractor shall be allowed to the extent that, in all the circumstances, the Authority approves, pursuant to article 4, paragraph 1, of this Annex, the debt-equity ratio and the rates of interest as reasonable, having regard to existing commercial practice.

(p) The costs referred to in this paragraph shall not be interpreted as including payments of corporate income taxes or similar charges levied by States in respect of the operations of the contractor.

7. (a) "Processed metals", referred to in paragraphs 5 and 6, means the metals in the most basic form in which they are customarily traded on international terminal markets. For this purpose, the Authority shall specify, in its financial rules, regulations and procedures, the relevant international terminal market. For the metals which are not traded on such markets, "processed metals" means the metals in the most basic form in which they are customarily traded in representative arm's length transactions.

(b) If the Authority cannot otherwise determine the quantity of the processed metals produced from the polymetallic nodules recovered from the area covered by the contract referred to in paragraphs 5(b) and 6(b), the quantity shall be determined on the basis of the metal content of the nodules, processing recovery efficiency and other relevant factors, in accordance with the rules, regulations and procedures of the Authority and in conformity with generally recognized accounting principles.

8. If an international terminal market provides a representative pricing mechanism for processed metals, polymetallic nodules and semi-processed metals from the nodules, the average price on that market shall be used. In all other cases, the Authority shall, after consulting the contractor, determine a fair price for the said products in accordance with paragraph 9.

9. (a) All costs, expenditures, proceeds and revenues and all determinations of price and value referred to in this article shall be the result of free market or arm's length transactions. In the absence thereof, they shall be determined by the Authority, after consulting the contractor, as though they were the result of free market or arm's length transactions, taking into account relevant transactions in other markets.

(b) In order to ensure compliance with and enforcement of the provisions of this paragraph, the Authority shall be guided by the principles adopted for, and the interpretation given to, arm's length transactions by the Commission on Transnational Corporations of the United Nations, the Group of Experts on Tax Treaties between Developing and Developed Countries and other international organizations, and shall, in its rules, regulations and procedures, specify uniform and internationally acceptable accounting rules and procedures, and the means of selection by the contractor of certified independent accountants acceptable to the Authority for the purpose of carrying out auditing in compliance with those rules, regulations and procedures.

10. The contractor shall make available to the accountants, in accordance with the financial rules, regulations and procedures of the Authority, such financial data as are required to determine compliance with this article.

11. All costs, expenditures, proceeds and revenues, and all prices and values referred to in this article, shall be determined in accordance with generally recognized accounting principles and the financial rules, regulations and procedures of the Authority.

12. Payments to the Authority under paragraphs 5 and 6 shall be made in freely usable currencies or currencies which are freely available and effectively usable on the major foreign exchange markets or, at the contractor's option, in the equivalents of processed metals at market value. The market value shall be determined in accordance with paragraph 5(b). The freely usable currencies and currencies which are freely available and effectively usable on the major foreign exchange

markets shall be defined in the rules, regulations and procedures of the Authority in accordance with prevailing international monetary practice.

13. All financial obligations of the contractor to the Authority, as well as all his fees, costs, expenditures, proceeds and revenues referred to in this article, shall be adjusted by expressing them in constant terms relative to a base year.

14. The Authority may, taking into account any recommendations of the Economic Planning Commission and the Legal and Technical Commission, adopt rules, regulations and procedures that provide for incentives, on a uniform and non-discriminatory basis, to contractors to further the objectives set out in paragraph 1.

15. In the event of a dispute between the Authority and a contractor over the interpretation or application of the financial terms of a contract, either party may submit the dispute to binding commercial arbitration, unless both parties agree to settle the dispute by other means, in accordance with article 188, paragraph 2.

Article 14   Transfer of data

1. The operator shall transfer to the Authority, in accordance with its rules, regulations and procedures and the terms and conditions of the plan of work, at time intervals determined by the Authority all data which are both necessary for and relevant to the effective exercise of the powers and functions of the principal organs of the Authority in respect of the area covered by the plan of work.

2. Transferred data in respect of the area covered by the plan of work, deemed proprietary, may only be used for the purposes set forth in this article. Data necessary for the formulation by the Authority of rules, regulations and procedures concerning protection of the marine environment and safety, other than equipment design data, shall not be deemed proprietary.

3. Data transferred to the Authority by prospectors, applicants for contracts or contractors, deemed proprietary, shall not be disclosed by the Authority to the Enterprise or to anyone external to the Authority, but data on the reserved areas may be disclosed to the Enterprise. Such data transferred by such persons to the Enterprise shall not be disclosed by the Enterprise to the Authority or to anyone external to the Authority.

Article 15   Training programmes

The contractor shall draw up practical programmes for the training of personnel of the Authority and developing States, including the participation of such personnel in all activities in the Area which are covered by the contract, in accordance with article 144, paragraph 2.

Article 16   Exclusive right to explore and exploit

The Authority shall, pursuant to Part XI and its rules, regulations and procedures, accord the operator the exclusive right to explore and exploit the area covered by the plan of work in respect of a specified category of resources and shall ensure that no other entity operates in the same area for a different category of resources in a manner which might interfere with the operations of the operator. The operator shall have security of tenure in accordance with article 153, paragraph 6.

Article 17   Rules, regulations and procedures of the Authority

1. The Authority shall adopt and uniformly apply rules, regulations and procedures in accordance with article 160, paragraph 2(f)(ii), and article 162, paragraph 2(o)(ii), for the exercise of its functions as set forth in Part XI on, *inter alia*, the following matters:

(a) administrative procedures relating to prospecting, exploration and exploitation in the Area;

(b) operations:

(i) size of area;

(ii) duration of operations;

(iii) performance requirements including assurances pursuant to article 4, paragraph 6(c), of this Annex;

(iv) categories of resources;

(v) renunciation of areas;

(vi) progress reports;

(vii) submission of data;

(viii) inspection and supervision of operations;

(ix) prevention of interference with other activities in the marine environment;

(x) transfer of rights and obligations by a contractor;

(xi) procedures for transfer of technology to developing States in accordance with article 144 and for their direct participation;

(xii) mining standards and practices, including those relating to operational safety, conservation of the resources and the protection of the marine environment;

(xiii) definition of commercial production;

(xiv) qualification standards for applicants;

(c) financial matters:

(i) establishment of uniform and non-discriminatory costing and accounting rules and the method of selection of auditors;

(ii) apportionment of proceeds of operations;

(iii) the incentives referred to in article 13 of this Annex;

(d) implementation of decisions taken pursuant to article 151, paragraph 10, and article 164, paragraph 2(d).

2. Rules, regulations and procedures on the following items shall fully reflect the objective criteria set out below:

(a) Size of areas:

The Authority shall determine the appropriate size of areas for exploration which may be up to twice as large as those for exploitation in order to permit intensive exploration operations. The size of area shall be calculated to satisfy the requirements of article 8 of this Annex on reservation of areas as well as stated production requirements consistent with article 151 in accordance with the terms of the contract taking into account the state of the art of technology then available for seabed mining and the relevant physical characteristics of the areas.

Areas shall be neither smaller nor larger than are necessary to satisfy this objective.

(b) Duration of operations:

(i) Prospecting shall be without time-limit;

(ii) Exploration should be of sufficient duration to permit a thorough survey of the specific area, the design and construction of mining equipment for the area and the design and construction of small and medium-size processing plants for the purpose of testing mining and processing systems;

(iii) The duration of exploitation should be related to the economic life of the mining project, taking into consideration such factors as the depletion of the ore, the useful life of mining equipment and processing facilities and commercial viability. Exploitation should be of sufficient duration to permit commercial extraction of minerals of the area and should include a reasonable time period for construction of commercial-scale mining and processing systems, during which period commercial production should not be required. The total duration of exploitation, however, should also be short enough to give the Authority an opportunity to amend the terms and conditions of the plan of work at the time it considers renewal in accordance with rules, regulations and procedures which it has adopted subsequent to approving the plan of work.

(c) Performance requirements:

The Authority shall require that during the exploration stage periodic expenditures be made by the operator which are reasonably related to the size of the area covered by the plan of work and the expenditures which would be expected of a *bona fide* operator who intended to bring the area into commercial production within the time-limits established by the Authority. The required expenditures should not be established at a level which would discourage prospective operators with less costly technology than is prevalently in use. The Authority shall establish a maximum time interval, after the exploration stage is completed and the exploitation stage begins, to achieve commercial production. To determine this interval, the Authority should take into consideration that construction of large-scale mining and processing systems cannot be initiated until after the termination of the exploration stage and the commencement of the exploitation stage. Accordingly, the interval to bring an area into commercial production should take into account the time necessary for this construction after the completion of the exploration stage and reasonable allowance should be made for unavoidable delays in the construction schedule. Once commercial production is achieved, the Authority shall within reasonable limits and taking into consideration all relevant factors require the operator to maintain commercial production throughout the period of the plan of work.

(d) Categories of resources:

In determining the category of resources in respect of which a plan of work may be approved, the Authority shall give emphasis *inter alia* to the following characteristics:

(i) that certain resources require the use of similar mining methods; and

(ii) that some resources can be developed simultaneously without undue interference between operators developing different resources in the same area. Nothing in this subparagraph shall preclude the Authority from approving a plan of work with respect to more than one category of resources in the same area to the same applicant.

(e) Renunciation of areas:

The operator shall have the right at any time to renounce without penalty the whole or part of his rights in the area covered by a plan of work.

(f) Protection of the marine environment:

Rules, regulations and procedures shall be drawn up in order to secure effective protection of the marine environment from harmful effects directly resulting from activities in the Area or from shipboard processing immediately above a mine site of minerals derived from that mine site, taking into account the extent to which such harmful effects may directly result from drilling, dredging, coring and excavation and from disposal, dumping and discharge into the marine environment of sediment, wastes or other effluents.

(g) Commercial production:

Commercial production shall be deemed to have begun if an operator engages in sustained large-scale recovery operations which yield a quantity of materials sufficient to indicate clearly that the principal purpose is large-scale production rather than production intended for information gathering, analysis or the testing of equipment or plant.

Article 18   Penalties

1. A contractor's rights under the contract may be suspended or terminated only in the following cases:

(a) if, in spite of warnings by the Authority, the contractor has conducted his activities in such a way as to result in serious, persistent and wilful violations of the fundamental terms of the contract, Part XI and the rules, regulations and procedures of the Authority; or

(b) if the contractor has failed to comply with a final binding decision of the dispute settlement body applicable to him.

2. In the case of any violation of the contract not covered by paragraph 1(a), or in lieu of suspension or termination under paragraph 1(a), the Authority may impose upon the contractor monetary penalties proportionate to the seriousness of the violation.

3. Except for emergency orders under article 162, paragraph 2(w), the Authority may not execute a decision involving monetary penalties, suspension or termination until the contractor has been accorded a reasonable opportunity to exhaust the judicial remedies available to him pursuant to Part XI, section 5.

Article 19   Revision of contract

1. When circumstances have arisen or are likely to arise which, in the opinion of either party, would render the contract inequitable or make it impracticable or impossible to achieve the objectives set out in the contract or in Part XI, the parties shall enter into negotiations to revise it accordingly.

2. Any contract entered into in accordance with article 153, paragraph 3, may be revised only with the consent of the parties.

Article 20   Transfer of rights and obligations

The rights and obligations arising under a contract may be transferred only with the consent of the Authority, and in accordance with its rules, regulations and procedures. The Authority shall not unreasonably withhold consent to the transfer if the proposed transferee is in all respects a qualified applicant and assumes all of the obligations of the transferor and if the transfer does not confer to the transferee a plan of work, the approval of which would be forbidden by article 6, paragraph 3(c), of this Annex.

Article 21   Applicable law

1. The contract shall be governed by the terms of the contract, the rules, regulations and procedures of the Authority, Part XI and other rules of international law not incompatible with this Convention.

2. Any final decision rendered by a court or tribunal having jurisdiction under this Convention relating to the rights and obligations of the Authority and of the contractor shall be enforceable in the territory of each State Party.

3. No State Party may impose conditions on a contractor that are inconsistent with Part XI. However, the application by a State Party to contractors sponsored by it, or to ships flying its flag, of environmental or other laws and regulations more stringent than those in the rules, regulations and procedures of the Authority adopted pursuant to article 17, paragraph 2(f), of this Annex shall not be deemed inconsistent with Part XI.

Article 22   Responsibility

The contractor shall have responsibility or liability for any damage arising out of wrongful acts in the conduct of its operations, account being taken of contributory acts or omissions by the Authority. Similarly, the Authority shall have responsibility or liability for any damage arising out of wrongful acts in the exercise of its powers and functions, including violations under article 168, paragraph 2, account being taken of contributory acts or omissions by the contractor. Liability in every case shall be for the actual amount of damage.

ANNEX IV   STATUTE OF THE ENTERPRISE

Article 1   Purposes

1. The Enterprise is the organ of the Authority which shall carry out activities in the Area directly, pursuant to article 153, paragraph 2 (a), as well as the transporting, processing and marketing of minerals recovered from the Area.

2. In carrying out its purposes and in the exercise of its functions, the Enterprise shall act in accordance with this Convention and the rules, regulations and procedures of the Authority.

3. In developing the resources of the Area pursuant to paragraph 1, the Enterprise shall, subject to this Convention, operate in accordance with sound commercial principles.

Article 2   Relationship to the Authority

1. Pursuant to article 170, the Enterprise shall act in accordance with the general policies of the Assembly and the directives of the Council.

2. Subject to paragraph l, the Enterprise shall enjoy autonomy in the conduct of its operations.

3. Nothing in this Convention shall make the Enterprise liable for the acts or obligations of the Authority, or make the Authority liable for the acts or obligations of the Enterprise.

Article 3   Limitation of liability

Without prejudice to article 11, paragraph 3, of this Annex, no member of the Authority shall be liable by reason only of its membership for the acts or obligations of the Enterprise.

Article 4   Structure

The Enterprise shall have a Governing Board, a Director-General and the staff necessary for the exercise of its functions.

Article 5   Governing Board

1. The Governing Board shall be composed of 15 members elected by the Assembly in accordance with article 160, paragraph 2(c). In the election of the members of the Board, due regard shall be paid to the principle of equitable geographical distribution. In submitting nominations of candidates for election to the Board, members of the Authority shall bear in mind the need to nominate candidates of the highest standard of competence, with qualifications in relevant fields, so as to ensure the viability and success of the Enterprise.

2. Members of the Board shall be elected for four years and may be re-elected; and due regard shall be paid to the principle of rotation of membership.

3. Members of the Board shall continue in office until their successors are elected. If the office of a member of the Board becomes vacant, the Assembly shall, in accordance with article 160, paragraph 2(c), elect a new member for the remainder of his predecessor's term.

4. Members of the Board shall act in their personal capacity. In the performance of their duties they shall not seek or receive instructions from any government or from any other source. Each member of the Authority shall respect the independent character of the members of the Board and shall refrain from all attempts to influence any of them in the discharge of their duties.

5. Each member of the Board shall receive remuneration to be paid out of the funds of the Enterprise. The amount of remuneration shall be fixed y the Assembly, upon the recommendation of the Council.

6. The Board shall normally function at the principal office of the Enterprise and shall meet as often as the business of the Enterprise may require.

7. Two thirds of the members of the Board shall constitute a quorum.

8. Each member of the Board shall have one vote. All matters before the Board shall be decided by a majority of its members. If a member has a conflict of interest on a matter before the Board he shall refrain from voting on that matter.

9. Any member of the Authority may ask the Board for information in respect of its operations which particularly affect that member. The Board shall endeavour to provide such information.

Article 6   Powers and functions of the Governing Board

The Governing Board shall direct the operations of the Enterprise. Subject to this Convention, the Governing Board shall exercise the powers necessary to fulfil the purposes of the Enterprise, including powers:

(a) to elect a Chairman from among its members;

(b) to adopt its rules of procedure;

(c) to draw up and submit formal written plans of work to the Council in accordance with article 153, paragraph 3, and article 162, paragraph 2(j);

(d) to develop plans of work and programmes for carrying out the activities specified in article 170;

(e) to prepare and submit to the Council applications for production authorizations in accordance with article 151, paragraphs 2 to 7;

(f) to authorize negotiations concerning the acquisition of technology, including those provided for in Annex III, article 5, paragraph 3(a), (c) and (d), and to approve the results of those negotiations;

(g) to establish terms and conditions, and to authorize negotiations, concerning joint ventures and other forms of joint arrangements referred to in Annex III, articles 9 and 11, and to approve the results of such negotiations;

(h) to recommend to the Assembly what portion of the net income of the Enterprise should be retained as its reserves in accordance with article 160, paragraph 2(f), and article 10 of this Annex;

(i) to approve the annual budget of the Enterprise;

(j) to authorize the procurement of goods and services in accordance with article 12, paragraph 3, of this Annex;

(k) to submit an annual report to the Council in accordance with article 9 of this Annex;

(l) to submit to the Council for the approval of the Assembly draft rules in respect of the organization, management, appointment and dismissal of the staff of the Enterprise and to adopt regulations to give effect to such rules;

(m) to borrow funds and to furnish such collateral or other security as it may determine in accordance with article 11, paragraph 2, of this Annex;

(n) to enter into any legal proceedings, agreements and transactions and to take any other actions in accordance with article 13 of this Annex;

(o) to delegate, subject to the approval of the Council, any non-discretionary powers to the Director-General and to its committees.

Article 7   Director-General and staff of the Enterprise

1. The Assembly shall, upon the recommendation of the Council and the nomination of the Governing Board, elect the Director-General of the Enterprise who shall not be a member of the Board. The Director-General shall hold office for a fixed term, not exceeding five years, and may be re-elected for further terms.

2. The Director-General shall be the legal representative and chief executive of the Enterprise and shall be directly responsible to the Board for the conduct of the operations of the Enterprise. He shall be responsible for the organization, management, appointment and dismissal of the staff of the Enterprise in accordance with the rules and regulations referred to in article 6, subparagraph (l), of this Annex. He shall participate, without the right to vote, in the meetings of the Board and may participate, without the right to vote, in the meetings of the Assembly and the Council when these organs are dealing with matters concerning the Enterprise.

3. The paramount consideration in the recruitment and employment of the staff and in the determination of their conditions of service shall be the necessity of securing the highest standards of efficiency and of technical competence. Subject to this consideration, due regard shall be

paid to the importance of recruiting the staff on an equitable
geographical basis.

4. In the performance of their duties the Director-General and the staff
shall not seek or receive instructions from any government or from any
other source external to the Enterprise. They shall refrain from any
action which might reflect on their position as international officials of
the Enterprise responsible only to the Enterprise. Each State Party
undertakes to respect the exclusively international character of the
responsibilities of the Director-General and the staff and not to seek to
influence them in the discharge of their responsibilities.

5. The responsibilities set forth in article 168, paragraph 2, are equally
applicable to the staff of the Enterprise.

Article 8   Location

The Enterprise shall have its principal office at the seat of the Authority.
The Enterprise may establish other offices and facilities in the territory of
any State Party with the consent of that State Party.

Article 9   Reports and financial statements

1. The Enterprise shall, not later than three months after the end of each
financial year, submit to the Council for its consideration an annual
report containing an audited statement of its accounts and shall transmit
to the Council at appropriate intervals a summary statement of its
financial position and a profit and loss statement showing the results of
its operations.

2. The Enterprise shall publish its annual report and such other reports
as it finds appropriate.

3. All reports and financial statements referred to in this article shall be
distributed to the members of the Authority.

Article 10   Allocation of net income

1. Subject to paragraph 3, the Enterprise shall make payments to the
Authority under Annex III, article 13, or their equivalent.

2. The Assembly shall, upon the recommendation of the Governing
Board, determine what portion of the net income of the Enterprise shall

be retained as reserves of the Enterprise. The remainder shall be transferred to the Authority.

3. During an initial period required for the Enterprise to become self-supporting, which shall not exceed 10 years from the commencement of commercial production by it, the Assembly shall exempt the Enterprise from the payments referred to in paragraph 1, and shall leave all of the net income of the Enterprise in its reserves.

Article 11   Finances

1. The funds of the Enterprise shall include:

(a) amounts received from the Authority in accordance with article 173, paragraph 2(b);

(b) voluntary contributions made by States Parties for the purpose of financing activities of the Enterprise;

(c) amounts borrowed by the Enterprise in accordance with paragraphs 2 and 3;

(d) income of the Enterprise from its operations;

(e) other funds made available to the Enterprise to enable it to commence operations as soon as possible and to carry out its functions.

2. (a) The Enterprise shall have the power to borrow funds and to furnish such collateral or other security as it may determine. Before making a public sale of its obligations in the financial markets or currency of a State Party, the Enterprise shall obtain the approval of that State Party. The total amount of borrowings shall be approved by the Council upon the recommendation of the Governing Board.

(b) States Parties shall make every reasonable effort to support applications by the Enterprise for loans on capital markets and from international financial institutions.

3. (a) The Enterprise shall be provided with the funds necessary to explore and exploit one mine site, and to transport, process and market the minerals recovered therefrom and the nickel, copper, cobalt and manganese obtained, and to meet its initial administrative expenses. The amount of the said funds, and the criteria and factors for its

adjustment, shall be included by the Preparatory Commission in the draft rules, regulations and procedures of the Authority.

(b) All States Parties shall make available to the Enterprise an amount equivalent to one half of the funds referred to in subparagraph (a) by way of long-term interest-free loans in accordance with the scale of assessments for the United Nations regular budget in force at the time when the assessments are made, adjusted to take into account the States which are not members of the United Nations. Debts incurred by the Enterprise in raising the other half of the funds shall be guaranteed by all States Parties in accordance with the same scale.

(c) If the sum of the financial contributions of States Parties is less than the funds to be provided to the Enterprise under subparagraph (a), the Assembly shall, at its first session, consider the extent of the shortfall and adopt by consensus measures for dealing with this shortfall, taking into account the obligation of States Parties under subparagraphs (a) and (b) and any recommendations of the Preparatory Commission.

(d) (i) Each State Party shall, within 60 days after the entry into force of this Convention, or within 30 days after the deposit of its instrument of ratification or accession, whichever is later, deposit with the Enterprise irrevocable, non-negotiable, non-interest-bearing promissory notes in the amount of the share of such State Party of interest-free loans pursuant to subparagraph (b).

(ii) The Board shall prepare, at the earliest practicable date after this Convention enters into force, and thereafter at annual or other appropriate intervals, a schedule of the magnitude and timing of its requirements for the funding of its administrative expenses and for activities carried out by the Enterprise in accordance with article 170 and article 12 of this Annex.

(iii) The States Parties shall, thereupon, be notified by the Enterprise, through the Authority, of their respective shares of the funds in accordance with subparagraph (b), required for such expenses. The Enterprise shall encash such amounts of the promissory notes as may be required to meet the expenditure referred to in the schedule with respect to interest-free loans.

(iv) States Parties shall, upon receipt of the notification, make available their respective shares of debt guarantees for the Enterprise in accordance with subparagraph (b).

(e) (i) If the Enterprise so requests, State Parties may provide debt guarantees in addition to those provided in accordance with the scale referred to in subparagraph (b).

(ii) In lieu of debt guarantees, a State Party may make a voluntary contribution to the Enterprise in an amount equivalent to that portion of the debts which it would otherwise be liable to guarantee.

(f) Repayment of the interest-bearing loans shall have priority over the repayment of the interest-free loans. Repayment of interest-free loans shall be in accordance with a schedule adopted by the Assembly, upon the recommendation of the Council and the advice of the Board. In the exercise of this function the Board shall be guided by the relevant provisions of the rules, regulations and procedures of the Authority, which shall take into account the paramount importance of ensuring the effective functioning of the Enterprise and, in particular, ensuring its financial independence.

(g) Funds made available to the Enterprise shall be in freely usable currencies or currencies which are freely available and effectively usable in the major foreign exchange markets.

These currencies shall be defined in the rules, regulations and procedures of the Authority in accordance with prevailing international monetary practice. Except as provided in paragraph 2, no State Party shall maintain or impose restrictions on the holding, use or exchange by the Enterprise of these funds.

(h) "Debt guarantee" means a promise of a State Party to creditors of the Enterprise to pay, *pro rata* in accordance with the appropriate scale, the financial obligations of the Enterprise covered by the guarantee following notice by the creditors to the State Party of a default by the Enterprise. Procedures for the payment of those obligations shall be in conformity with the rules, regulations and procedures of the Authority.

4. The funds, assets and expenses of the Enterprise shall be kept separate from those of the Authority. This article shall not prevent the Enterprise from making arrangements with the Authority regarding facilities, personnel and services and arrangements for reimbursement of administrative expenses paid by either on behalf of the other.

5. The records, books and accounts of the Enterprise, including its annual financial statements, shall be audited annually by an independent auditor appointed by the Council.

Article 12   Operations

1. The Enterprise shall propose to the Council projects for carrying out activities in accordance with article 170. Such proposals shall include a formal written plan of work for activities in the Area in accordance with article 153, paragraph 3, and all such other information and data as may be required from time to time for its appraisal by the Legal and Technical Commission and approval by the Council.

2. Upon approval by the Council, the Enterprise shall execute the project on the basis of the formal written plan of work referred to in paragraph 1.

3. (a) If the Enterprise does not possess the goods and services required for its operations it may procure them. For that purpose, it shall issue invitations to tender and award contracts to bidders offering the best combination of quality, price and delivery time.

(b) If there is more than one bid offering such a combination, the contract shall be awarded in accordance with:

(i) the principle of non-discrimination on the basis of political or other considerations not relevant to the carrying out of operations with due diligence and efficiency; and

(ii) guidelines approved by the Council with regard to the preferences to be accorded to goods and services originating in developing States, including the land-locked and geographically disadvantaged among them.

(c) The Governing Board may adopt rules determining the special circumstances in which the requirement of invitations to bid may, in the best interests of the Enterprise, be dispensed with.

4. The Enterprise shall have title to all minerals and processed substances produced by it.

5. The Enterprise shall sell its products on a non-discriminatory basis. It shall not give non-commercial discounts.

6. Without prejudice to any general or special power conferred on the Enterprise under any other provision of this Convention, the Enterprise shall exercise such powers incidental to its business as shall be necessary.

7. The Enterprise shall not interfere in the political affairs of any State Party; nor shall it be influenced in its decisions by the political character of the State Party concerned. Only commercial considerations shall be relevant to its decisions, and these considerations shall be weighed impartially in order to carry out the purposes specified in article 1 of this Annex.

Article 13   Legal status, privileges and immunities

1. To enable the Enterprise to exercise its functions, the status, privileges and immunities set forth in this article shall be accorded to the Enterprise in the territories of States Parties. To give effect to this principle the Enterprise and States Parties may, where necessary, enter into special agreements.

2. The Enterprise shall have such legal capacity as is necessary for the exercise of its functions and the fulfilment of its purposes and, in particular, the capacity:

(a) to enter into contracts, joint arrangements or other arrangements, including agreements with States and international organizations;

(b) to acquire, lease, hold and dispose of immovable and movable property;

(c) to be a party to legal proceedings.

3. (a) Actions may be brought against the Enterprise only in a court of competent jurisdiction in the territory of a State Party in which the Enterprise:

(i) has an office or facility;

(ii) has appointed an agent for the purpose of accepting service or notice of process;

(iii) has entered into a contract for goods or services;

(iv) has issued securities; or

(v) is otherwise engaged in commercial activity.

(b) The property and assets of the Enterprise, wherever located and by whomsoever held, shall be immune from all forms of seizure, attachment or execution before the delivery of final judgment against the Enterprise.

4. (a) The property and assets of the Enterprise, wherever located and by whomsoever held, shall be immune from requisition, confiscation, expropriation or any other form of seizure by executive or legislative action.

(b) The property and assets of the Enterprise, wherever located and by whomsoever held, shall be free from discriminatory restrictions, regulations, controls and moratoria of any nature.

(c) The Enterprise and its employees shall respect local laws and regulations in any State or territory in which the Enterprise or its employees may do business or otherwise act.

(d) States Parties shall ensure that the Enterprise enjoys all rights, privileges and immunities accorded by them to entities conducting commercial activities in their territories. These rights, privileges and immunities shall be accorded to the Enterprise on no less favourable a basis than that on which they are accorded to entities engaged in similar commercial activities. If special privileges are provided by States Parties for developing States or their commercial entities, the Enterprise shall enjoy those privileges on a similarly preferential basis.

(e) States Parties may provide special incentives, rights, privileges and immunities to the Enterprise without the obligation to provide such incentives, rights, privileges and immunities to other commercial entities.

5. The Enterprise shall negotiate with the host countries in which its offices and facilities are located for exemption from direct and indirect taxation.

6. Each State Party shall take such action as is necessary for giving effect in terms of its own law to the principles set forth in this Annex and shall inform the Enterprise of the specific action which it has taken.

7. The Enterprise may waive any of the privileges and immunities conferred under this article or in the special agreements referred to in paragraph 1 to such extent and upon such conditions as it may determine.

ANNEX V   CONCILIATION

SECTION 1   CONCILIATION PROCEDURE PURSUANT TO SECTION 1 OF PART XV

Article 1   Institution of proceedings

If the parties to a dispute have agreed, in accordance with article 284, to submit it to conciliation under this section, any such party may institute the proceedings by written notification addressed to the other party or parties to the dispute.

Article 2   List of conciliators

A list of conciliators shall be drawn up and maintained by the Secretary-General of the United Nations. Every State Party shall be entitled to nominate four conciliators, each of whom shall be a person enjoying the highest reputation for fairness, competence and integrity. The names of the persons so nominated shall constitute the list. If at any time the conciliators nominated by a State Party in the list so constituted shall be fewer than four, that State Party shall be entitled to make further nominations as necessary.

The name of a conciliator shall remain on the list until withdrawn by the State Party which made the nomination, provided that such conciliator shall continue to serve on any conciliation commission to which that conciliator has been appointed until the completion of the proceedings before that commission.

Article 3   Constitution of conciliation commission

The conciliation commission shall, unless the parties otherwise agree, be constituted as follows:

(a) Subject to subparagraph (g), the conciliation commission shall consist of five members.

(b) The party instituting the proceedings shall appoint two conciliators to be chosen preferably from the list referred to in article 2 of this Annex, one of whom may be its national, unless the parties otherwise agree. Such appointments shall be included in the notification referred to in article 1 of this Annex.

(c) The other party to the dispute shall appoint two conciliators in the manner set forth in subparagraph (b) within 21 days of receipt of the notification referred to in article 1 of this Annex. If the appointments are not made within that period, the party instituting the proceedings may, within one week of the expiration of that period, either terminate the proceedings by notification addressed to the other party or request the Secretary-General of the United Nations to make the appointments in accordance with subparagraph (e).

(d) Within 30 days after all four conciliators have been appointed, they shall appoint a fifth conciliator chosen from the list referred to in article 2 of this Annex, who shall be chairman. If the appointment is not made within that period, either party may, within one week of the expiration of that period, request the Secretary-General of the United Nations to make the appointment in accordance with subparagraph (e).

(e) Within 30 days of the receipt of a request under subparagraph (c) or (d), the Secretary-General of the United Nations shall make the necessary appointments from the list referred to in article 2 of this Annex in consultation with the parties to the dispute.

(f) Any vacancy shall be filled in the manner prescribed for the initial appointment.

(g) Two or more parties which determine by agreement that they are in the same interest shall appoint two conciliators jointly. Where two or more parties have separate interests or there is a disagreement as to whether they are of the same interest, they shall appoint conciliators separately.

(h) In disputes involving more than two parties having separate interests, or where there is disagreement as to whether they are of the same interest, the parties shall apply subparagraphs (a) to (f) in so far as possible.

Article 4   Procedure

The conciliation commission shall, unless the parties otherwise agree, determine its own procedure. The commission may, with the consent of the parties to the dispute, invite any State Party to submit to it its views orally or in writing. Decisions of the commission regarding procedural matters, the report and recommendations shall be made by a majority vote of its members.

Article 5   Amicable settlement

The commission may draw the attention of the parties to any measures which might facilitate an amicable settlement of the dispute.

Article 6   Functions of the commission

The commission shall hear the parties, examine their claims and objections, and make proposals to the parties with a view to reaching an amicable settlement.

Article 7   Report

1. The commission shall report within 12 months of its constitution. Its report shall record any agreements reached and, failing agreement, its conclusions on all questions of fact or law relevant to the matter in dispute and such recommendations as the commission may deem appropriate for an amicable settlement. The report shall be deposited with the Secretary-General of the United Nations and shall immediately be transmitted by him to the parties to the dispute.

2. The report of the commission, including its conclusions or recommendations, shall not be binding upon the parties.

Article 8   Termination

The conciliation proceedings are terminated when a settlement has been reached, when the parties have accepted or one party has rejected the recommendations of the report by written notification addressed to the Secretary-General of the United Nations, or when a period of three months has expired from the date of transmission of the report to the parties.

Article 9   Fees and expenses

The fees and expenses of the commission shall be borne by the parties to the dispute.

Article 10   Right of parties to modify procedure

The parties to the dispute may by agreement applicable solely to that dispute modify any provision of this Annex.

SECTION 2   COMPULSORY SUBMISSION TO CONCILIATION PROCEDURE PURSUANT TO SECTION 3 OF PART XV

Article 11   Institution of proceedings

1. Any party to a dispute which, in accordance with Part XV, section 3, may be submitted to conciliation under this section, may institute the proceedings by written notification addressed to the other party or parties to the dispute.

2. Any party to the dispute, notified under paragraph 1, shall be obliged to submit to such proceedings.

Article 12   Failure to reply or to submit to conciliation

The failure of a party or parties to the dispute to reply to notification of institution of proceedings or to submit to such proceedings shall not constitute a bar to the proceedings.

Article 13   Competence

A disagreement as to whether a conciliation commission acting under this section has competence shall be decided by the commission.

Article 14   Application of section 1

Articles 2 to 10 of section 1 of this Annex apply subject to this section.

**ANNEX VI   STATUTE OF THE INTERNATIONAL TRIBUNAL
FOR THE LAW OF THE SEA**

Article 1   General provisions

1. The International Tribunal for the Law of the Sea is constituted and shall function in accordance with the provisions of this Convention and this Statute.

2. The seat of the Tribunal shall be in the Free and Hanseatic City of Hamburg in the Federal Republic of Germany.

3. The Tribunal may sit and exercise its functions elsewhere whenever it considers this desirable.

4. A reference of a dispute to the Tribunal shall be governed by the provisions of Parts XI and XV.

SECTION 1   ORGANIZATION OF THE TRIBUNAL

Article 2   Composition

1. The Tribunal shall be composed of a body of 21 independent members, elected from among persons enjoying the highest reputation for fairness and integrity and of recognized competence in the field of the law of the sea.

2. In the Tribunal as a whole the representation of the principal legal systems of the world and equitable geographical distribution shall be assured.

Article 3   Membership

1. No two members of the Tribunal may be nationals of the same State. A person who for the purposes of membership in the Tribunal could be regarded as a national of more than one State shall be deemed to be a national of the one in which he ordinarily exercises civil and political rights.

2. There shall be no fewer than three members from each geographical group as established by the General Assembly of the United Nations.

Article 4   Nominations and elections

1. Each State Party may nominate not more than two persons having the qualifications prescribed in article 2 of this Annex. The members of the Tribunal shall be elected from the list of persons thus nominated.

2. At least three months before the date of the election, the Secretary-General of the United Nations in the case of the first election and the Registrar of the Tribunal in the case of subsequent elections shall address a written invitation to the States Parties to submit their nominations for members of the Tribunal within two months. He shall prepare a list in alphabetical order of all the persons thus nominated, with an indication of the States Parties which have nominated them, and shall submit it to the States Parties before the seventh day of the last month before the date of each election.

3. The first election shall be held within six months of the date of entry into force of this Convention.

4. The members of the Tribunal shall be elected by secret ballot. Elections shall be held at a meeting of the States Parties convened by the Secretary-General of the United Nations in the case of the first election and by a procedure agreed to by the States Parties in the case of subsequent elections. Two thirds of the States Parties shall constitute a quorum at that meeting. The persons elected to the Tribunal shall be those nominees who obtain the largest number of votes and a two-thirds majority of the States Parties present and voting, provided that such majority includes a majority of the States Parties.

Article 5   Term of office

1. The members of the Tribunal shall be elected for nine years and may be re-elected; provided, however, that of the members elected at the first election, the terms of seven members shall expire at the end of three years and the terms of seven more members shall expire at the end of six years.

2. The members of the Tribunal whose terms are to expire at the end of the above-mentioned initial periods of three and six years shall be chosen by lot to be drawn by the Secretary-General of the United Nations immediately after the first election.

3. The members of the Tribunal shall continue to discharge their duties until their places have been filled. Though replaced, they shall finish any proceedings which they may have begun before the date of their replacement.

4. In the case of the resignation of a member of the Tribunal, the letter of resignation shall be addressed to the President of the Tribunal. The place becomes vacant on the receipt of that letter.

Article 6   Vacancies

1. Vacancies shall be filled by the same method as that laid down for the first election, subject to the following provision: the Registrar shall, within one month of the occurrence of the vacancy, proceed to issue the invitations provided for in article 4 of this Annex, and the date of the election shall be fixed by the President of the Tribunal after consultation with the States Parties.

2. A member of the Tribunal elected to replace a member whose term of office has not expired shall hold office for the remainder of his predecessor's term.

Article 7   Incompatible activities

1. No member of the Tribunal may exercise any political or administrative function, or associate actively with or be financially interested in any of the operations of any enterprise concerned with the exploration for or exploitation of the resources of the sea or the seabed or other commercial use of the sea or the seabed.

2. No member of the Tribunal may act as agent, counsel or advocate in any case.

3. Any doubt on these points shall be resolved by decision of the majority of the other members of the Tribunal present.

Article 8   Conditions relating to participation of members in a particular case

1. No member of the Tribunal may participate in the decision of any case in which he has previously taken part as agent, counsel or advocate for one of the parties, or as a member of a national or international court or tribunal, or in any other capacity.

2. If, for some special reason, a member of the Tribunal considers that he should not take part in the decision of a particular case, he shall so inform the President of the Tribunal.

3. If the President considers that for some special reason one of the members of the Tribunal should not sit in a particular case, he shall give him notice accordingly.

4. Any doubt on these points shall be resolved by decision of the majority of the other members of the Tribunal present.

Article 9   Consequences of ceasing to fulfil required conditions

If, in the unanimous opinion of the other members of the Tribunal, a member has ceased to fulfil the required conditions, the President of the Tribunal shall declare the seat vacant.

Article 10   Privileges and immunities

The members of the Tribunal, when engaged on the business of the Tribunal, shall enjoy diplomatic privileges and immunities.

Article 11   Solemn declaration by members

Every member of the Tribunal shall, before taking up his duties, make a solemn declaration in open session that he will exercise his powers impartially and conscientiously.

Article 12   President, Vice-President and Registrar

1. The Tribunal shall elect its President and Vice-President for three years; they may be re-elected.

2. The Tribunal shall appoint its Registrar and may provide for the appointment of such other officers as may be necessary.

3. The President and the Registrar shall reside at the seat of the Tribunal.

Article 13   Quorum

1. All available members of the Tribunal shall sit; a quorum of 11 elected members shall be required to constitute the Tribunal.

2. Subject to article 17 of this Annex, the Tribunal shall determine which members are available to constitute the Tribunal for the consideration of a particular dispute, having regard to the effective functioning of the chambers as provided for in articles 14 and 15 of this Annex.

3. All disputes and applications submitted to the Tribunal shall be heard and determined by the Tribunal, unless article 14 of this Annex applies, or the parties request that it shall be dealt with in accordance with article 15 of this Annex.

Article 14   Seabed Disputes Chamber

A Seabed Disputes Chamber shall be established in accordance with the provisions of section 4 of this Annex. Its jurisdiction, powers and functions shall be as provided for in Part XI, section 5.

Article 15   Special Chambers

1. The Tribunal may form such chambers, composed of three or more of its elected members, as it considers necessary for dealing with particular categories of disputes.

2. The Tribunal shall form a chamber for dealing with a particular dispute submitted to it if the parties so request. The composition of such a chamber shall be determined by the Tribunal with the approval of the parties.

3. With a view to the speedy dispatch of business, the Tribunal shall form annually a chamber composed of five of its elected members which may hear and determine disputes by summary procedure. Two alternative members shall be selected for the purpose of replacing members who are unable to participate in a particular proceeding.

4. Disputes shall be heard and determined by the chambers provided for in this article if the parties so request.

5. A judgment given by any of the chambers provided for in this article and in article 14 of this Annex shall be considered as rendered by the Tribunal.

Article 16   Rules of the Tribunal

The Tribunal shall frame rules for carrying out its functions. In particular it shall lay down rules of procedure.

Article 17   Nationality of members

1. Members of the Tribunal of the nationality of any of the parties to a dispute shall retain their right to participate as members of the Tribunal.

2. If the Tribunal, when hearing a dispute, includes upon the bench a member of the nationality of one of the parties, any other party may choose a person to participate as a member of the Tribunal.

3. If the Tribunal, when hearing a dispute, does not include upon the bench a member of the nationality of the parties, each of those parties may choose a person to participate as a member of the Tribunal.

4. This article applies to the chambers referred to in articles 14 and 15 of this Annex. In such cases, the President, in consultation with the parties, shall request specified members of the Tribunal forming the chamber, as many as necessary, to give place to the members of the Tribunal of the nationality of the parties concerned, and, failing such, or if they are unable to be present, to the members specially chosen by the parties.

5. Should there be several parties in the same interest, they shall, for the purpose of the preceding provisions, be considered as one party only. Any doubt on this point shall be settled by the decision of the Tribunal.

6. Members chosen in accordance with paragraphs 2, 3 and 4 shall fulfil the conditions required by articles 2, 8 and 11 of this Annex. They shall participate in the decision on terms of complete equality with their colleagues.

Article 18   Remuneration of members

1. Each elected member of the Tribunal shall receive an annual allowance and, for each day on which he exercises his functions, a special allowance, provided that in any year the total sum payable to any member as special allowance shall not exceed the amount of the annual allowance.

2. The President shall receive a special annual allowance.

3. The Vice-President shall receive a special allowance for each day on which he acts as President.

4. The members chosen under article 17 of this Annex, other than elected members of the Tribunal, shall receive compensation for each day on which they exercise their functions.

5. The salaries, allowances and compensation shall be determined from time to time at meetings of the States Parties, taking into account the workload of the Tribunal. They may not be decreased during the term of office.

6. The salary of the Registrar shall be determined at meetings of the States Parties, on the proposal of the Tribunal.

7. Regulations adopted at meetings of the States Parties shall determine the conditions under which retirement pensions may be given to members of the Tribunal and to the Registrar, and the conditions under which members of the Tribunal and Registrar shall have their travelling expenses refunded.

8. The salaries, allowances, and compensation shall be free of all taxation.

Article 19   Expenses of the Tribunal

1. The expenses of the Tribunal shall be borne by the States Parties and by the Authority on such terms and in such a manner as shall be decided at meetings of the States Parties.

2. When an entity other than a State Party or the Authority is a party to a case submitted to it, the Tribunal shall fix the amount which that party is to contribute towards the expenses of the Tribunal.

SECTION 2   COMPETENCE

Article 20   Access to the Tribunal

1. The Tribunal shall be open to States Parties.

2. The Tribunal shall be open to entities other than States Parties in any case expressly provided for in Part XI or in any case submitted pursuant to any other agreement conferring jurisdiction on the Tribunal which is accepted by all the parties to that case.

Article 20   Jurisdiction

The jurisdiction of the Tribunal comprises all disputes and all applications submitted to it in accordance with this Convention and all matters specifically provided for in any other agreement which confers jurisdiction on the Tribunal.

Article 22   Reference of disputes subject to other agreements

If all the parties to a treaty or convention already in force and concerning the subject-matter covered by this Convention so agree, any disputes concerning the interpretation or application of such treaty or convention may, in accordance with such agreement, be submitted to the Tribunal.

Article 23   Applicable law

The Tribunal shall decide all disputes and applications in accordance with article 293.

SECTION 3   PROCEDURE

Article 24   Institution of proceedings

1. Disputes are submitted to the Tribunal, as the case may be, either by notification of a special agreement or by written application, addressed to the Registrar. In either case, the subject of the dispute and the parties shall be indicated.

2. The Registrar shall forthwith notify the special agreement or the application to all concerned.

3. The Registrar shall also notify all States Parties.

Article 25   Provisional measures

1. In accordance with article 290, the Tribunal and its Seabed Disputes Chamber shall have the power to prescribe provisional measures.

2. If the Tribunal is not in session or a sufficient number of members is not available to constitute a quorum, the provisional measures shall be prescribed by the chamber of summary procedure formed under article 15, paragraph 3, of this Annex. Notwithstanding article 15, paragraph 4, of this Annex, such provisional measures may be adopted at the request

of any party to the dispute. They shall be subject to review and revision by the Tribunal.

Article 26   Hearing

1. The hearing shall be under the control of the President or, if he is unable to preside, of the Vice-President. If neither is able to preside, the senior judge present of the Tribunal shall preside.

2. The hearing shall be public, unless the Tribunal decides otherwise or unless the parties demand that the public be not admitted.

Article 27   Conduct of case

The Tribunal shall make orders for the conduct of the case, decide the form and time in which each party must conclude its arguments, and make all arrangements connected with the taking of evidence.

Article 28   Default

When one of the parties does not appear before the Tribunal or fails to defend its case, the other party may request the Tribunal to continue the proceedings and make its decision. Absence of a party or failure of a party to defend its case shall not constitute a bar to the proceedings. Before making its decision, the Tribunal must satisfy itself not only that it has jurisdiction over the dispute, but also that the claim is well founded in fact and law.

Article 29   Majority for decision

1. All questions shall be decided by a majority of the members of the Tribunal who are present.

2. In the event of an equality of votes, the President or the member of the Tribunal who acts in his place shall have a casting vote.

Article 30   Judgment

1. The judgment shall state the reasons on which it is based.

2. It shall contain the names of the members of the Tribunal who have taken part in the decision.

3. If the judgment does not represent in whole or in part the unanimous opinion of the members of the Tribunal, any member shall be entitled to deliver a separate opinion.

4. The judgment shall be signed by the President and by the Registrar. It shall be read in open court, due notice having been given to the parties to the dispute.

Article 31   Request to intervene

1. Should a State Party consider that it has an interest of a legal nature which may be affected by the decision in any dispute, it may submit a request to the Tribunal to be permitted to intervene.

2. It shall be for the Tribunal to decide upon this request.

3. If a request to intervene is granted, the decision of the Tribunal in respect of the dispute shall be binding upon the intervening State Party in so far as it relates to matters in respect of which that State Party intervened.

Article 32   Right to intervene in cases of interpretation or application

1. Whenever the interpretation or application of this Convention is in question, the Registrar shall notify all States Parties forthwith.

2. Whenever pursuant to article 21 or 22 of this Annex the interpretation or application of an international agreement is in question, the Registrar shall notify all the parties to the agreement.

3. Every party referred to in paragraphs 1 and 2 has the right to intervene in the proceedings; if it uses this right, the interpretation given by the judgment will be equally binding upon it.

Article 33   Finality and binding force of decisions

1. The decision of the Tribunal is final and shall be complied with by all the parties to the dispute.

2. The decision shall have no binding force except between the parties in respect of that particular dispute.

3. In the event of dispute as to the meaning or scope of the decision, the Tribunal shall construe it upon the request of any party.

Article 34   Costs

Unless otherwise decided by the Tribunal, each party shall bear its own costs.

SECTION 4   SEABED DISPUTES CHAMBER

Article 35   Composition

1. The Seabed Disputes Chamber referred to in article 14 of this Annex shall be composed of 11 members, selected by a majority of the elected members of the Tribunal from among them.

2. In the selection of the members of the Chamber, the representation of the principal legal systems of the world and equitable geographical distribution shall be assured. The Assembly of the Authority may adopt recommendations of a general nature relating to such representation and distribution.

3. The members of the Chamber shall be selected every three years and may be selected for a second term.

4. The Chamber shall elect its President from among its members, who shall serve for the term for which the Chamber has been selected.

5. If any proceedings are still pending at the end of any three-year period for which the Chamber has been selected, the Chamber shall complete the proceedings in its original composition.

6. If a vacancy occurs in the Chamber, the Tribunal shall select a successor from among its elected members, who shall hold office for the remainder of his predecessor's term.

7. A quorum of seven of the members selected by the Tribunal shall be required to constitute the Chamber.

Article 36   Ad hoc chambers

1. The Seabed Disputes Chamber shall form an ad hoc chamber, composed of three of its members, for dealing with a particular dispute submitted to it in accordance with article 188, paragraph 1(b). The

composition of such a chamber shall be determined by the Seabed Disputes Chamber with the approval of the parties.

2. If the parties do not agree on the composition of an ad hoc chamber, each party to the dispute shall appoint one member, and the third member shall be appointed by them in agreement. If they disagree, or if any party fails to make an appointment, the President of the Seabed Disputes Chamber shall promptly make the appointment or appointments from among its members, after consultation with the parties.

3. Members of the ad hoc chamber must not be in the service of, or nationals of, any of the parties to the dispute.

Article 37   Access

The Chamber shall be open to the States Parties, the Authority and the other entities referred to in Part XI, section 5.

Article 38   Applicable law

In addition to the provisions of article 293, the Chamber shall apply:

(a) the rules, regulations and procedures of the Authority adopted in accordance with this Convention; and

(b) the terms of contracts concerning activities in the Area in matters relating to those contracts.

Article 39   Enforcement of decisions of the Chamber

The decisions of the Chamber shall be enforceable in the territories of the States Parties in the same manner as judgments or orders of the highest court of the State Party in whose territory the enforcement is sought.

Article 40   Applicability of other sections of this Annex

1. The other sections of this Annex which are not incompatible with this section apply to the Chamber.

2. In the exercise of its functions relating to advisory opinions, the Chamber shall be guided by the provisions of this Annex relating to procedure before the Tribunal to the extent to which it recognizes them to be applicable.

SECTION 5   AMENDMENTS

Article 41   Amendments

1. Amendments to this Annex, other than amendments to section 4, may be adopted only in accordance with article 313 or by consensus at a conference convened in accordance with this Convention.

2. Amendments to section 4 may be adopted only in accordance with article 314.

3. The Tribunal may propose such amendments to this Statute as it may consider necessary, by written communications to the States Parties for their consideration in conformity with paragraphs 1 and 2.

ANNEX VII   ARBITRATION

Article 1   Institution of proceedings

Subject to the provisions of Part XV, any party to a dispute may submit the dispute to the arbitral procedure provided for in this Annex by written notification addressed to the other party or parties to the dispute. The notification shall be accompanied by a statement of the claim and the grounds on which it is based.

Article 2   List of arbitrators

1. A list of arbitrators shall be drawn up and maintained by the Secretary-General of the United Nations. Every State Party shall be entitled to nominate four arbitrators, each of whom shall be a person experienced in maritime affairs and enjoying the highest reputation for fairness, competence and integrity. The names of the persons so nominated shall constitute the list.

2. If at any time the arbitrators nominated by a State Party in the list so constituted shall be fewer than four, that State Party shall be entitled to make further nominations as necessary.

3. The name of an arbitrator shall remain on the list until withdrawn by the State Party which made the nomination, provided that such arbitrator shall continue to serve on any arbitral tribunal to which that arbitrator has been appointed until the completion of the proceedings before that arbitral tribunal.

Article 3   Constitution of arbitral tribunal

For the purpose of proceedings under this Annex, the arbitral tribunal shall, unless the parties otherwise agree, be constituted as follows:

(a) Subject to subparagraph (g), the arbitral tribunal shall consist of five members.

(b) The party instituting the proceedings shall appoint one member to be chosen preferably from the list referred to in article 2 of this Annex, who may be its national. The appointment shall be included in the notification referred to in article 1 of this Annex.

(c) The other party to the dispute shall, within 30 days of receipt of the notification referred to in article 1 of this Annex, appoint one member to be chosen preferably from the list, who may be its national. If the appointment is not made within that period, the party instituting the proceedings may, within two weeks of the expiration of that period, request that the appointment be made in accordance with subparagraph (e).

(d) The other three members shall be appointed by agreement between the parties. They shall be chosen preferably from the list and shall be nationals of third States unless the parties otherwise agree. The parties to the dispute shall appoint the President of the arbitral tribunal from among those three members. If, within 60 days of receipt of the notification referred to in article 1 of this Annex, the parties are unable to reach agreement on the appointment of one or more of the members of the tribunal to be appointed by agreement, or on the appointment of the President, the remaining appointment or appointments shall be made in accordance with subparagraph (e), at the request of a party to the dispute. Such request shall be made within two weeks of the expiration of the aforementioned 60-day period.

(e) Unless the parties agree that any appointment under subparagraphs (c) and (d) be made by a person or a third State chosen by the parties, the President of the International Tribunal for the Law of the Sea shall make the necessary appointments. If the President is unable to act under this subparagraph or is a national of one of the parties to the dispute, the appointment shall be made by the next senior member of the International Tribunal for the Law of the Sea who is available and is not a national of one of the parties. The appointments referred to in this subparagraph shall be made from the list referred to in article 2 of this Annex within a period of 30 days of the receipt of the request and in consultation with the parties. The members so appointed shall be of different nationalities and may not be in the service of, ordinarily resident in the territory of, or nationals of, any of the parties to the dispute.

(f) Any vacancy shall be filled in the manner prescribed for the initial appointment.

(g) Parties in the same interest shall appoint one member of the tribunal jointly by agreement. Where there are several parties having separate interests or where there is disagreement as to whether they are of the same interest, each of them shall appoint one member of the tribunal. The number of members of the tribunal appointed separately by the parties shall always be smaller by one than the number of members of the tribunal to be appointed jointly by the parties.

(h) In disputes involving more than two parties, the provisions of subparagraphs (a) to (f) shall apply to the maximum extent possible.

Article 4   Functions of arbitral tribunal

An arbitral tribunal constituted under article 3 of this Annex shall function in accordance with this Annex and the other provisions of this Convention.

Article 5   Procedure

Unless the parties to the dispute otherwise agree, the arbitral tribunal shall determine its own procedure, assuring to each party a full opportunity to be heard and to present its case.

Article 6   Duties of parties to a dispute

The parties to the dispute shall facilitate the work of the arbitral tribunal and, in particular, in accordance with their law and using all means at their disposal, shall:

(a) provide it with all relevant documents, facilities and information; and

(b) enable it when necessary to call witnesses or experts and receive their evidence and to visit the localities to which the case relates.

Article 7   Expenses

Unless the arbitral tribunal decides otherwise because of the particular circumstances of the case, the expenses of the tribunal, including the remuneration of its members, shall be borne by the parties to the dispute in equal shares.

Article 8   Required majority for decisions

Decisions of the arbitral tribunal shall be taken by a majority vote of its members. The absence or abstention of less than half of the members shall not constitute a bar to the tribunal reaching a decision. In the event of an equality of votes, the President shall have a casting vote.

Article 9   Default of appearance

If one of the parties to the dispute does not appear before the arbitral tribunal or fails to defend its case, the other party may request the tribunal to continue the proceedings and to make its award. Absence of a party or failure of a party to defend its case shall not constitute a bar to the proceedings. Before making its award, the arbitral tribunal must satisfy itself not only that it has jurisdiction over the dispute but also that the claim is well founded in fact and law.

Article 10   Award

The award of the arbitral tribunal shall be confined to the subject-matter of the dispute and state the reasons on which it is based. It shall contain the names of the members who have participated and the date of the award. Any member of the tribunal may attach a separate or dissenting opinion to the award.

Article 11   Finality of award

The award shall be final and without appeal, unless the parties to the dispute have agreed in advance to an appellate procedure. It shall be complied with by the parties to the dispute.

Article 12   Interpretation of implementation of award

1. Any controversy which may arise between the parties to the dispute as regards the interpretation or manner of implementation of the award may be submitted by either party for decision to the arbitral tribunal which made the award. For this purpose, any vacancy in the tribunal shall be filled in the manner provided for in the original appointments of the members of the tribunal.

2. Any such controversy may be submitted to another court or tribunal under article 287 by agreement of all the parties to the dispute.

Article 13   Application to entities other than States Parties

The provisions of this Annex shall apply *mutatis mutandis* to any dispute involving entities other than States Parties.

ANNEX VIII   SPECIAL ARBITRATION

Article 1   Institution of proceedings

Subject to Part XV, any party to a dispute concerning the interpretation or application of the articles of this Convention relating to (1) fisheries, (2) protection and preservation of the marine environment, (3) marine scientific research, or (4) navigation, including pollution from vessels and by dumping, may submit the dispute to the special arbitral procedure provided for in this Annex by written notification addressed to the other party or parties to the dispute. The notification shall be accompanied by a statement of the claim and the grounds on which it is based.

Article 2   Lists of experts

1. A list of experts shall be established and maintained in respect of each of the fields of (1) fisheries, (2) protection and preservation of the marine environment, (3) marine scientific research, and (4) navigation, including pollution from vessels and by dumping.

2. The lists of experts shall be drawn up and maintained, in the field of fisheries by the Food and Agriculture Organization of the United Nations, in the field of protection and preservation of the marine environment by the United Nations Environment Programme, in the field of marine scientific research by the Intergovernmental Oceanographic Commission, in the field of navigation, including pollution from vessels and by dumping, by the International Maritime Organization, or in each case by the appropriate subsidiary body concerned to which such organization, programme or commission has delegated this function.

3. Every State Party shall be entitled to nominate two experts in each field whose competence in the legal, scientific or technical aspects of such field is established and generally recognized and who enjoy the highest reputation for fairness and integrity. The names of the persons so nominated in each field shall constitute the appropriate list.

4. If at any time the experts nominated by a State Party in the list so constituted shall be fewer than two, that State Party shall be entitled to make further nominations as necessary.

5. The name of an expert shall remain on the list until withdrawn by the State Party which made the nomination, provided that such expert shall continue to serve on any special arbitral tribunal to which that expert has been appointed until the completion of the proceedings before that special arbitral tribunal.

Article 3   Constitution of special arbitral tribunal

For the purpose of proceedings under this Annex, the special arbitral tribunal shall, unless the parties otherwise agree, be constituted as follows:

(a) Subject to subparagraph (g), the special arbitral tribunal shall consist of five members.

(b) The party instituting the proceedings shall appoint two members to be chosen preferably from the appropriate list or lists referred to in article 2 of this Annex relating to the matters in dispute, one of whom may be its national. The appointments shall be included in the notification referred to in article 1 of this Annex.

(c) The other party to the dispute shall, within 30 days of receipt of the notification referred to in article 1 of this Annex, appoint two members to be chosen preferably from the appropriate list or lists relating to the matters in dispute, one of whom may be its national. If the appointments are not made within that period, the party instituting the proceedings may, within two weeks of the expiration of that period, request that the appointments be made in accordance with subparagraph (e).

(d) The parties to the dispute shall by agreement appoint the President of the special arbitral tribunal, chosen preferably from the appropriate list, who shall be a national of a third State, unless the parties otherwise agree. If, within 30 days of receipt of the notification referred to in article 1 of this Annex, the parties are unable to reach agreement on the appointment of the President, the appointment shall be made in accordance with subparagraph (e), at the request of a party to the dispute. Such request shall be made within two weeks of the expiration of the aforementioned 30-day period.

(e) Unless the parties agree that the appointment be made by a person or a third State chosen by the parties, the Secretary-General of the United Nations shall make the necessary appointments within 30 days of receipt of a request under subparagraphs (c) and (d). The appointments referred to in this subparagraph shall be made from the appropriate list or lists of experts referred to in article 2 of this Annex and in consultation with the parties to the dispute and the appropriate international organization. The members so appointed shall be of different nationalities and may not be in the service of, ordinarily resident in the territory of, or nationals of, any of the parties to the dispute.

(f) Any vacancy shall be filled in the manner prescribed for the initial appointment.

(g) Parties in the same interest shall appoint two members of the tribunal jointly by agreement. Where there are several parties having separate interests or where there is disagreement as to whether they are of the same interest, each of them shall appoint one member of the tribunal.

(h) In disputes involving more than two parties, the provisions of subparagraphs (a) to (f) shall apply to the maximum extent possible.

Article 4   General provisions

Annex VII, articles 4 to 13, apply *mutatis mutandis* to the special arbitration proceedings in accordance with this Annex.

Article 5   Fact finding

1. The parties to a dispute concerning the interpretation or application of the provisions of this Convention relating to (1) fisheries, (2) protection and preservation of the marine environment, (3) marine scientific research, or (4) navigation, including pollution from vessels and by dumping, may at any time agree to request a special arbitral tribunal constituted in accordance with article 3 of this Annex to carry out an inquiry and establish the facts giving rise to the dispute.

2. Unless the parties otherwise agree, the findings of fact of the special arbitral tribunal acting in accordance with paragraph 1, shall be considered as conclusive as between the parties.

3. If all the parties to the dispute so request, the special arbitral tribunal may formulate recommendations which, without having the force of a decision, shall only constitute the basis for a review by the parties of the questions giving rise to the dispute.

4. Subject to paragraph 2, the special arbitral tribunal shall act in accordance with the provisions of this Annex, unless the parties otherwise agree.

ANNEX IX   PARTICIPATION BY INTERNATIONAL
            ORGANIZATIONS

Article 1   Use of terms

For the purposes of article 305 and of this Annex, "international
organization" means an intergovernmental organization constituted by
States to which its member States have transferred competence over
matters governed by this Convention, including the competence to enter
into treaties in respect of those matters.

Article 2   Signature

An international organization may sign this Convention if a majority of its
member States are signatories of this Convention. At the time of signature
an international organization shall make a declaration specifying the
matters governed by this Convention in respect of which competence has
been transferred to that organization by its member States which are
signatories, and the nature and extent of that competence.

Article 3   Formal confirmation and accession

1. An international organization may deposit its instrument of formal
confirmation or of accession if a majority of its member States deposit or
have deposited their instruments of ratification or accession.

2. The instruments deposited by the international organization shall
contain the undertakings and declarations required by articles 4 and 5 of
this Annex.

Article 4   Extent of participation and rights and obligations

1. The instrument of formal confirmation or of accession of an
international organization shall contain an undertaking to accept the rights
and obligations of States under this Convention in respect of matters
relating to which competence has been transferred to it by its member
States which are Parties to this Convention.

2. An international organization shall be a Party to this Convention to the
extent that it has competence in accordance with the declarations,
communications of information or notifications referred to in article 5 of
this Annex.

3. Such an international organization shall exercise the rights and perform the obligations which its member States which are Parties would otherwise have under this Convention, on matters relating to which competence has been transferred to it by those member States. The member States of that international organization shall not exercise competence which they have transferred to it.

4. Participation of such an international organization shall in no case entail an increase of the representation to which its member States which are States Parties would otherwise be entitled, including rights in decision-making.

5. Participation of such an international organization shall in no case confer any rights under this Convention on member States of the organization which are not States Parties to this Convention.

6. In the event of a conflict between the obligations of an international organization under this Convention and its obligations under the agreement establishing the organization or any acts relating to it, the obligations under this Convention shall prevail.

Article 5   Declarations, notifications and communications

l. The instrument of formal confirmation or of accession of an international organization shall contain a declaration specifying the matters governed by this Convention in respect of which competence has been transferred to the organization by its member States which are Parties to this Convention.

2. A member State of an international organization shall, at the time it ratifies or accedes to this Convention or at the time when the organization deposits its instrument of formal confirmation or of accession, whichever is later, make a declaration specifying the matters governed by this Convention in respect of which it has transferred competence to the organization.

3. States Parties which are member States of an international organization which is a Party to this Convention shall be presumed to have competence over all matters governed by this Convention in respect of which transfers of competence to the organization have not been specifically declared, notified or communicated by those States under this article.

4. The international organization and its member States which are States Parties shall promptly notify the depositary of this Convention of any changes to the distribution of competence, including new transfers of competence, specified in the declarations under paragraphs 1 and 2.

5. Any State Party may request an international organization and its member States which are States Parties to provide information as to which, as between the organization and its member States, has competence in respect of any specific question which has arisen. The organization and the member States concerned shall provide this information within a reasonable time. The international organization and the member States may also, on their own initiative, provide this information.

6. Declarations, notifications and communications of information under this article shall specify the nature and extent of the competence transferred.

Article 6   Responsibility and liability

1. Parties which have competence under article 5 of this Annex shall have responsibility for failure to comply with obligations or for any other violation of this Convention.

2. Any State Party may request an international organization or its member States which are States Parties for information as to who has responsibility in respect of any specific matter. The organization and the member States concerned shall provide this information. Failure to provide this information within a reasonable time or the provision of contradictory information shall result in joint and several liability.

Article 7   Settlement of disputes

1. At the time of deposit of its instrument of formal confirmation or of accession, or at any time thereafter, an international organization shall be free to choose, by means of a written declaration, one or more of the means for the settlement of disputes concerning the interpretation or application of this Convention, referred to in article 287, paragraph 1(a), (c) or (d).

2. Part XV applies *mutatis mutandis* to any dispute between Parties to this Convention, one or more of which are international organizations.

3. When an international organization and one or more of its member States are joint parties to a dispute, or parties in the same interest, the organization shall be deemed to have accepted the same procedures for the settlement of disputes as the member States; when, however, a member State has chosen only the International Court of Justice under article 287, the organization and the member State concerned shall be deemed to have accepted arbitration in accordance with Annex VII, unless the parties to the dispute otherwise agree.

Article 8   Applicability of Part XVII

Part XVII applies *mutatis mutandis* to an international organization, except in respect of the following:

(a) the instrument of formal confirmation or of accession of an international organization shall not be taken into account in the application of article 308, paragraph l;

(b) (i) an international organization shall have exclusive capacity with respect to the application of articles 312 to 315, to the extent that it has competence under article 5 of this Annex over the entire subject-matter of the amendment;

(ii) the instrument of formal confirmation or of accession of an international organization to an amendment, the entire subject-matter over which the international organization has competence under article 5 of this Annex, shall be considered to be the instrument of ratification or accession of each of the member States which are States Parties, for the purposes of applying article 316, paragraphs 1, 2 and 3;

(iii) the instrument of formal confirmation or of accession of the international organization shall not be taken into account in the application of article 316, paragraphs 1 and 2, with regard to all other amendments;

(c) (i) an international organization may not denounce this Convention in accordance with article 317 if any of its member States is a State Party and if it continues to fulfil the qualifications specified in article 1 of this Annex;

(ii) an international organization shall denounce this Convention when none of its member States is a State Party or if the international organization no longer fulfils the qualifications specified in article 1 of this Annex. Such denunciation shall take effect immediately.

ANNEX I [to the Final Act]

RESOLUTION I

ESTABLISHMENT OF THE PREPARATORY COMMISSION FOR THE INTERNATIONAL SEA-BED AUTHORITY AND FOR THE INTERNATIONAL TRIBUNAL FOR THE LAW OF THE SEA

The Third United Nations Conference on the Law of the Sea,

Having adopted the Convention on the Law of the Sea which provides for the establishment of the International Seabed Authority and the International Tribunal for the Law of the Sea,

Having decided to take all possible measures to ensure the entry into effective operation without undue delay of the Authority and the Tribunal and to make the necessary arrangements for the commencement of their functions,

Having decided that a Preparatory Commission should be established for the fulfilment of these purposes,

Decides as follows:

1. There is hereby established the Preparatory Commission for the International Seabed Authority and for the International Tribunal for the Law of the Sea. Upon signature of or accession to the Convention by 50 States, the Secretary-General of the United Nations shall convene the Commission, and it shall meet no sooner than 60 days and no later than 90 days thereafter.

2. The Commission shall consist of the representatives of States and of Namibia, represented by the United Nations Council for Namibia, which have signed the Convention or acceded to it. The representatives of signatories of the Final Act may participate fully in the deliberations of the Commission as observers but shall not be entitled to participate in the taking of decisions.

3. The Commission shall elect its Chairman and other officers.

4. The Rules of Procedure of the Third United Nations Conference on the Law of the Sea shall apply *mutatis mutandis* to the adoption of the rules of procedure of the Commission.

5. The Commission shall:

(a) prepare the provisional agenda for the first session of the Assembly and of the Council and, as appropriate, make recommendations relating to items thereon;

(b) prepare draft rules of procedure of the Assembly and of the Council;

(c) make recommendations concerning the budget for the first financial period of the Authority;

(d) make recommendations concerning the relationship between the Authority and the United Nations and other international organizations;

(e) make recommendations concerning the Secretariat of the Authority in accordance with the relevant provisions of the Convention;

(f) undertake studies, as necessary, concerning the establishment of the headquarters of the Authority, and make recommendations relating thereto;

(g) prepare draft rules, regulations and procedures, as necessary, to enable the Authority to commence its functions, including draft regulations concerning the financial management and the internal administration of the Authority;

(h) exercise the powers and functions assigned to it by resolution II of the Third United Nations Conference on the Law of the Sea relating to preparatory investment;

(i) undertake studies on the problems which would be encountered by developing land-based producer States likely to be most seriously affected by the production of minerals derived from the Area with a view to minimizing their difficulties and helping them to make the necessary economic adjustment, including studies on the establishment of a compensation fund, and submit recommendations to the Authority thereon.

6. The Commission shall have such legal capacity as may be necessary for the exercise of its functions and the fulfilment of its purposes as set forth in this resolution.

7. The Commission may establish such subsidiary bodies as are necessary for the exercise of its functions and shall determine their functions and rules of procedure. It may also make use, as appropriate, of outside sources of expertise in accordance with United Nations practice to facilitate the work of bodies so established.

8. The Commission shall establish a special commission for the Enterprise and entrust to it the functions referred to in paragraph 12 of resolution II of the Third United Nations Conference on the Law of the Sea relating to preparatory investment. The special commission shall take all measures necessary for the early entry into effective operation of the Enterprise.

9. The Commission shall establish a special commission on the problems which would be encountered by developing land-based producer States likely to be most seriously affected by the production of minerals derived from the Area and entrust to it the functions referred to in paragraph 5(i).

10. The Commission shall prepare a report containing recommendations for submission to the meeting of the States Parties to be convened in accordance with Annex VI, article 4, of the Convention regarding practical arrangements for the establishment of the International Tribunal for the Law of the Sea.

11. The Commission shall prepare a final report on all matters within its mandate, except as provided in paragraph 10, for the presentation to the Assembly at its first session. Any action which may be taken on the basis of the report must be in conformity with the provisions of the Convention concerning the powers and functions entrusted to the respective organs of the Authority.

12. The Commission shall meet at the seat of the Authority if facilities are available; it shall meet as often as necessary for the expeditious exercise of its functions.

13. The Commission shall remain in existence until the conclusion of the first session of the Assembly, at which time its property and records shall be transferred to the Authority.

14. The expenses of the Commission shall be met from the regular budget of the United Nations, subject to the approval of the General Assembly of the United Nations.

15. The Secretary-General of the United Nations shall make available to the Commission such secretariat services as may be required.

16. The Secretary-General of the United Nations shall bring this resolution, in particular paragraphs 14 and 15, to the attention of the General Assembly for necessary action.

RESOLUTION II

GOVERNING PREPARATORY INVESTMENT IN PIONEER ACTIVITIES RELATING TO POLYMETALLIC NODULES

The Third United Nations Conference on the Law of the Sea,

Having adopted the Convention on the Law of the Sea (the "Convention"),

Having established by resolution I the Preparatory Commission for the International Seabed Authority and for the International Tribunal for the Law of the Sea (the "Commission") and directed it to prepare draft rules, regulations and procedures, as necessary to enable the Authority to commence its functions, as well as to make recommendations for the early entry into effective operation of the Enterprise,

Desirous of making provision for investments by States and other entities made in a manner compatible with the international regime set forth in Part XI of the Convention and the Annexes relating thereto, before the entry into force of the Convention,

Recognizing the need to ensure that the Enterprise will be provided with the funds, technology and expertise necessary to enable it to keep pace with the States and other entities referred to in the preceding paragraph with respect to activities in the Area,

Decides as follows:

1. For the purposes of this resolution:

   (a) "pioneer investor" refers to:

   (i) France, India, Japan and the Union of Soviet Socialist Republics, or a state enterprise of each of those States or one natural or juridical person which possesses the nationality of or is effectively controlled by each of those States, or their nationals, provided that the State concerned signs the Convention and the State or state enterprise or natural or juridical person has expended, before 1 January 1983, an amount equivalent to at least $US 30 million (United States dollars calculated in constant dollars relative to 1982) in pioneer activities and has expended no less than 10 per cent of that amount in the location, survey and evaluation of the area referred to in paragraph 3(a);

(ii) four entities, whose components being natural or juridical persons[1] possess the nationality of one or more of the following States, or are effectively controlled by one or more of them or their nationals: Belgium, Canada, the Federal Republic of Germany, Italy, Japan, the Netherlands, the United Kingdom of Great Britain and Northern Ireland, and the United States of America, provided that the certifying State or States sign the Convention and the entity concerned has expended, before 1 January 1983, the levels of expenditure for the purpose stated in subparagraph (i);

(iii) any developing State which signs the Convention or any state enterprise or natural or juridical person which possesses the nationality of such State or is effectively controlled by it or its nationals, or any group of the foregoing, which, before 1 January 1985, has expended the levels of expenditure for the purpose stated in subparagraph (i);

The rights of the pioneer investor may devolve upon its successor in interest.

(b) "pioneer activities" means undertakings, commitments of financial and other assets, investigations, findings, research, engineering development and other activities relevant to the identification, discovery, and systematic analysis and evaluation of polymetallic nodules and to the determination of the technical and economic feasibility of exploitation. Pioneer activities include:

(i) any at-sea observation and evaluation activity which has as its objective the establishment and documentation of the nature, shape, concentration, location and grade of polymetallic nodules and of the

---

[1] For their identity and composition see "Seabed mineral resource development: recent activities of the international Consortia" and addendum, published by the Department of International Economic and Social Affairs of the United Nations (ST/ESA/107 and Add.1). [This footnote in the original]

environmental, technical and other appropriate factors which must be taken into account before exploitation;

(ii) the recovery from the Area of polymetallic nodules with a view to the designing, fabricating and testing of equipment which is intended to be used in the exploitation of polymetallic nodules;

(c) "certifying State" means a State which signs the Convention, standing in the same relation to a pioneer investor as would a sponsoring State pursuant to Annex III, article 4, of the Convention and which certifies the levels of expenditure specified in subparagraph (a);

(d) "polymetallic nodules" means one of the resources of the Area consisting of any deposit or accretion of nodules, on or just below the surface of the deep seabed, which contain manganese, nickel, cobalt and copper;

(e) "pioneer area" means an area allocated by the Commission to a pioneer investor for pioneer activities pursuant to this resolution. A pioneer area shall not exceed 150,000 square kilometres. The pioneer investor shall relinquish portions of the pioneer area to revert to the Area, in accordance with the following schedule:

(i) 20 per cent of the area allocated by the end of the third year from the date of the allocation;

(ii) an additional 10 per cent of the area allocated by the end of the fifth year from the date of the allocation;

(iii) an additional 20 per cent of the area allocated or such larger amount as would exceed the exploitation area decided upon by the Authority in its rules, regulations and procedures, after eight years from the date of the allocation of the area or the date of the award of a production authorization, whichever is earlier;

(f) "Area", "Authority", "activities in the Area" and "resources" have the meanings assigned to those terms in the Convention.

2. As soon as the Commission begins to function, any State which has signed the Convention may apply to the Commission on its behalf or on behalf of any state enterprise or entity or natural or juridical person specified in paragraph 1(a) for registration as a pioneer investor. The

Commission shall register the applicant as a pioneer investor if the application:

(a) is accompanied, in the case of a State which has signed the Convention, by a statement certifying the level of expenditure made in accordance with paragraph 1(a), and, in all other cases, a certificate concerning such level of expenditure issued by a certifying State or States; and

(b) is in conformity with the other provisions of this resolution, including paragraph 5.

3. (a) Every application shall cover a total area which need not be a single continuous area, sufficiently large and of sufficient estimated commercial value to allow two mining operations. The application shall indicate the coordinates of the area defining the total area and dividing it into two parts of equal estimated commercial value and shall contain all the data available to the applicant with respect to both parts of the area. Such data shall include, *inter alia*, information relating to mapping, testing, the density of polymetallic nodules and their metal content. In dealing with such data, the Commission and its staff shall act in accordance with the relevant provisions of the Convention and its Annexes concerning the confidentiality of data.

(b) Within 45 days of receiving the data required by subparagraph (a), the Commission shall designate the part of the area which is to be reserved in accordance with the Convention for the conduct of activities in the Area by the Authority through the Enterprise or in association with developing States. The other part of the area shall be allocated to the pioneer investor as a pioneer area.

4. No pioneer investor may be registered in respect of more than one pioneer area. In the case of a pioneer investor which is made up of two or more components, none of such components may apply to be registered as a pioneer investor in its own right or under paragraph 1(a)(iii).

5. (a) Any State which has signed the Convention and which is a prospective certifying State shall ensure, before making applications to the Commission under paragraph 2, that areas in respect of which applications are made do not overlap one another or areas previously allocated as pioneer areas. The States concerned shall keep the Commission currently and fully informed of any efforts to resolve conflicts with respect to overlapping claims and of the results thereof.

(b) Certifying States shall ensure, before the entry into force of the Convention, that pioneer activities are conducted in a manner compatible with it.

(c) The prospective certifying States, including all potential claimants, shall resolve their conflicts as required under subparagraph (a) by negotiations within a reasonable period. If such conflicts have not been resolved by 1 March 1983, the prospective certifying States shall arrange for the submission of all such claims to binding arbitration in accordance with UNCITRAL Arbitration Rules to commence not later than 1 May 1983 and to be completed by 1 December 1984. If one of the States concerned does not wish to participate in the arbitration, it shall arrange for a juridical person of its nationality to represent it in the arbitration. The arbitral tribunal may, for good cause, extend the deadline for the making of the award for one or more 30-day periods.

(d) In determining the issue as to which applicant involved in a conflict shall be awarded all or part of each area in conflict, the arbitral tribunal shall find a solution which is fair and equitable, having regard, with respect to each applicant involved in the conflict, to the following factors:

(i) the deposit of the list of relevant coordinates with the prospective certifying State or States not later than the date of adoption of the Final Act or 1 January 1983, whichever is earlier;

(ii) the continuity and extent of past activities relevant to each area in conflict and to the application area of which it is a part;

(iii) the date on which each pioneer investor concerned or predecessor in interest or component organization thereof commenced activities at sea in the application area;

(iv) the financial cost of activities measured in constant United States dollars relevant to each area in conflict and to the application area of which it is a part; and

(v) the time when those activities were carried out and the quality of activities.

6. A pioneer investor registered pursuant to this resolution shall, from the date of registration, have the exclusive right to carry out pioneer activities in the pioneer area allocated to it.

7. (a) Every applicant for registration as a pioneer investor shall pay to the Commission a fee of $US 250,000. When the pioneer investor applies to the Authority for a plan of work for exploration and exploitation the fee referred to in Annex III, article 13, paragraph 2, of the Convention shall be $US 250,000.

(b) Every registered pioneer investor shall pay an annual fixed fee of $US 1 million commencing from the date of the allocation of the pioneer area. The payments shall be made by the pioneer investor to the Authority upon the approval of its plan of work for exploration and exploitation. The financial arrangements undertaken pursuant to such plan of work shall be adjusted to take account of the payments made pursuant to this paragraph.

(c) Every registered pioneer investor shall agree to incur periodic expenditures, with respect to the pioneer area allocated to it, until approval of its plan of work pursuant to paragraph 8, of an amount to be determined by the Commission. The amount should be reasonably related to the size of the pioneer area and the expenditures which would be expected of a *bona fide* operator who intends to bring that area into commercial production within a reasonable time.

8. (a) Within six months of the entry into force of the Convention and certification by the Commission in accordance with paragraph 11, of compliance with this resolution, the pioneer investor so registered shall apply to the Authority for approval of a plan of work for exploration and exploitation, in accordance with the Convention. The plan of work in respect of such application shall comply with and be governed by the relevant provisions of the Convention and the rules, regulations and procedures of the Authority, including those on the operational requirements, the financial requirements and the undertakings concerning the transfer of technology. Accordingly, the Authority shall approve such application.

(b) When an application for approval of a plan of work is submitted by an entity other than a State, pursuant to subparagraph (a), the certifying State or States shall be deemed to be the sponsoring State for the purposes of Annex III, article 4, of the Convention, and shall thereupon assume such obligations.

(c) No plan of work for exploration and exploitation shall be approved unless the certifying State is a Party to the Convention. In the case of the entities referred to in paragraph 1(a)(ii), the plan of work for exploration and exploitation shall not be approved unless all the States whose natural or juridical persons comprise those entities are Parties to the Convention. If any such State fails to ratify the Convention within six months after it has received a notification from the Authority that an application by it, or sponsored by it, is pending, its status as a pioneer investor or certifying State, as the case may be, shall terminate, unless the Council, by a majority of three fourths of its members present and voting, decides to postpone the terminal date for a period not exceeding six months.

9. (a) In the allocation of production authorizations, in accordance with article 151 and Annex III, article 7, of the Convention, the pioneer investors who have obtained approval of plans of work for exploration and exploitation shall have priority over all applicants other than the Enterprise which shall be entitled to production authorizations for two mine sites including that referred to in article 151, paragraph 5, of the Convention. After each of the pioneer investors has obtained production authorization for its first mine site, the priority for the Enterprise contained in Annex III, article 7, paragraph 6, of the Convention shall apply.

(b) Production authorizations shall be issued to each pioneer investor within 30 days of the date on which that pioneer investor notifies the Authority that it will commence commercial production within five years. If a pioneer investor is unable to begin production within the period of five years for reasons beyond its control, it shall apply to the Legal and Technical Commission for an extension of time. That Commission shall grant the extension of time, for a period not exceeding five years and not subject to further extension, if it is satisfied that the pioneer investor cannot begin on an economically viable basis at the time originally planned. Nothing in this subparagraph shall prevent the Enterprise or any other pioneer applicant, who has notified the Authority that it will commence commercial production within five years, from being given a priority over any applicant who has obtained an extension of time under this subparagraph.

(c) If the Authority, upon being given notice, pursuant to subparagraph (b), determines that the commencement of commercial production within five years would exceed the production ceiling in article 151, paragraphs 2 to 7, of the Convention, the applicant shall hold a priority over any other applicant for the award of the next production authorization allowed by the production ceiling.

(d) If two or more pioneer investors apply for production authorizations to begin commercial production at the same time and article 151, paragraphs 2 to 7, of the Convention, would not permit all such production to commence simultaneously, the Authority shall notify the pioneer investors concerned. Within three months of such notification, they shall decide whether and, if so, to what extent they wish to apportion the allowable tonnage among themselves.

(e) If, pursuant to subparagraph (d), the pioneer investors concerned decide not to apportion the available production among themselves they shall agree on an order of priority for production authorizations and all subsequent applications for production authorizations will be granted after those referred to in this subparagraph have been approved.

(f) If, pursuant to subparagraph (d), the pioneer investors concerned decide to apportion the available production among themselves, the Authority shall award each of them a production authorization for such lesser quantity as they have agreed. In each case the stated production requirements of the applicant will be approved and their full production will be allowed as soon as the production ceiling admits of additional capacity sufficient for the applicants involved in the competition. All subsequent applications for production authorizations will only be granted after the requirements of this subparagraph have been met and the applicant is no longer subject to the reduction of production provided for in this subparagraph.

(g) If the parties fail to reach agreement within the stated time period, the matter shall be decided immediately by the means provided for in paragraph 5(c) in accordance with the criteria set forth in Annex III, article 7, paragraphs 3 and 5, of the Convention.

10. (a) Any rights acquired by entities or natural or juridical persons which possess the nationality of or are effectively controlled by a State or States whose status as certifying State has been terminated, shall lapse unless the pioneer investor changes its nationality and sponsorship within six months of the date of such termination, as provided for in subparagraph (b).

(b) A pioneer investor may change its nationality and sponsorship from that existing at the time of its registration as a pioneer investor to that of any State Party to the Convention which has effective control over the pioneer investor in terms of paragraph l(a).

(c) Changes of nationality and sponsorship pursuant to this paragraph shall not affect any right or priority conferred on a pioneer investor pursuant to paragraphs 6 and 8.

11. The Commission shall:

(a) provide each pioneer investor with the certificate of compliance with the provisions of this resolution referred to in paragraph 8; and

(b) include in its final report required by paragraph 11 of resolution I of the Conference details of all registrations of pioneer investors and allocations of pioneer areas pursuant to this resolution.

12. In order to ensure that the Enterprise is able to carry out activities in the Area in such a manner as to keep pace with States and other entities:

(a) every registered pioneer investor shall:

(i) carry out exploration, at the request of the Commission, in the area reserved, pursuant to paragraph 3 in connection with its application, for activities in the Area by the Authority through the Enterprise or in association with developing States, on the basis that the costs so incurred plus interest thereon at the rate of 10 per cent per annum shall be reimbursed;

(ii) provide training at all levels for personnel designated by the Commission;

(iii) undertake before the entry into force of the Convention, to perform the obligations prescribed in the Convention relating to transfer of technology;

(b) every certifying State shall:

(i) ensure that the necessary funds are made available to the Enterprise in a timely manner in accordance with the Convention, upon its entry into force; and

(ii) report periodically to the Commission on the activities carried out by it, by its entities or natural or juridical persons.

13. The Authority and its organs shall recognize and honour the rights and obligations arising from this resolution and the decisions of the Commission taken pursuant to it.

14. Without prejudice to paragraph 13, this resolution shall have effect until the entry into force of the Convention.

15. Nothing in this resolution shall derogate from Annex III, article 6, paragraph 3(c), of the Convention.

RESOLUTION III

The Third United Nations Conference on the Law of the Sea,

Having regard to the Convention on the Law of the Sea,

Bearing in mind the Charter of the United Nations, in particular Article 73,

1. *Declares* that:

(a) In the case of a territory whose people have not attained full independence or other self-governing status recognized by the United Nations, or a territory under colonial domination, provisions concerning rights and interests under the Convention shall be implemented for the benefit of the people of the territory with a view to promoting their well-being and development.

 (b) Where a dispute exists between States over the sovereignty of a territory to which this resolution applies, in respect of which the United Nations has recommended specific means of settlement, there shall be consultations between the parties to that dispute regarding the exercise of the rights referred to in subparagraph (a). In such consultations the interests of the people of the territory concerned shall be a fundamental consideration. Any exercise of those rights shall take into account the relevant resolutions of the United Nations and shall be without prejudice to the position of any party to the dispute. The States concerned shall make every effort to enter into provisional arrangements of a practical nature and shall not jeopardize or hamper the reaching of a final settlement of the dispute.

2. *Requests* the Secretary-General of the United Nations to bring this resolution to the attention of all Members of the United Nations and the other participants in the Conference, as well as the principal organs of the United Nations, and to request their compliance with it.

RESOLUTION IV

The Third United Nations Conference on the Law of the Sea,

Bearing in mind that national liberation movements have been invited to participate in the Conference as observers in accordance with rule 62 of its rules of procedure,

Decides that the national liberation movements, which have been participating in the Third United Nations Conference on the Law of the Sea, shall be entitled to sign the Final Act of the Conference, in their capacity as observers.

ANNEX II   STATEMENT OF UNDERSTANDING
CONCERNING A SPECIFIC METHOD TO BE USED
IN ESTABLISHING THE OUTER EDGE OF THE
CONTINENTAL MARGIN

The Third United Nations Conference on the Law of the Sea,

Considering the special characteristics of a State's continental margin where: (1) the average distance at which the 200 metre isobath occurs is not more than 20 nautical miles; (2) the greater proportion of the sedimentary rock of the continental margin lies beneath the rise; and

Taking into account the inequity that would result to that State from the application to its continental margin of article 76 of the Convention, in that, the mathematical average of the thickness of sedimentary rock along a line established at the maximum distance permissible in accordance with the provisions of paragraph 4(a)(i) and (ii) of that article as representing the entire outer edge of the continental margin would not be less than 3.5 kilometres; and that more than half of the margin would be excluded thereby;

Recognizes that such State may, notwithstanding the provisions of article 76, establish the outer edge of its continental margin by straight lines not exceeding 60 nautical miles in length connecting fixed points, defined by latitude and longitude, at each of which the thickness of sedimentary rock is not less than 1 kilometre,

Where a State establishes the outer edge of its continental margin by applying the method set forth in the preceding paragraph of this statement, this method may also be utilized by a neighbouring State for delineating the outer edge of its continental margin on a common geological feature, where its outer edge would lie on such feature on a line established at the maximum distance permissible in accordance with article 76, paragraph 4(a)(i) and (ii), along which the mathematical average of the thickness of sedimentary rock is not less than 3.5 kilometres,

The Conference requests the Commission on the Limits of the Continental Shelf set up pursuant to Annex II of the Convention, to be governed by the terms of this Statement when making its recommendations on matters related to the establishment of the outer edge of the continental margins of these States in the southern part of the Bay of Bengal.

ANNEX III   TRIBUTE TO SIMON BOLIVAR THE LIBERATOR

The Third United Nations Conference on the Law of the Sea,

Considering that 24 July 1974 marks a further anniversary of the birth of Simón Bolivar, the Liberator, a man of vision and early champion of international organization, and a historic figure of universal dimensions,

Considering further that the work of Simón Bolivar the Liberator, based on the concepts of liberty and justice as foundations for the peace and progress of peoples, has left an indelible mark on history and constitutes a source of constant inspiration,

Decides to pay a public tribute of admiration and respect to Simón Bolivar the Liberator, in the plenary meeting of the Third United Nations Conference on the Law of the Sea.

ANNEX IV   RESOLUTION EXPRESSING GRATITUDE TO THE PRESIDENT, THE GOVERNMENT AND OFFICIALS OF VENEZUELA

The Third United Nations Conference on the Law of the Sea,

Bearing in mind that its second session was held in the city of Caracas, cradle of Simón Bolivar, Liberator of five nations, who devoted his life to fighting for the self-determination of peoples, equality among States and justice as the expression of their common destiny,

Acknowledging with keen appreciation the extraordinary effort made by the Government and the people of Venezuela, which enabled the Conference to meet in the most favourable spirit of brotherhood and in unparalleled material conditions,

Decides

1. To express to His Excellency the President of the Republic of Venezuela, the President and members of the Organizing Committee of the Conference and the Government and people of Venezuela its deepest gratitude for the unforgettable hospitality which they have offered it;

2. To give voice to its hope that the ideals of social justice, equality among nations and solidarity among peoples advocated by the Liberator Simón Bolivar will serve to guide the future work of the Conference.

ANNEX V   TRIBUTE TO THE AMPHICTYONIC CONGRESS OF PANAMA

The Third United Nations Conference on the Law of the Sea, at its fifth session,

Considering that the current year 1976 marks the one hundred and fiftieth anniversary of the Amphictyonic Congress of Panama, convoked by the Liberator Simón Bolivar for the laudable and visionary purpose of uniting the Latin American peoples,

Considering likewise that a spirit of universality prevailed at the Congress of Panama, which was ahead of its time and which foresaw that only on the basis of union and reciprocal co-operation is it possible to guarantee peace and promote the development of nations,

Considering further that the Congress of Panama evoked the prestigious and constructive Greek Amphictyony and anticipated the ecumenical and creative image of the United Nations,

Decides to render to the Amphictyonic Congress of Panama, in a plenary meeting of the Third United Nations Conference on the Law of the Sea, at its fifth session, a public tribute acknowledging its expressive historic significance.

ANNEX VI   RESOLUTION ON DEVELOPMENT OF NATIONAL MARINE SCIENCE, TECHNOLOGY AND OCEAN SERVICE INFRASTRUCTURES

The Third United Nations Conference on the Law of the Sea,

Recognizing that the Convention on the Law of the Sea is intended to establish a new regime for the seas and oceans which will contribute to the realization of a just and equitable international economic order through making provision for the peaceful use of ocean space, the equitable and efficient management and utilization of its resources, and the study, protection and preservation of the marine environment,

Bearing in mind that the new regime must take into account, in particular, the special needs and interests of the developing countries, whether coastal, land-locked, or geographically disadvantaged,

Aware of the rapid advances being made in the field of marine science and technology, and the need for the developing countries, whether coastal, land-locked, or geographically disadvantaged, to share in these achievements if the aforementioned goals are to be met,

Convinced that, unless urgent measures are taken, the marine scientific and technological gap between the developed and the developing countries will widen further and thus endanger the very foundations of the new regime,

Believing that optimum utilization of the new opportunities for social and economic development offered by the new regime will be facilitated through action at the national and international level aimed at strengthening national capabilities in marine science, technology and ocean services, particularly in the developing countries, with a view to ensuring the rapid absorption and efficient application of technology and scientific knowledge available to them,

Considering that national and regional marine scientific and technological centres would be the principal institutions through which States and, in particular, the developing countries, foster and conduct marine scientific research, and receive and disseminate marine technology,

Recognizing the special role of the competent international organizations envisaged by the Convention on the Law of the Sea, especially in relation to the establishment and development of national and regional marine scientific and technological centres,

Noting that present efforts undertaken within the United Nations system in training, education and assistance in the field of marine science and technology and ocean services are far below current requirements and would be particularly inadequate to meet the demands generated through operation of the Convention on the Law of the Sea,

Welcoming recent initiatives within international organizations to promote and coordinate their major international assistance programmes aimed at strengthening marine science infrastructures in developing countries,

1. *Calls upon* all Member States to determine appropriate priorities in their development plans for the strengthening of their marine science, technology and ocean services;

2. *Calls upon* the developing countries to establish programmes for the promotion of technical cooperation among themselves in the field of marine science, technology and ocean service development;

3. *Urges* the industrialized countries to assist the developing countries in the preparation and implementation of their marine science, technology and ocean service development programmes;

4. *Recommends* that the World Bank, the regional banks, the United Nations Development Programme, the United Nations Financing System for Science and Technology and other multilateral funding agencies augment and coordinate their operations for the provision of funds to developing countries for the preparation and implementation of major programmes of assistance in strengthening their marine science, technology and ocean services;

5. *Recommends* that all competent international organizations within the United Nations system expand programmes within their respective fields of competence for assistance to developing countries in the field of marine science, technology and ocean services and coordinate their efforts on a system-wide basis in the implementation of such programmes, paying particular attention to the special needs of the developing countries, whether coastal, land-locked or geographically disadvantaged;

6. *Requests* the Secretary-General of the United Nations to transmit this resolution to the General Assembly at its thirty-seventh session.

States Parties as of 1 January 2009

State	Signed	Entered into Force	Acceded, Ratified or Succeeded
Afghanistan	18 Mar 1983		
Albania		23 Jun 2003	Acceded
Algeria	10 Dec 1982	11 Jun 1996	Ratified
Angola	10 Dec 1982	5 Dec 1990	Ratified
Antigua and Barbuda	7 Feb 1983	2 Feb 1989	Ratified
Argentina	5 Oct 1984	1 Dec 1995	Ratified
Armenia[1]	10 Dec 1982	9 Dec 2002	Acceded
Australia	10 Dec 1982	5 Oct 1994	Ratified
Austria	10 Dec 1982	14 Jul 1995	Ratified
Azerbaijan[2]	10 Dec 1982		
Bahamas	10 Dec 1982	29 Jul 1983	Ratified
Bahrain	10 Dec 1982	30 May 1985	Ratified
Bangladesh	10 Dec 1982	27 Jul 2001	Ratified
Barbados	10 Dec 1982	12 Oct 1993	Ratified
Belarus[3]	10 Dec 1982	30 Aug 2006	Ratified
Belgium	5 Dec 1984	13 Nov 1998	Ratified
Belize	10 Dec 1982	13 Aug 1983	Ratified
Benin	30 Aug 1983	16 Oct 1997	Ratified
Bhutan	10 Dec 1982		
Bolivia	27 Nov 1984	28 Apr 1995	Ratified
Bosnia and Herzegovina[4]	10 Dec 1982	5 May 1986 / 12 Jan 1994	Ratified / Succeeded
Botswana	5 Dec 1984	2 May 1990	Ratified
Brazil	10 Dec 1982	22 Dec 1988	Ratified
Brunei Darussalam	5 Dec 1984	5 Nov 1996	Ratified
Bulgaria	10 Dec 1982	15 May 1996	Ratified
Burkina Faso	10 Dec 1982	25 Jan 2005	Ratified
Burundi	10 Dec 1982		

[1] The former Union of Soviet Socialist Republics signed on 10 December 1982 but did not ratify.
[2] *See supra* note 1 regarding the USSR.
[3] In the name of the "Byelorussian Soviet Socialist Republic". *Also see supra* note 1 regarding the former USSR.
[4] The former Soviet Federal Socialist Republic of Yugoslavia signed on 10 December 1982 and ratified on 5 May 1986.

Cambodia	1 Jul 1983		
Cameroon	10 Dec 1982	19 Nov 1985	Ratified
Canada	10 Dec 1982	7 Nov 2003	Ratified
Cape Verde	10 Dec 1982	10 Aug 1987	Ratified
Central African Republic	4 Dec 1984		
Chad	10 Dec 1982		
Chile	10 Dec 1982	25 Aug 1997	Ratified
China	10 Dec 1982	7 Jun 1996	Ratified
Colombia	10 Dec 1982	10 Apr 1985	Ratified
Comoros	6 Dec 1984	21 Jun 1994	Ratified
Congo[5]	10 Dec 1982	9 Jul 2008	Ratified
Congo, Dem. Rep. of the	22 Aug 1983	17 Feb 1989	Ratified
Cook Islands[6]	10 Dec 1982	15 Feb 1995	Ratified
Costa Rica	10 Dec 1982	21 Sep 1992	Ratified
Côte d'Ivoire[7]	10 Dec 1982	26 Mar 1984	Ratified
Croatia[8]	10 Dec 1982	5 May 1986	Ratified
		5 Apr 1995	Succeeded
Cuba	10 Dec 1982	15 Aug 1984	Ratified
Cyprus	10 Dec 1982	12 Dec 1988	Ratified
Czech Rep.[9]	10 Dec 1982		Succeeded
	22 Feb 1993	21 Jun 1996	Ratified
Denmark	10 Dec 1982	16 Nov 2004	Ratified
Djibouti	10 Dec 1982	8 Oct 1991	Ratified
Dominica	28 Mar 1983	24 Oct 1991	Ratified
Dominican Rep.	10 Dec 1982		
Ecuador	10 Dec 1982		
Egypt	10 Dec 1982	26 Aug 1983	Ratified
El Salvador	5 Dec 1984		
Equatorial Guinea	30 Jan 1984	21 Jul 1997	Ratified
Estonia[10]	10 Dec 1982	26 Aug 2005	Acceded
Ethiopia	10 Dec 1982		
European Community[11]	7 Dec 1984	1 Apr 1998	Confirmed

---

[5] In the name of "Zaire".

[6] The Cook Islands signed on 10 December 1982 as a self-governing associated State. *See* Art. 305(1)(c).

[7] In the name "Ivory Coast".

[8] *See supra* note 4 regarding the former Yugoslavia.

[9] The former Czechoslovak Socialist Republic signed on 10 December 1982.

[10] *See supra* note 1 regarding the former USSR.

Fiji	10 Dec 1982	10 Dec 1982	Ratified
Finland	10 Dec 1982		
France	10 Dec 1982	21 Jun 1996	Ratified
Gabon	10 Dec 1982	11 Mar 1998	Ratified
Gambia	10 Dec 1982	22 May 1984	Ratified
Georgia[12]	10 Dec 1982	21 Mar 1996	Acceded
Germany[13]	10 Dec 1982	14 Oct 1994	Acceded
Ghana	10 Dec 1982	7 Jun 1983	Ratified
Greece	10 Dec 1982	21 Jul 1995	Ratified
Grenada	10 Dec 1982	25 Apr 1991	Ratified
Guatemala	8 Jul 1983	11 Feb 1997	Ratified
Guinea	4 Oct 1984	6 Sep 1985	Ratified
Guinea-Bissau	10 Dec 1982	25 Aug 1986	Ratified
Guyana	10 Dec 1982	16 Nov 1993	Ratified
Haiti	10 Dec 1982	31 Jul 1996	Ratified
Holy See	10 Dec 1982		
Honduras	10 Dec 1982	5 Oct 1993	Ratified
Hungary	10 Dec 1982	5 Feb 2002	Ratified
Iceland	10 Dec 1982	21 Jun 1985	Ratified
India	10 Dec 1982	29 Jun 1995	Ratified
Indonesia	10 Dec 1982	3 Feb 1986	Ratified
Iran	10 Dec 1982		
Iraq	10 Dec 1982	30 Jul 1985	Ratified
Ireland	10 Dec 1982	21 Jun 1996	Ratified
Israel	10 Dec 1982		
Italy	7 Dec 1984	13 Jan 1995	Ratified
Jamaica	10 Dec 1982	21 Mar 1983	Ratified
Japan	7 Feb 1983	20 Jun 1996	Ratified
Jordan	10 Dec 1982	27 Nov 1995	Acceded
Kazakhstan[14]	10 Dec 1982		
Kenya	10 Dec 1982	2 Mar 1989	Ratified
Kiribati		24 Feb 2003	Acceded
Korea, Dem. People's Rep of	10 Dec 1982		
Korea, Rep. of	14 Mar 1983	29 Jan 1996	Ratified
Kuwait	10 Dec 1982	2 May 1986	Ratified
Kyrgyzstan[15]	10 Dec 1982		

[11] The European Economic Community signed on 10 December 1982 as an international organization. *See* Art. 305(1)(f); Annex IX, Art. 1.
[12] *See supra* note 1 regarding the former USSR.
[13] The former German Democratic Republic also signed on 10 December 1982.
[14] *See supra* note 1 regarding the former USSR.

Laos	10 Dec 1982	5 Jun 1998	Ratified
Latvia[16]	10 Dec 1982	23 Dec 2004	Acceded
Lebanon	7 Dec 1984	5 Jan 1995	Ratified
Lesotho	10 Dec 1982	31 May 2007	Ratified
Liberia	10 Dec 1982	25 Sep 2008	Ratified
Libya	3 Dec 1984		
Liechtenstein	30 Nov 1984		
Lithuania[17]	10 Dec 1982	12 Nov 2003	Acceded
Luxembourg	5 Dec 1984	5 Oct 2000	Ratified
Macedonia[18]	10 Dec 1982	5 May 1986	Ratified
		8 Jul 1999	Succeeded
Madagascar	25 Feb 1983	22 Aug 2001	Ratified
Malawi	7 Dec 1984		
Malaysia	10 Dec 1982	14 Oct 1996	Ratified
Maldives	10 Dec 1982	7 Sep 2000	Ratified
Mali	19 Oct 1983	16 Jul 1985	Ratified
Malta	10 Dec 1982	20 May 1993	Ratified
Marshall Isls[19]	10 Dec 1982	9 Aug 1991	Acceded
Mauritania	10 Dec 1982	17 Jul 1996	Ratified
Mauritius	10 Dec 1982	4 Nov 1994	Ratified
Mexico	10 Dec 1982	18 Mar 1983	Ratified
Micronesia[20]	10 Dec 1982	29 Apr 1991	Acceded
Moldova[21]	10 Dec 1982	6 Feb 2007	Acceded
Monaco	10 Dec 1982	20 Mar 1996	Ratified
Mongolia	10 Dec 1982	13 Aug 1996	Ratified
Montenegro[22]	10 Dec 1982	5 May 1986	Ratified
		23 Oct 2006	Succeeded
Morocco	10 Dec 1982	31 May 2007	Ratified
Mozambique	10 Dec 1982	13 Mar 1997	Ratified
Myanmar[23]	10 Dec 1982	21 May 1996	Ratified
Namibia[24]	10 Dec 1982	18 Apr 1983	Ratified

[15] *See supra* note 1 regarding the former USSR.

[16] *See supra* note 1 regarding the former USSR.

[17] *See supra* note 1 regarding the former USSR.

[18] *See supra* note 4 regarding the former Yugoslavia.

[19] The Trust Territory of the Pacific Islands signed on 10 December 1982 as an observer. *See* UN GA Res. 3334 (XXIX).

[20] *See supra* note 19 regarding the Trust Territory of the Pacific Islands.

[21] *See supra* note 1 regarding the former USSR.

[22] *See supra* note 2 4 regarding the former Yugoslavia.

[23] In the name of "Burma".

[24] The United Nations Council for Namibia signed on 10 December 1982 in the name of Namibia. *See* Art. 305(1)(b). Also the South West Africa People's Organization signed on 10

Nauru	10 Dec 1982	23 Jan 1996	Ratified
Nepal	10 Dec 1982	2 Nov 1998	Ratified
Netherlands[25]	10 Dec 1982	28 Jun 1996	Ratified
New Zealand	10 Dec 1982	19 Jul 1996	Ratified
Nicaragua	9 Dec 1984	3 May 2000	Ratified
Niger	10 Dec 1982		
Nigeria	10 Dec 1982	14 Aug 1986	Ratified
Niue	5 Dec 1984	11 Oct 2006	Ratified
Norway	10 Dec 1982	24 Jun 1996	Ratified
Oman	1 Jul 1983	17 Aug 1989	Ratified
Pakistan	10 Dec 1982	26 Feb 1997	Ratified
Palau		30 Sep 1996	Acceded
Palestine[26]	10 Dec 1982		
Panama	10 Dec 1982	1 Jul 1996	Ratified
Papua New Guinea	10 Dec 1982	14 Jan 1997	Ratified
Paraguay	10 Dec 1982	26 Sep 1986	Ratified
Peru	10 Dec 1982		
Philippines	10 Dec 1982	8 May 1984	Ratified
Poland	10 Dec 1982	13 Nov 1998	Ratified
Portugal	10 Dec 1982	3 Nov 1997	Ratified
Qatar	27 Nov 1984	9 Dec 2002	Ratified
Romania	10 Dec 1982	17 Dec 1996	Ratified
Russia[27]	10 Dec 1982	12 Mar 1997	Ratified
Rwanda	10 Dec 1982		
Samoa	28 Sep 1984	14 Aug 1995	Ratified
São Tomé and Príncipe	13 Jul 1983	3 Nov 1987	Ratified
Saudi Arabia	7 Dec 1984	24 Apr 1996	Ratified
Senegal	10 Dec 1982	25 Oct 1984	Ratified
Serbia[28]	10 Dec 1982	5 May 1986 12 Mar 2001	Ratified Succeeded
Seychelles	10 Dec 1982	16 Sep 1991	Ratified
Sierra Leone	10 Dec 1982	12 Dec 1994	Ratified
Singapore	10 Dec 1982	17 Nov 1994	Ratified

December 1982 as a National Liberation Movement. *See* Resolution IV, Rules of Procedure, Rule 62.

[25] The Netherlands Antilles signed on 10 December 1982 as an observer. *See* UN GA Res. 3334 (XXIX).

[26] The Palestine Liberation Organization signed on 10 December 1982 as a National Liberation Movement. *See* Resolution IV, Rules of Procedure, Rule 62.

[27] *See supra* note 1 regarding the former USSR.

[28] *See supra* note 4 regarding the former Yugoslavia.

Slovakia[29]	10 Dec 1982	28 May 1993	Succeeded
		8 May 1996	Ratified
Slovenia[30]	10 Dec 1982	5 May 1986	Ratified
		16 Jun 1995	Succeeded
Solomon Isls	10 Dec 1982	23 Jun 1997	Ratified
Somalia	10 Dec 1982	24 Jul 1989	Ratified
South Africa[31]	5 Dec 1984	23 Dec 1997	Ratified
Spain	4 Dec 1984	15 Jan 1997	Ratified
Sri Lanka	10 Dec 1982	19 Jul 1994	Ratified
St. Kitts and Nevis	7 Dec 1984	7 Jan 1993	Ratified
St. Lucia	10 Dec 1982	27 Mar 1985	Ratified
St. Vincent and the Grenadines	10 Dec 1982	1 Oct 1993	Ratified
Sudan	10 Dec 1982	23 Jan 1985	Ratified
Suriname	10 Dec 1982	9 Jul 1998	Ratified
Swaziland	18 Jan 1984		
Sweden	10 Dec 1982	25 Jun 1996	Ratified
Switzerland	17 Oct 1984	1 May 2009	Ratified
Tajikistan[32]	10 Dec 1982		
Tanzania	10 Dec 1982	30 Sep 1985	Ratified
Thailand	10 Dec 1982		
Togo	10 Dec 1982	16 Apr 1985	Ratified
Tonga		2 Aug 1995	Acceded
Trinidad and Tobago	10 Dec 1982	25 Apr 1986	Ratified
Tunisia	10 Dec 1982	24 Apr 1985	Ratified
Turkmenistan[33]	10 Dec 1982		
Tuvalu	10 Dec 1982	9 Dec 2002	Ratified
Uganda	10 Dec 1982	9 Nov 1990	Ratified
Ukraine[34]	10 Dec 1982	26 Jul 1999	Ratified
United Arab Emirates	10 Dec 1982		
United Kingdom[35]		25 Jul 1997	Acceded

[29] *See supra* note 4.

[30] *See supra* note 4 regarding the former Yugoslavia.

[31] The African National Congress signed on 10 December 1982 as a National Liberation Movement. *See* Resolution IV, Rules of Procedure, Rule 62.

[32] *See supra* note 1 regarding the former USSR.

[33] *See supra* note 1 regarding the former USSR.

[34] In the name "Ukrainian Soviet Socialist Republic". *Also see supra* note 1 regarding the former USSR.

United States	10 Dec 1982		
Uruguay	10 Dec 1982	10 Dec 1992	Ratified
Uzbekistan[36]	10 Dec 1982		
Vanuatu	10 Dec 1982	10 Aug 1999	Ratified
Venezuela	10 Dec 1982		
Vietnam	10 Dec 1982	25 Jul 1994	Ratified
Yemen[37]	10 Dec 1982	21 Jul 1987	Ratified
Zambia	10 Dec 1982	7 Mar 1983	Ratified
Zimbabwe	10 Dec 1982	24 Feb 1993	Ratified

[35] The United Kingdom acceded and declared that the convention applied to certain territories for which it was internationally responsible. *See* Declaration of the United Kingdom, *infra.*

[36] *See supra* note 1 regarding the former USSR.

[37] The Yemen Arab Republic also signed on 10 December 1982 in the name of "Democratic Yemen".

Declarations, Reservations, Objections and Communications[38]

Algeria

Declaration:

"It is the view of the Government of Algeria that its signing the Final Act and the United Nations Convention on the Law of the Sea does not entail any change in its position on the non-recognition of certain other signatories, nor any obligation to co-operate in any field whatsoever with those signatories."

Reservation:

"The People's Democratic Republic of Algeria does not consider itself bound by the provisions of article 287, paragraph 1 (b), of the [said Convention] dealing with the submission of disputes to the International Court of Justice.

The People's Democratic Republic of Algeria declares that, in order to submit a dispute to the International Court of Justice, prior agreement between all the Parties concerned is necessary in each case.

The Algerian Government declares that, in conformity with the provisions of Part II, Section 3, Subsections A and C of the Convention, the passage of warships in the territorial sea of Algeria is subject to an authorization fifteen (15) days in advance, except in cases of *force majeure* as provided for in the Convention."

Angola

Declaration:

"The Government of the People's Republic of Angola reserves the right to interpret any and all articles of the Convention in the context of and with due regard to Angolan Sovereignty and territorial integrity as it applies to land, space and sea. Details of these interpretations will be placed on record at the time of ratification of the Convention.

---

[38] All declarations, reservations and objections are in conenction with UNCLOS unless otherwise noted.

The present signature is without prejudice to the position taken by the Government of Angola or to be taken by it on the Convention at the time of ratification."

Argentina

Declaration:

"The signing of the Convention by the Argentine Government does not imply acceptance of the Final Act of the Third United Nations Conference on the Law of the Sea. In that regard, the Argentine Republic, as in its written statement of 8 December 1982 (A/CONF.62/WS/35), places on record its reservation to the effect that resolution III, in annex I to the final Act, in no way affects the 'Question of the Falkland Islands (Malvinas)', which is governed by the following specific resolutions of the General Assembly: 2065 (XX), 3160 (XXVIII), 31/49, 37/9 and 38/12, adopted within the framework of the decolonization process.

In this connection, and bearing in mind that the Malvinas and the South Sandwich and South Georgia Islands form an integral part of Argentine territory, the Argentine Government declares that it neither recognizes nor will it recognize the title of any other State, community or entity or the exercise by it of any right of maritime jurisdiction which is claimed to be protected under any interpretation of resolution III that violates the rights of Argentina over the Malvinas and the South Sandwich and South Georgia Islands and their respective maritime zones.

Consequently, it likewise neither recognizes nor will recognize and will consider null and void any activity or measure that may be carried out or adopted without its consent with regard to this question, which the Argentine Government considers to be of major importance.

The Argentine Government will accordingly interpret the occurrence of acts of the kind referred to above as contrary to the aforementioned resolutions adopted by the United Nations, the patent objective of which is the peaceful settlement of the sovereignty dispute concerning the islands by means of bilateral negotiations and through the good offices of the Secretary-General of the United Nations.

Furthermore, it is the understanding of the Argentine Republic that, wheres the Final Act states in paragraph 42 that the Convention 'together with resolutions I to IV, [forms] an integral whole', it is merely describing the procedure that was followed at the Conference to avoid a series of separate votes on the Convention and the resolutions. The

Convention itself clearly establishes in article 318 that only the Annexes form an integral part of the Convention; thus, any other instrument or document, even one adopted by the Conference, does not form an integral part of the United Nations Convention on the Law of the Sea."

Reservation:

"(a) With regard to those provisions of the Convention which deal with innocent passage through the territorial sea, it is the intention of the Government of the Argentine Republic to continue to apply the regime currently in force to the passage of foreign warships through the Argentine territorial sea, since that regime is totally compatible with the provisions of the Convention.

(b) With regard to Part III of the Convention, the Argentine Government declares that in the Treaty of Peace and Friendship signed with the Republic of Chile on 29 November 1984, which entered into force on 2 May 1985 and was registered with the United Nations Secretariat in accordance with Article 102 of the Charter of the United Nations, both States reaffirmed the validity of article V of the Boundary Treaty of 1881 whereby the Strait of Magellan (Estrecho de Magallanes) is neutralized forever with free navigation assured for the flags of all nations. The aforementioned Treaty of Peace and Friendship includes regulations for vessels flying the flags of third countries in the Beagle Channel and other straits and channels of the Tierra del Fuego archipelago.

(c) The Argentine Republic accepts the provisions on the conservation and management of the living resources of the high seas, but considers that they are insufficient, particularly the provisions relating to straddling fish stocks or highly migratory fish stocks, and that they should be supplemented by an effective and binding multilateral regime which, *inter alia* , would facilitate cooperation to prevent and avoid over-fishing, and would permit the monitoring of the activities of fishing vessels on the high seas and of the use of fishing methods and gear.

The Argentine Government, bearing in mind its priority interest in conserving the resources of its exclusive economic zone and the area of the high seas adjacent thereto, considers that, in accordance with the provisions of the Convention, where the same stock or stocks of associated species occur both within the exclusive economic zone and in the area of the high seas adjacent thereto, the Argentine Republic, as the coastal State, and other States fishing for such stocks in the area adjacent to its exclusive economic zone should agree upon the measures necessary for the conservation of those stocks or stocks of associated species in the highs seas.

Independently of this, it is the understanding of the Argentine Government, that in order to comply with the obligation laid down in the Convention concerning the conservation of the living resources in its exclusive economic zone and the area adjacent thereto, it is authorized to adopt, in accordance with international law, all the measures it may deem necessary for the purpose.

(d) The ratification of the Convention by the Argentine Republic does not imply acceptance of the Final Act of the Third United Nations Conference on the Law of the Sea. In that regard, the Argentine Republic, as in its written statement of 8 December 1982 (A/CONF.62/WS/35), places on record its reservation to the effect that resolution III, in annex I to the Final Act, in no way affects the 'Question of the Falkland Islands (Malvinas)', which is governed by the following specific resolutions of the General Assembly: 2065 (XX), 3160 (XXVIII), 31/49, 37/9, 38/12, 39/6, 40/21, 41/40, 42/19, 43/25, 44/406, 45/424, 46/406, 47/408 and 48/408, adopted within the framework of the decolonization process.

The Argentine Republic reaffirms its legitimate and inalienable sovereignty over the Malvinas and the South Sandwich Islands and their respective maritime and island zones, which form an integral part of its national territory. The recovery of those territories and the full exercise of sovereignty, respecting the way of life of the inhabitants of the territories and in accordance with the principles of international law, constitute a permanent objective of the Argentine people that cannot be renounced.

Furthermore, it is the understanding of the Argentine Republic that the Final Act, in referring in paragraph 42 to the Convention together with resolutions I to IV as forming an integral whole, is merely describing the procedure that was followed at the Conference to avoid a series of separate votes on the Convention and the resolutions. The Convention itself clearly establishes in article 318 that only the Annexes form an integral part of the Convention; thus, any other instrument or document, even one adopted by the Conference, does not form an integral part of the United Nations Convention on the Law of the Sea.

(e) The Argentine Republic fully respects the right of free navigation as embodied in the Convention, however, it considers that the transit by sea of vessels carrying highly radioactive substances must be duly regulated.

The Argentine Government accepts the provisions on prevention of pollution of the marine environment contained in Part XII of the

Convention, but considers that, in the light of events subsequent to the adoption of that international instrument, the measures to prevent, control and minimize the effects of the pollution of the sea by noxious and potentially dangerous substances and highly active radioactive substances must be supplemented and reinforced.

(f) In accordance with the provisions of article 287, the Argentine Government declares that it accepts, in order of preference, the following means for the settlement of disputes concerning the interpretation or application of the Convention: (a) the International Tribunal for the Law of the Sea; (b) an arbitral tribunal constituted in accordance with Annex VIII for questions relating to fisheries, protection and preservation of the marine environment, marine scientific research, and navigation, in accordance with Annex VIII, article 1. The Argentine Government also declares that it does not accept the procedures provided for in Part XV, section 2, with respect to the disputes specified in article 298, paragraph 1 (a), (b) and (c)."

Objection by the UK

" [(a) – (b), (d) omitted]

(c) *The Falkland Islands*

With regard to paragraph (d) of the Declaration made upon ratification of the Convention by the Government of the Argentine Republic, the Government of the United Kingdom has no doubt about the sovereignty of the United Kingdom over the Falkland Islands and over South Georgia and the South Sandwich Islands. The Government of the United Kingdom, as the administering authority of both Territories, has extended the United Kingdom's accession to the Falkland Islands and to South Georgia and the South Sandwich Islands. The Government of the United Kingdom, therefore, rejects as unfounded paragraph (d) of the Argentine declaration."

Australia

Declaration:

"The Government of Australia declares, under paragraph 1 of article 287 of the United Nations Convention on the Law of the Sea done at Montego Bay on the tenth day of December one thousand nine hundred and eighty-two that it chooses the following means for the settlement of disputes concerning the interpretation or application of the Convention, without specifying that one has precedence over the other:

(a) the International Tribunal for the Law of the Sea established in accordance with Annex VI of the Convention; and
(b) the International Court of Justice.

The Government of Australia further declares, under paragraph 1 (a) of article 298 of the United Nations Convention on the Law of the Sea done at Montego Bay on the tenth day of December one thousand nine hundred and eighty-two, that it does not accept any of the procedures provided for in section 2 of Part XV (including the procedures referred to in paragraphs (a) and (b) of this declaration) with respect to disputes concerning the interpretation or application of articles 15, 74 and 83 relating to sea boundary delimitations as well as those involving historic bays or titles.

These declarations by the Government of Australia are effective immediately."

Austria[39]

Declaration:

"In the absence of any other peaceful means to which it would give preference the Government of the Republic of Austria hereby chooses one of the following means for the settlement of disputes concerning the interpretation or application of the two Conventions in accordance with article 287 of the [Convention], in the following order:

1. The international Tribunal for the Law of the Sea established in accordance with Annex VI;
2. A special arbitral tribunal constituted in accordance with Annex VIII;
3. The International Court of Justice.

Also in the absence of any other peaceful means, the Government of the Republic of Austria hereby recognizes as of today the validity of special arbitration for any dispute concerning the interpretation or application of the Convention on the Law of the Sea relating to fisheries,

---

[39] *Also see* the reservation entered by the European Community, *infra.*

protection and preservation of the marine environment, marine scientific research and navigation, including pollution from vessels and by dumping."

Bangladesh

Declaration:

"1. The Government of the People's Republic of Bangladesh understands that the provisions of the Convention do not authorise other States to carry out in the exclusive economic zone and on the continental shelf military exercise or manoeuvres, in particular, those involving the use of weapons or explosives, without the consent of the coastal State.

2. The Bangladesh Government is not bound by any domestic legislation or by any declaration issued by other States upon signature or ratification of this Convention. Bangladesh reserves the right to state its position concerning all such legislation or declarations at the appropriate time. In particular, Bangladesh ratification of the Convention in no way constitutes recognition of the maritime claims of any other State having signed or ratified the Convention, where such claims are inconsistent with the relevant principles of international law and which are prejudicial to the sovereign rights and jurisdiction of Bangladesh in its maritime areas.

3. The exercise of the right of innocent passage of warships through the territorial sea of other States should also be perceived to be a peaceful one. Effective and speedy means of communication are easily available and make the prior notification of the exercise of the right of innocent passage of warships reasonable and not incompatible with the Convention. Such notification is already required by some States. Bangladesh reserves the right to legislate on this point.

4. Bangladesh is of the view that such a notification requirement is needed in respect of nuclear-powered ships or ships carrying nuclear or other inherently dangerous or noxious substances. Furthermore, no such ships shall be allowed within Bangladesh waters without the necessary authorisation.

5. Bangladesh is of the view that the sovereign immunity as envisaged in article 236 does not relieve a State from the obligation, moral or otherwise, in accepting responsibility and liability for compensation and

relief in respect of damage caused by pollution of the marine environment by any warship, naval auxiliary, other vessels or aircraft owned or operated by the State and used on government non-commercial service.

6. Ratification of the Convention by Bangladesh does not ipso facto imply recognition or acceptance of any territorial claim made by a State party to the Convention, nor automatic recognition of any land or sea border.

7. The Bangladesh Government does not consider itself bound by any of the declarations or statements, however phrased or named, made by other States when signing, accepting, ratifying or acceding to the Convention and that it reserves the right to state its position on any of those declarations or statements at any time.

8. The Bangladesh Government declares, without prejudice to article 303 of the Convention on the Law of the Sea, that any objects of an archaeological and historical nature found within the marine areas over which it exercises sovereignty or jurisdiction shall not be removed, without its prior notification and consent.

9. The Government of Bangladesh shall, at an appropriate time, make declarations provided for in articles 287 and 298 relating to the settlement of disputes.

10. The Government of Bangladesh intends to undertake a comprehensive review of existing domestic laws and regulations with a view to harmonizing them with the provisions of the Convention."

Belarus

Declaration:

"1. The Byelorussian Soviet Socialist Republic declares that, in accordance with article 287 of the United Nations Convention on the Law of the Sea, it accepts, as the basic means for the settlement of disputes concerning the interpretation or application of the Convention, an arbitral tribunal constituted in accordance with Annex VII. For the consideration of questions relating to fisheries, the protection and preservation of the marine environment, marine scientific research and navigation, including pollution from vessels and by dumping, the

Byelorussian Soviet Socialist Republic chooses a special arbitral tribunal constituted in accordance with Annex VIII. The Byelorussian Soviet Socialist Republic recognizes the competence of the International Tribunal for the Law of the Sea in relation to questions of the prompt release of detained vessels or their crews, as envisaged in article 292.

2. The Byelorussian Soviet Socialist Republic declares that, in accordance with article 298 of the Convention, it does not accept compulsory procedures entailing binding decisions in the consideration of disputes concerned with the delimitation of marine limits, disputes relating to military activity and disputes in relation to which the United Nations Security Council performs functions entrusted to it under the United Nations Charter."

Declaration:

"1. In accordance with article 287 of the Convention, the Republic of Belarus accepts as the basic means for the settlement of disputes concerning the interpretation or application of the Convention an arbitral tribunal constituted in accordance with Annex VII. For the settlement of disputes concerning fisheries, protection and preservation of the marine environment, marine scientific research or navigation, including pollution from vessels and by dumping, the Republic of Belarus will use a special arbitral tribunal constituted in accordance with Annex VIII. The Republic of Belarusecognizes the jurisdiction of the International Tribunal for the Law of the Sea over questions concerning the prompt release of detained vessels or their crews, as envisaged in article 292 of the Convention; 2. In accordance with article 298 of the Convention, the Republic of Belarus does not accept compulsory procedures entailing binding decisions for the consideration of disputes concerning military activities, including by government vessels and aircraft engaged in non-commercial service, or disputes concerning law enforcement activities in regard to the exercise of sovereign rights or jurisdiction, or disputes in respect of which the Security Council of the United Nations is exercising the functions assigned to it by the Charter of the United Nations."

Belgium[40]

Declaration:

"[A] [41] The Government of the Kingdom of Belgium has decided to sign the United Nations Convention on the Law of the Sea because the Convention has a very large number of positive features and achieves a compromise on them which is acceptable to most States. Nevertheless, with regard to the status of maritime space, it regrets that the concept of equity, adopted for the delimitation of the continental shelf and the exclusive economic zone, was not applied again in the provisions for delimiting the territorial sea. It welcomes, however, the distinctions established by the Convention between the nature of the rights which riparian States exercise over their territorial sea, on the one hand, and over the continental shelf and their exclusive economic zone, on the other.

[B] It is common knowledge that the Belgian Government cannot declare itself also satisfied with certain provisions of the international régime of the sea-bed which, though based on a principle that it would not think of challenging, seems not to have chosen the most suitable way of achieving the desired result as quickly and surely as possible, at the risk of jeopardizing the success of a generous undertaking which Belgium consistently encourages and supports. Indeed, certain provisions of Part XI and of Annexes III and IV appear to it to be marred by serious defects and shortcomings which explain why consensus was not reached on this text at the last session of the Third   United Nations Conference on the Law of the Sea, in New York, in April 1982. These shortcomings and defects concern in particular the restriction of access to the Area, the limitations on production and certain procedures for the transfer of technology, not to mention the vexatious implications of the cost and financing of the future International Sea-Bed Authority and the first mine site of the Enterprise. The Belgian Government sincerely hopes that these shortcomings and defects will in fact be rectified b the rules, regulations and procedures which the Preparatory Commission should draw up with the twofold intent of facilitating acceptance of the new régime by the whole international community and enabling the common heritage of mankind to be properly exploited for the benefit of all and, preferably, for the benefit of the least favoured countries. The Government of the Kingdom of Belgium is not alone in thinking that the success of this new régime, the effective establishment of the

---

[40] *Also see* the reservation entered by the European Community, *infra.*
[41] Paragraph numbers added for the reader's reference. They do not constitute a part of the communication.

International Sea-Bed Authority and the economic viability of the Enterprise will depend to a large extent on the quality and seriousness of the Preparatory Commission's work: it therefore considers that all decisions of the Commission should be adopted by consensus, that being the only way of protecting the legitimate interests of all.

[C] As the representatives of France and the Netherlands pointed out two years ago, the Belgian Government wishes to make it abundantly clear that, notwithstanding its decision to sign the Convention today, the Kingdom of Belgium is not here and now determined to ratify it. It will take a separate decision on this point at a later date, which will take account of what the Preparatory Commission has accomplished to make the international régime of the sea-bed acceptable to all, focusing mainly on the questions to which attention has been drawn above.

[D] The Belgian Government also wishes to recall that Belgium is a member of the European Economic Community, to which it has transferred powers in certain areas covered by the Convention; detailed declarations on the nature and extent of the powers transferred will be made in due course, in accordance with the provisions of Annex IX of the Convention.

[E] It also wishes to draw attention formally to several points which it considers particularly crucial. For example, it attaches great importance to the conditions to which Articles 21 and 23 of the Convention subject the right of innocent passage through the territal sea, and it intends to ensure that the criteria prescribed by the relevant international agreements are strictly applied, whether the flag States are parties thereto or not. The limitation of the breadth of the territorial sea, as established by Article 3 of the Convention, confirms and codifies a widely observed customary practice which it is incumbent on every State to respect, as it is the only one admitted by international law: the Government of the Kingdom of Belgium will not therefore recognize, as territorial sea, waters which are, or may be, claimed to be such beyond 12 nautical miles measured from baselines determined by the riparian State in accordance with the Convention. Having underlined the close linkage which it perceives between Article 33, paragraph 1 (a), and Article 27, paragraph 2, of the Convention, the Government of the Kingdom of Belgium intends to reserve the right, in emergencies and especially in cases of blatant violation, to exercise the powers accorded to the riparian State by the latter text, without notifying beforehand a diplomatic agent or consular officer of the flag State, on the understanding that such notification shall be given as soon as it is physically possible. Finally, everyone will understand that the Government of the Kingdom of Belgium chooses to emphasize those provisions of the Convention which entitle it to protect itself, beyond the limit of the territorial sea, against any threat of pollution and, *a fortiori*, against any existing pollution resulting from an accident at sea, as well as those provisions which recognize the validity of rights and obligations deriving from specific conventions and agreements concluded previously or which may be concluded subsequently in furtherance of the general principles set forth in the Convention.

[F] In the absence of any other peaceful means to which it obviously gives priority, the Government of the Kingdom of Belgium deems it expedient to choose alternatively, and in order of preference, as Article 287 of the Convention leaves it free to do, the following means of settling disputes concerning the interpretation or application of the Convention:

1. an arbitral tribunal constituted in accordance with Annex VIII;
2. the International Tribunal for the Law of the Sea established in accordance with Annex VI;
3. the International Court of Justice.

[G] Still in the absence of any other peaceful means, the Government of the Kingdom of Belgium wishes here and now to recognize the validity of the special arbitration procedure for any dispute concerning the interpretation or application of the provisions of the Convention in respect of fisheries, protection and preservation of the marine environment, marine scientific research or navigation, including pollution from vessels and by dumping.

[H] For the time being, the Belgian Government does not wish to make any declaration in accordance with Article 298, confining itself to the one made above in accordance with Article 287. Finally, the Government of the Kingdom of Belgium does not consider itself bound by any of the declarations which other States have made, or may make, upon signing or ratifying the Convention, reserving the right, as necessary, to determine its position with regard to each of them at the appropriate time."

Declaration:

"The Kingdom of Belgium Notes that, as a State member of the European Community, it has transferred competence to the Community for some matters provided for in the Convention, which are listed in the declaration made by the European Community upon formal confirmation of the Convention by the European Community on 1st April 1998.

In accordance with article 287 of the Convention, the Kingdom of Belgium hereby declares that it chooses, as a means for the settlement of disputes concerning the interpretation or application of the Convention, in view of its preference for pre-established jurisdictions, either the

International Tribunal for the Law of the Sea established in accordance with Annex VI (art. 287.1 (a)) or the International Court of Justice (art. 287.1(b)), in the absence of any other means of peaceful settlement of disputes that it might prefer."

Bolivia

Declaration:

"On signing the United Nations Convention on the Law of the Sea, the Government of Bolivia hereby makes the following declaration before the International community:

1. The Convention on the Law of the Sea is a perfectible instrument and, according to its own provisions, is subject to revision. As a party to it, Bolivia will, when the time comes, put forward proposals and revisions which are in keeping with its national interests.

2. Bolivia is confident that the Convention will ensure, in the near future, the joint development of the resources of the sea-bed, with equal opportunities and rights for all nations, especially developing countries.

3. Freedom of access to and from the sea, which the Convention grants to land-locked nations, is a right that Bolivia has been exercising by virtue of bilateral treaties and will continue to exercise by virtue of the norms of positive international law contained in the Convention.

4. Bolivia wishes to place on record that it is a country that has no maritime sovereignty as a result of a war and not as a result of its natural geographic position and that it will assert all the rights of coastal States under the Convention once it recovers the legal status in question as a consequence of negotiations on the restoration to Bolivia of its own sovereign outlet to the Pacific Ocean."

Bosnia[42]

Declaration:

"1. Proceeding from the right that State Parties have on the basis of article 310 of the United Nations Convention on the Law of the Sea, the Government of the Socialist Federal Republic of Yugoslavia considers that a coastal State may, by its laws and regulations, subject the passage of foreign warships to the requirement of previous notification to the respective coastal State and limit the number of ships simultaneously passing, on the basis of the international customary law and in compliance with the right of innocent passage (articles 17-32 of the Convention).

2. The Government of the Socialist Federal Republic of Yugoslavia also considers that it may, on the basis of article 38, para. 1, and article 45, para. 1 (a) of the Convention, determine by its laws and regulations which of the straits used for international navigation in the territorial sea of the Socialist Federal Republic of Yugoslavia will retain the regime of innocent passage, as appropriate.

3. Due to the fact that the provisions of the Convention relating to the contiguous zone (article 33) do not provide rules on the delimitation of the contiguous zone between States with opposite or adjacent coasts, the Government of the Socialist Federal Republic of Yugoslavia considers that the principles of the customary international law, codified in article 24, para. 3, of the Convention on the Territorial Sea and the Contiguous Zone, signed in Geneva on 29 April 1958, will apply to the delimitation of the contiguous zone between the Parties to the United Nations Convention on the Law of the Sea."

Brazil

Declaration:

"I. Signature by Brazil is *ad referendum*, subject to ratification of the Convention in conformity with Brazilian constitutional procedures, which include approval by the National Congress.

---

[42] Entered by the former Yugoslavia.

II. The Brazilian Government understands that the régime which is applied in practice in maritime areas adjacent to the coast of Brazil is compatible with the provisions of the Convention.

III. The Brazilian Government understands that the provision of article 301, which prohibits 'any threat or use of force against the territorial integrity or political independence of any State, or in any other manner inconsistent with the principles of international law embodied in the Charter of the United Nations', apply, in particular, to the maritime areas under the sovereignty or the jurisdiction of the coastal State.

IV. The Brazilian Government understands that the provisions of the Convention do not authorize other States to carry out in the exclusive economic zone military exercises or manoeuvres, in particular those that imply the use of weapons or explosives, without the consent of the coastal State.

V. The Brazilian Government understands that, in accordance with the provisions of the Convention, the coastal State has, in the exclusive economic zone and on the continental shelf, the exclusive right to construct and to authorize and regulate the construction, operation and use of all types of installations and structures, without exception, whatever their nature or purpose.

VI. Brazil exercises sovereignty rights over the continental shelf, beyond the distance of two hundred nautical miles from the baselines, up to the outer edge of the continental margin, as defined in article 76.

VII. The Brazilian Government reserves the right to make at the appropriate time the declarations provided for in articles 287 and 298, concerning the settlement of disputes."

Declaration:

"I. The Brazilian Government understands that the provisions of article 301 prohibiting 'any threat or use of force against the territorial integrity of any State, or in other manner inconsistent with the principles of international law embodied in the Charter of the United Nations' apply in particular to the maritime areas under the sovereignty or jurisdiction of the coastal State.

II. The Brazilian Government understands that the provisions of the Convention do not authorize other States to carry out military exercises or manoeuvres, in particular those involving the use of weapons or explosives, in the Exclusive Economic Zone without the consent of the coastal State.

III. The Brazilian Government understands that in accordance with the provisions of the Convention the coastal State has, in the Exclusive Economic Zone and on the continental shelf, the exclusive right to construct and to authorize and to regulate the construction, operation and use of all kinds of installations and structures, without exception, whatever their nature or purpose."

Objection by Italy [omitted][43]

Bulgaria [None][44]

Canada

Declaration:

"With regard to article 287 of the Convention on the Law of the Sea, the Government of Canada hereby chooses the following means for the settlement of disputes concerning the interpretation or application of the Convention without specifying that one has precedence over the other:

(a) the International Tribunal for the Law of the Sea established in accordance with Annex VI of the Convention; and
(b) an arbitral tribunal constituted in accordance with Annex VII of the Convention.

With regard to Article 298, paragraph 1 of the Convention on the Law of the Sea, Canada does not accept any of the procedures provided for in Part XV, section 2, with respect to the following disputes:

- Disputes concerning the interpretation or application of articles 15, 74 and 83 relating to sea boundary delimitations, or those involving historic bays or titles;

- Disputes concerning military activities, including military activities by government vessels and aircraft engaged in non-commercial service,

---

[43] *See* objection by Italy to the reservation by Brazil *supra*.
[44] *Also see* the reservation entered by the European Community, *supra*.

and disputes concerning law enforcement activities in regard to the exercise of sovereign rights or jurisdiction excluded from the jurisdiction of a court or tribunal under article 297, paragraph 2 or 3;

- Disputes in respect of which the Security Council of the United Nations is exercising the functions assigned to it by the Charter of the United Nations, unless the Security Council decides to remove the matter from its agenda or calls upon the parties to settle it by the means provided for in the Convention.

According to Article 309 of the Convention on the Law of the Sea, no reservations or exceptions may be made to the Convention unless expressly permitted by other articles of the Convention. A declaration or statement made pursuant to article 310 of the Convention cannot purport to exclude or to modify the legal effect of the provisions of the Convention in their application to the state, entity or international organization making it. Consequently, the Goernment of Canada declares that it does not consider itself bound by declarations or statements that have been made or will be made by other states, entities and international organizations pursuant to article 310 of the Convention and that exclude or modify the legal effect of the provisions of the Convention and their application to the State, entity or international organization making it. Lack of response by the Government of Canada to any declaration or statement shall not be interpreted as tacit acceptance of that declaration or statement. The Government of Canada reserves the right at any time to take a position on any declaration or statement in the manner deemed appropriate."

Cape Verde

Declaration:

"The Government of the Republic of Cape Verde signs the United Nations Convention on the Law of the Sea with the following understandings:

I. This Convention recognizes the right of coastal States to adopt measures to safeguard their security interests, including the right to adopt laws and regulations relating to the innocent passage of foreign warships through their territorial sea or archipelagic waters. This right is in full conformity with articles 19 and 25 of the Convention, as it was clearly stated in the Declaration made by the President of the Third

United Nations Conference on the Law of the Sea in the plenary meeting of the Conference on April 26, 1982.

II. The provisions of the Convention relating to the archipelagic waters, territorial sea, exclusive economic zone and continental shelf are compatible with the fundamental objectives and aims that inspire the legislation of the Republic of Cape Verde concerning its sovereignty and jurisdiction over the sea adjacent to and within its coasts and over the seabed and subsoil thereof up to the limit of 200 miles.

III. The legal nature of the exclusive economic zone as defined in the Convention and the scope of the rights recognized therein to the coastal state leave no doubt as to its character of a *sui generis* zone of national jurisdiction different from the territorial sea and which is not a part of the high seas.

IV. The regulations of the uses or activities which are not expressly provided for in the Convention but are related to the sovereign rights and to the jurisdiction of the coastal State in its exclusive economic zone falls within the competence of the said State, provided that such regulation does not hinder the enjoyment of the freedoms of international communication which are recognized to other States.

V. In the exclusive economic zone, the enjoyment of the freedoms of international communication, in conformity with its definition and with other relevant provisions of the Convention, excludes any non-peaceful use without the consent of the coastal State, such as exercises with weapons or other activities which may affect the rights or interests of the said state; and it also excludes the threat or use of force against the territorial integrity, political independence, peace or security of the coastal State.

VI. This Convention does not entitle any State to construct, operate or use installations or structures in the exclusive economic zone of another State, either those provided for in the Convention or those of any other nature, without the consent of the coastal State.

VII. In accordance with all the relevant provisions of the Convention, where the same stock or stocks of associated species occur both within the exclusive economic zone and in an area beyond and adjacent to the zone, the States fishing for such stocks in the adjacent area are duty bound to enter into arrangements with the coastal State upon the measures necessary for the conservation of these stock or stocks of associated species."

Declaration:

I. [omitted]

II. The Republic of Cape Verde declares, without prejudice of article 303 of the United Nations Convention on the Law of the Sea, that any objects of an archaeological and historical nature found within the maritime areas over which it exerts sovereignty or jurisdiction, shall not be removed without its prior notification and consent.

III. The Republic of Cape Verde declares that, in the absence of or failing any other peaceful means, it chooses, in order of preference and in accordance with article 287 of the United Nations Convention on the Law of the Sea, the following procedures for the settlement of disputes regarding the interpretation or application of the said Convention:

a) the International Tribunal for the Law of the Sea;
b) the International Court of Justice

IV. The Republic of Cape Verde, in accordance with article 298 of the United Nations Convention on the Law of the Sea, declares that it does not accept the procedures provided for in Part XV, Section 2, of the said Convention for the settlement of disputes concerning military activities, including military activities by government operated vessels and aircraft engaged in non-commercial service, as well as disputes concerning law enforcement activities in regard to the exercise of sovereign rights or jurisdiction excluded from the jurisdiction of a court or tribunal under article 297, paragraphs 2 and 3 of the aforementioned Convention."

Objection by Italy [omitted][45]

---

[45] See objection by Italy to the declaration of Brazil.

Chile

Declaration:

"In exercise of the right conferred by article 310 of the Convention, the delegation of Chile wishes first of all to reiterate in its entirety the statement it made at last April's meeting when the Convention was adopted. That statement is reproduced in document A/CONF.62/SR.164 [...] in particular to the Convention's pivotal legal concept, that of the 200 mile exclusive economic zone to the elaboration of which [the Government] country made an important contribution, having been the first to declare such a concept, 35 years ago in 1947, and having subsequently helped to define and earn it international acceptance. The exclusive economic zone has a *sui generis* legal character distinct from that of the territorial sea and the high seas. It is a zone under national jurisdiction, over which the coastal State exercises economic sovereignty and in which third States enjoy freedom of navigation and overflight and the freedoms inherent in international communication. The Convention defines it as a maritime space under the jurisdiction of the coastal State, bound to the latters' territorial sovereignty and actual territory, on terms similar to those governing other maritime spaces, namely the territorial sea and the continental shelf. With regard to straits used for international navigation, the delegation of Chile wishes to reaffirm and reiterate in full the statement made last April, as reproduced in document A/CONF.62/SR.164 referred to above, as well as the content of the supplementary written statement dated 7 April 1982 contained in document A/CONF.62/WS/19.

With regard to the international sea-bed régime, [the Government wishes] to reiterate the statement made by the Group of 77 at last April's meeting regarding the legal concept of the common heritage of mankind, the existence of which was solemnly confirmed by consensus by the General Assembly in 1970 and which the present Convention defines as a part of *jus cogens*. Any action taken in contravention of this principle and outside the framework of the sea-bed régime would, as last April's debate showed, be totally invalid and illegal."

Declaration:

1. [omitted]

2. The Republic of Chile declares that the Treaty of Peace and Friendship signed with the Argentine Republic on 29 November 1984, which entered into force on 2 May 1985, shall define the boundaries

between the respective sovereignties over the sea, seabed and subsoil of the Argentine Republic and the Republic of Chile in the sea of the southern zone in the terms laid down in articles 7 to 9.

3. With regard to part II of the Convention:

(a) In accordance with article 13 of the Treaty of Peace and Friendship of 1984, the Republic of Chile, in exercise of its sovereign rights, grants to the Argentine Republic the navigation facilities through Chilean internal waters described in that Treaty, which are specified in annex 2, articles 1 to 9.

In addition, the Republic of Chile declares that by virtue of this Treaty, ships flying the flag of third countries may navigate without obstacles through the internal waters along the routes specified in annex 2, articles 1 and 8, subject to the relevant Chilean regulations.

In the Treaty of Peace and Friendship of 1984, the two Parties agreed on the system of navigation and pilotage in the Beagle Channel defined in annex 2, articles 11 to 16. The provisions on navigation set forth in that annex replace any previous agreement on the subjectthat might exist between the Parties.

We reiterate that the navigation systems and facilities referred to in this paragraph were established in the 1984 Treaty of Peace and Friendship for the sole purpose of facilitating maritime communication between specific maritime points and areas, along the specific routes indicated, so that they do not apply to other routes existing in the zone which have not ben specifically agreed on.

b) The Republic of Chile reaffirms the full validity and force of Supreme Decree No. 416 of 1977, of the Ministry of Foreign Affairs, which, in accordance with the principles of article 7 of the Convention -- which have been fully recognized by Chile -- established the straight baselines which were confirmed in article 11 of the 1984 Treaty of Peace and Friendship.

c) In cases in which the State places restrictions on the right of innocent passage for foreign warships, the Republic of Chile reserves the right to apply similar restrictive measures.

4. With regard to part III of the Convention, it should be noted that in accordance with article 35 (c), the provisions of this part do not affect the legal regime of the Strait of Magellan, since passage through that strait is 'regulated by long-standing international conventions in force specifically relating to such straits' such as the 1881 Boundary Treaty, a regime which is reaffirmed in the Treaty of Peace and Friendship of 1984.

In article 10 of the latter Treaty, Chile and Argentina agreed on the boundary at the eastern end of the Strait of Magellan and agreed that this boundary in no way alters the provisions of the 1881 Boundary Treaty, whereby, as Chile declared unilaterally in 1873, the Strait of Magellan is neutralized forever with free navigation assured for the flags of all nations under the terms laid down in article V. For its part, the Argentine Republic undertook to maintain, at any time and in whatever circumstances, the right of ships of all flags to navigate expeditiously and without obstacles through its jurisdictional waters to and from the Strait of Magellan.

Furthermore, we reiterate that Chilean maritime traffic to and from the north through the Estrecho de Le Maire shall enjoy the facilities laid down in annex 2, article 10 of the 1984 Treaty of Peace and Friendship.

5. Having regard for its interest in the conservation of the resources in its exclusive economic zone and the adjacent area of the high seas, the Republic of Chile believes that, in accordance with the provisions of the Convention, where the same stock or stocks of associated species occur both within the exclusive economic zone and in the adjacent area of the high seas, the Republic of Chile, as the coastal State, and the States fishing for such stocks in the area adjacent to its exclusive economic zone must agree upon the measures necessary for the conservation in the high seas of these stocks or associated species. In the absence of such agreement, Chile reserves the right to exercise its rights under article 116 and other provisions of the [said Convention], and the other rights accorded to it under international law.

6. With reference to part XI of the Convention and its supplementary Agreement, it is Chile's understanding that, in respect of the prevention of pollution in exploration and exploitation activities, the Authority must apply the general criterion that underwater mining shall be subject to standards which are at least as stringent as comparable standards on land.

7. With regard to part XV of the Convention, the Republic of Chile declares that:

(a) In accordance with article 287 of the Convention, it accepts, in order of preference, the following means for the settlement of disputes concerning the interpretation or application of the Convention:

i) The International Tribunal for the Law of the Sea established in accordance with annex VI;

ii) A special arbitral tribunal, established in accordance with annex VIII, for the categories of disputes specified therein relating to fisheries, protection and preservation of the marine environment, and marine scientific research and navigation, including pollution from vessels and by dumping.

(b) In accordance with articles 280 to 282 of the Convention, the choice of means for the settlement of disputes indicated in the preceding paragraph shall in no way affect the obligations deriving from the general, regional or bilateral agreements to which the Republic of Chile is a party concerning the peaceful settlement of disputes.

(c) In accordance with article 298 of the Convention, Chile declares that it does not accept any of the procedures provided for in part XV, section 2 with respect to the disputes referred to in article 298, paragraphs 1(a), (b) and (c) of the Convention."

China

Declaration:

1. In accordance with the provisions of the United Nations Convention on the Law of the Sea, the People's Republic of China shall enjoy sovereign rights and jurisdiction over an exclusive economic zone of 200 nautical miles and the continental shelf.

2. The People's Republic of China will effect, through consultations, the delimitation of boundary of the maritime jurisdiction with the states with coasts opposite or adjacent to China respectively on the basis of international law and in accordance with the equitable principle.

3. The People's Republic of China reaffirms its sovereignty over all its archipelagoes and islands as listed in article 2 of the Law of the People's Republic of China on the Territorial Sea and Contiguous Zone which was promulgated on 25 February 1992.

4. The People's Republic of China reaffirms that the provisions of the United Nations Convention on the Law of the Sea concerning innocent passage through the territorial sea shall not prejudice the right of a coastal state to request, in accordance with its laws and regulations, a foreign state to obtain advance approval from or give prior notification

to the coastal state for the passage of its warships through the territorial sea of the coastal state."

Declaration:

"The Government of the People's Republic of China does not accept any of the procedures provided for in Section 2 of Part XV of the Convention with respect to all the categories of disputes referred to in paragraph 1 (a) (b) and (c) of Article 298 of the Convention."

Communication [of 12 June 1985]:

"The so-called Kalayaan Islands are part of the Nansha Islands, which have always been Chinese territory. The Chinese Government has stated on many occasions that China has indisputable sovereignty over the Nansha Islands and at the adjacent waters and resources."

Objection by Vietnam[46]

" [...] The Republic of the Philippines, upon its signature and ratification of the 1982 U.N. Convention on the Law of the Sea, has claimed sovereignty over the islands called by the Philippines as the Kalaysan [see paragraph 4 of the Philippine declaration]. The People's Republic of China has likewise claimed that the islands, called by the Philippines as the Kalaysan, constitute part of the Nansha Islands which are Chinese territory. The so-called 'Kalaysan Islands' or 'Nansha Islands' mentioned above are in fact the Truong Sa Archipelago which has always been under the sovereignty of the Socialist Republic of Vietnam. The Socialist Republic of Vietnam has so far published two White Books confirming the legality of its sovereignty over the Hoang Sa and Truong Sa Archipelagoes.

The Socialist Republic of Vietnam once again reaffirms its indisputable sovereignty over the Truong Sa Archipelago and hence its determination to defend its territorial integrity."

Declaration by Vietnam:

"1. The People's Republic of China's establishment of the territorial baselines of the Hoang Sa archipelago (Paracel), part of the territory of Viet Nam, constitutes a serious violation of the Vietnamese sovereignty over the archipelago. The Socialist Republic of Viet Nam has on many occasions reaffirmed its indisputable sovereignty over the Hoang Sa as

---

[46] *See* communication and declaration of Vietnam *infra.*

well as the Tuong Sa (Spratly) archipelagoes. The above-mentioned act of the People's Republic of China which runs counter to the international law, is absolutely null and void. Furthermore, the People's Republic of China correspondingly violated the provisions of the 1982 United Nations Law of the Sea by giving the Hoang Sa archipelago the status of an archipelagic state to illegally annex a vast sea area into the so-called internal water of the archipelago.

2. In drawing the baseline at the segment east of the Leishou peninsula from point 31 to point 32, the People's Republic of China has also failed to comply with the provisions, particularly articles 7 and 38, of the 1982 United Nations Law of the Sea. By so drawing, the People's Republic of China has turned a considerable sea area into its internal water which obstructs the rights and freedom of international navigation including those of Vietnam through the Qiongzhou strait. This is totally unacceptable to the Socialist Republic of Viet Nam."

Costa Rica

Declaration:

"The Government of Costa Rica declares that the provisions of Costa Rican law under which foreign vessels must pay for licences to fish in its exclusive economic zone, shall apply also to fishing for highly migratory species, pursuant to the provisions of articles 62 and 64, paragraph 2, of the Convention."

Croatia[47]

Declaration:

"The Republic of Croatia considers that, in accordance with article 53 the Vienna Convention on the Law of Treaties of 29 May 1969, there is no peremptory norm of general international law, which would forbid a coastal state to request by its laws and regulations foreign warships to notify their intention of innocent passage through its territorial waters, and to limit the number of warships allowed to exercise the right of innocent passage at the same time (articles 17-32 of the Convention)."

---

[47] *Also see* the declaration entered by the former Yugoslavia listed under Bosnia *supra*.

Declaration:

"In implementation of article 287 of the [Convention], the Government of Croatia [declares] that, for the settlement of disputes concerning the application or interpretation of the Convention and of the Agreement adopted on 28 July 1994 relating to the Implementation of Part XI, it chooses, in order of preference, the following means:

i) The International Tribunal for the Law of the Sea established in accordance with annex VI;
ii) The International Court of Justice."

Cuba

Declaration:

"At the time of signing the Convention on the Law of the Sea, the Cuban Delegation declares that, having gained possession of the definitive text of the Convention just a few hours ago, it will leave for the time of the ratification of the Convention the issuing of any statement it deems pertinent with respect to articles:

287 -- on the election of the procedure for the settlement of controversies pertaining to the interpretation or implementation of the Convention;

292 -- on the prompt release of ships and their crews;

298 -- on the optional exceptions to the applicability of Section 2;

as well as whatever statement or declaration it might deem appropriate to make in conformity with article 310 of the Convention."

Declaration:

"With regard to article 287 on the choice of procedure for the settlement of disputes concerning the interpretation or application of the Convention, the Government of the Republic of Cuba declares that it does not accept the jurisdiction of the International Court of Justice and, consequently, will not accept either the jurisdiction of the Court with respect to the provisions of either article 297 or 298.

With regard to article 292, the Government of the Republic of Cuba considers that once financial security has been posted, the detaining State should proceed promptly and without delay to release the vessel and its crew and declares that where this procedure is not followed with respect to its vessels or members of their crew it will not agree to submit the matter to the International Court of Justice.

Cyprus [None][48]

Czech Republic [None][49]

Denmark[50]

Declaration:

"The Kingdom of Denmark makes the following declaration: It is the position of the Government of the Kingdom of Denmark that the exception from the transit passage regime provided for in article 35(c) of the Convention applies to the specific regime in the Danish straits (the Great Belt, the Little Belt and the Danish part of the Sound), which has developed on the basis of the Copenhagen Treaty of 1857. The present legal regime of the Danish straits will therefore remain unchanged.

The Government of the Kingdom of Denmark declares pursuant to article 287 of the Convention that it chooses the International Court of Justice for the settlement of disputes concerning the interpretation or application of the Convention.

The Government of the Kingdom of Denmark declares pursuant to article 298 of the Convention that it does not accept an arbitral tribunal constituted in accordance with Annex VII for any of the categories of disputes mentioned in article 298.

The Government of the Kingdom of Denmark declares, in accordance with article 310 of the Convention, its objection to any declaration or position excluding or amending the legal scope of the provisions of the Convention. Passivity with respect to such declarations or positions shall be interpreted neither as acceptance nor rejection of such declarations or positions.

---

[48] *Also see* the reservation entered by the European Community, *supra*.
[49] *Also see* the reservation entered by the European Community, *infra*.
[50] *Also see* the reservation entered by the European Community, *infra*.

The Kingdom of Denmark recalls that, as a member of the European Community, it has transferred competence in respect of certain matters governed by the Convention. In accordance with the provisions of Annex IX of the Convention, a detailed declaration on the nature and ex tent of the competence transferred to the European Community was made by the European Community upon deposit of its instrument of formal confirmation. This transfer of competence does not extend to the Faroe Islands and Greenland."

Ecuador

Declaration [in connection with the Final Act]

"On 30 April 1982, in New York, the Convention on the Law of the Sea was adopted by a vote. On that occasion the delegation of Ecuador made an official declaration saying that it had decided not to participate in the vote and stating, for the record, the reasons behind that decision. [The delegation also wishes] to recall the official declarations made by the delegation of Ecuador, particularly at the tenth and eleventh sessions of the Conference, clearly setting for the position of Ecuador.

On this occasion, [the delegation of Ecuador] must state for the record that, notwithstanding the significant progress made in the negotiations carried out during the Third United Nations Conference on the Law of the Sea and notwithstanding the establishment in the Convention of fundamental principles and rights of developing coastal States, and of the international community in general, the Convention which is today being opened for signature by States does not fully meet Ecuador's rights and interests. Ecuador has always exercised and will continue to exercise such rights in accordance with its national legislation. That legislation was drawn up without violating any principle or norm of international law long before any of the three conferences held under the auspices of the United Nations was convened.

Recognition of the exclusive rights of sovereignty and jurisdiction over all the living and non-living resources contained in the adjacent seas up to a distance of 200 miles and their respective beds, constitutes a victory for the coastal States, one that began with the visionary Declaration of Santiago of 1952. The territorialist group, which is coordinated on a permanent basis by the delegation of Ecuador, has played an important role in this achievement.

[Ecuador] has participated actively in the negotiations of the Third United Nations Conference on the Law of the Sea, spanning an eight-year period, and in the preparatory meetings and, given the importance of the issue because of Ecuador's long continental and island shorelines and its rich sea-beds Ecuador will remain attached to that evolving law of the sea in the interest of better defence and promotion of national rights. In affirmation of this it is signing the Final Act of the Third United Nations Conference on the Law of the Sea.

On the occasion of the signing of the Final Act and notwithstanding the progress made in the law of the sea [the Delegation of Ecuador] wishes to reiterate its position in defence of its territorial sea of 200 miles.

Egypt

Declaration [I]:

"1. The Arab Republic of Egypt establishes the breadth of its territorial sea at 12 nautical miles, pursuant to article 5 of the Ordinance of 18 January 1951 as amended by the Decree of 17 February 1958, in line with the provisions of article 3 of the Convention.

2. The Arab Republic of Egypt will publish, at the earliest opportunity, charts showing the baselines from which the breadth of its territorial sea in the Mediterranean Sea and in the Red Sea is measured, as well as the lines marking the outer limit of the territorial sea, in accordance with usual practice."

Declaration [II]:

"The Arab Republic of Egypt has decided that its contiguous zone (as defined in the Ordinance of 18 January 1951 as amended by the Presidential Decree of 17 February 1958) extends to 24 nautical miles from the baselines from which the breadth of the territorial sea is measured, as provided for in article 33 of the Convention."

Declaration [III]:

"Pursuant to the provisions of the Convention relating to the right of the coastal State to regulate the passage of ships through its territorial sea and whereas the passage of foreign nuclear-powered ships and ships carrying nuclear or other inherently dangerous and noxious substances poses a number of hazards,

Whereas article 23 of the Convention stipulates that the ships in question shall, when exercising the right of innocent passage through the territorial sea, carry documents and observe special precautionary measures established for such ships by international agreements, the Government of the Arab Republic of Egypt declares that it will require the aforementioned ships to obtain authorization before entering the territorial sea of Egypt, until such international agreements are concluded and Egypt becomes a party to them."

Declaration [IV]:

"Warships shall be ensured innocent passage through the territorial sea of Egypt, subject to prior notification."

Declaration [V]:

"The provisions of the 1979 Peace Treaty between Egypt and Israel concerning passage through the Strait of Tiran and the Gulf of Aqaba come within the framework of the general régime of waters forming straits referred to in part III of the Convention, wherein it is stipulated that the general régime shall not affect the legal status of waters forming straits and shall include certain obligations with regard to security and the maintenance of order in the State bordering the strait."

Declaration [VI]:

"The Arab Republic of Egypt will exercise as from this day the rights attributed to it by the provisions of parts V and VI of the United Nations Convention on the Law of the Sea in the exclusive economic zone situated beyond and adjacent to its territorial sea in the Mediterranean Sea and in the Red Sea.

The Arab Republic of Egypt will also exercise its sovereign rights in this zone for the purpose of exploring and exploiting, conserving and managing the natural resources, whether living or non-living, of the sea-bed and subsoil and the super-adjacent waters, and with regard to all other activities for the economic exploration and exploitation of the zone, such as the production of energy from the water, currents and winds.

The Arab Republic of Egypt will exercise its jurisdiction over the exclusive economic zone according to the modalities laid down in the Convention with regard to the establishment and use of artificial islands, installations and structures, marine scientific research, the protection and pservation of the marine environment and the other rights and duties provided for in the Convention.

The Arab Republic of Egypt proclaims that, in exercising its rights and performing its duties under the Convention in the exclusive economic zone, it will have due regard for the rights and duties of other States and will act in a manner compatible with the provisions of the Convention.

The Arab Republic of Egypt undertakes to establish the outer limits of its exclusive economic zone in accordance with the rules, criteria and modalities laid down in the Convention.

[...] Egypt declares that it will take the necessary action and make the necessary arrangements to regulate all matters relating to its exclusive economic zone."

Declaration [VII]:

"[...] the Arab Republic of Egypt declares that it accepts the arbitral procedure, the modalities of which are defined in annex VII to the Convention, as the procedure for the settlement of any dispute which might arise between Egypt and any other State relating to the interpretation or application of the Convention.

The Arab Republic of Egypt further declares that it excludes from the scope of application of this procedure those disputes contemplated in article 297 of the Convention."

Statement:

"The Government of the Arab Republic of Egypt is gratified that the Third United Nations Conference on the Law of the Sea adopted the new Convention in six languages, including Arabic, with all the texts being equally authentic, thus establishing absolute equality between all the versions and preventing any one from prevailing over another.

However, when the official Arabic version of the Convention is compared with the other official versions, it becomes clear that, in some cases, the official Arabic text does not exactly correspond to the other versions, in that it fails to reflect precisely the content of certain provisions of the Convention which were found acceptable and adopted by the States in establishing a legal régime governing the seas.

For these reasons, the Government of the Arab Republic of Egypt takes the opportunity afforded by the deposit of the instrument of ratification of the United Nations Convention on the Law of the Sea to declare that it will adopt the interpretation which is best corroborated by the various official texts of the Convention.

Objection by Israel

"The concerns of the Government of Israel, with regard to the law of the sea, relate principally to ensuring maximum freedom of navigation and overflight everywhere and particularly through straits used for international navigation.

In this regard, the Government of Israel states that the regime of navigation and overflight, confirmed by the 1979 Treaty of Peace between Israel and Egypt, in which the Strait of Tiran and the Gulf of Aqaba are considered by the Parties to be international waterways open to all nations for unimpeded and non-suspendable freedom of navigation and overflight, is applicable to the said areas. Moreover, being fully compatible with the United Nations Convention on the Law of the Sea, the regime of the Peace Treaty will continue to prevail and to be applicable to the said areas.

It is the understanding of the Government of Israel that the declaration of the Arab Republic of Egypt in this regard, upon its ratification of [this] Convention, is consonant with the above declaration [by Egypt]."

Equatorial Guinea

Declaration:

"The Government of the Republic of Equatorial Guinea hereby enters a reservation and declares that, under article 298, paragraph 1, of the United Nations Convention of 1982 on the Law of the Sea, it does not recognize as mandatory ipso facto with respect to any other State any of the procedures provided for in part XV, section 2, of the Convention as regards the categories of disputes set forth in article 298, paragraph 1(a)."

Estonia[51]

Declaration :

"1. As a member state of the European Community, the Republic of Estonia has transferred competence in certain matters governed by the Convention to the European Community according to the declaration

---

[51] *Also see* the reservation entered by the European Community, *infra*.

made by the European Community on April 1, 1998 while acceding to the United Nations Convention on the Law of the Sea.

2. Pursuant to Article 287, paragraph 1 of the Convention the Republic of Estonia chooses the International Tribunal for the Law of the Sea established in accordance with Annex VI and the International Court of Justice as means for the settlement of disputes concerning the interpretation or application of this Convention."

European Community

Declaration [I]:

"[A] [52] On signing the United Nations Convention on the Law of the Sea, the European Economic Community declares that it considers that the Convention constitutes, within the framework of the Law of the Sea, a major effort in the codification and progressive development of international law in the fields to which its declaration pursuant to Article 2 of Annex IX of the Convention refers. The Community would like to express the hope that this development will become a useful means for promoting co-operation and stable relations between all countries in these fields.

[B] The Community, however, considers that significant provisions of Part XI of the Convention are not conducive to the development of the activities to which that Part refers in view of the fact that several Member States of the Community have already expressed their position that this Part contains considerable deficiencies and flaws which require rectification. The Community recognises the importance of the work which remains to be done and hopes that conditions for the implementation of a sea bed mining regime, which are generally acceptable and which are therefore likely to promote activities in the international sea bed area, can be agreed. The Community, within the limits of its competence, will play a full part in contributing to the task of finding satisfactory solutions.

[C] A separate decision on formal confirmation (*) will have to be taken at a later stage. It will be taken in the light of the results of the efforts made to attain a universally acceptable Convention."

---

52 Paragraph numbers added for the reader's reference. They do not constitute a part of the communication.

(*) Formal confirmation is the term used in the Convention for ratification by international organisations (see Article 306 and Annex IX, Article 3). [Footnote in the original.]

Declaration [II]:

"[A] [53] Competence of the European Communities with regard to matters governed by the Convention on the Law of the Sea (Declaration made pursuant to article 2 of Annex IX to the Convention)

[B] Article 2 of Annex IX to the Convention on the Law of the Sea stipulates that the participation of an international organisation shall be subject to a declaration specifying the matters governed by the Convention in respect of which competence has been transferred to the organisation by its member states.

[C] The European Communities were established by the Treaties of Paris and of Rome, signed on 18 April 1951 and 25 1957, respectively. After being ratified by the Signatory States the Treaties entered into force on 25 July 1952 and 1 January 1958 (**).

[D] In accordance with the provisions referred to above this declaration indicates the competence of the European Economic Community in matters governed by the Convention.

[E] The Community points out that its Member States have transferred competence to it with regard to the conservation and management of sea fishing resources. Hence, in the field of sea fishing it is for the Community to adopt the relevant rules and regulations (which

---

[53] Paragraph numbers added for the reader's reference. They do not constitute a part of the communication.

(**) The Treaty of Paris establishing the European Coal and Steel Community was registered at the Secretariat of the United Nations on 15.3.1957 under No. 3729; the Treaties of Rome establishing the European Economic Community and the European Atomic Energy Community (Euratom) were registered on 21 April and 24 April 1958, respectively under Nos 4300 and 4301. The current members of the Communities are the Kingdom of Belgium, the Kingdom of Denmark, the Federal Republic of Germany, the Hellenic Republic, the French Republic, Ireland,the Italian Republic, the Grand Duchy of Luxembourg, the Kingdom of the Netherlands and the United Kingdom of Great Britain and Northern Ireland. The United Nations Convention on the Law of the Sea shall apply, with regard to matters transferred to the European Economic Community, to the territories in which the Treaty establishing the European Economic Community is applied and under the cditions laid down in that Treaty.

Furthermore, with regard to rules and regulations for the protection and preservation of the marine environment, the Member States have transferred to the Community competences as formulated in provisions adopted by the Community and as reflected by its participation in certain international agreements (see Annex).

With regard to the provisions of Part X, the Community has certain powers as its purpose is to bring about an economic union based on a customs union.

With regard to the provisions of Part XI, the Community enjoys competence in matters of commercial policy, including the control of unfair economic practices.

The exercise of the competence that the Member States have transferred to the Community under the Treaties is, by its very nature, subject to continuous development. As a result the Community reserves the right to make new declarations at a later date. [Footnote in the original.]

are enforced by the Member States) and to enter into external undertakings with third states or competent international organisations."

Annex [I]

"Community texts applicable in the sector of the protection and preservation of the marine environment and relating directly to subjects covered by the Convention

[1] Council Decision of 3 December 1981 establishing a Community information system for the control and reduction of pollution caused by hydrocarbons discharged at sea (81/971/EEC) (OJ No L 355, 10.12.1981, p. 52).

[2] Council Directive of 4 May 1976 on pollution caused by certain dangerous substances discharged into the aquatic environment of the Community (76/464/EEC) (OJ No L 129, 18.5.1976, p. 23).

[3] Council Directive of 16 June 1975 on the disposal of waste oils (75/439/EEC)(OJ No L 194, 25.7.1975, p. 23).

[4] Council Directive of 20 February 1978 on waste from the titanium dioxide industry (78/176/EEC) (OJ No L 54, 25.2.1978, p. 19).

[5] Council Directive of 30 October 1979 on the quality required of shellfish waters (79/923/EEC) (OJ No L 281, 10.11.1979, p. 47).

[6] Council Directive of 22 March 1982 on limit values and quality objectives for mercury discharges by the chlor-alkali electrolysis industry (82/176/EEC) (OJ No L 81, 27.3.1982, p. 29).

[7] Council Directive of 26 September 1983 on limit values and quality objectives for cadmium discharges (83/513/EEC) (OJ No L 291, 24.10.1983, p. 1 et seq.).

[8] Council Directive of 8 March 1984 on limit values and quality objectives for mercury discharges by sectors other than the chlor-alkali electrolysis industry (84/156/EEC) (OJ No L 74, 17.3.1984, p. 49 et seq.)."

Annex [II]

"The Community has also concluded the following Conventions:

[1] Convention for the prevention of marine pollution from land-based sources (Council Decision 75/437/EEC of 3 March 1975 published in OJ No L 194, 25.7.1975, p. 5).

[2] Convention on long-range transboundary air pollution (Council Decision of 11 June 1981 published in OJ No L 171, 27.6.1981, p. 11).

[3] Convention for the protection of the Mediterranean Sea against pollution and the Protocol for the prevention of pollution of the Mediterranean Sea by dumping from ships and aircraft (Council Decision 77/585/EEC of 25 July 1977 published in OJ No L 240, 19.9.1977, p. 1).

[4] Protocol concerning co-operation in combating pollution of the Mediterranean Sea by oil and other harmful substances in cases of emergency (Council Decision 81/420/EEC of 19 May 1981 published in OJ No L 162, 19.6.1981, p. 4).

[5] Protocol of 2 and 3 April 1983 concerning Mediterranean specially protected areas (OJ No L 68/36, 10.3.1984)."

Declaration [III]:

"[A] [54] By depositing [the instrument of formal confirmation], the Community has the honour of declaring its acceptance, in respect of matters for which competence has been transferred to it by those of its Members States which are parties to the Convention, of the rights and obligations laid down for States in the Convention and the Agreement. The declaration concerning the competence provided for in Article 5(1) of Annex IX to the Convention [follows below].
[B] The Community also wishes to declare, in accordance with Article 310 of the Convention, its objection to any declaration or position excluding or amending the legal scope of the provisions of [this Convention], and in particular those relating to fishing activities. The Community does not consider the Convention to recognize the rights or jurisdiction of coastal States regarding the exploitation, conservation and

---

54 Paragraph numbers added for the reader's reference. They do not constitute a part of the communication.

management of fishery resources other than sedentary species outside their exclusive economic zone.

[C] The Community reserves the right to make subsequent declarations in respect of the Convention and the Agreement and in response to future declarations and positions.

[D] Declaration concerning the competence of the European Community with regard to matters governed by the United Nations Convention on the Law of the Sea of 10 December 1982 and the Agreement of 28 July 1994 relating to the implementation of Part XI of the Convention (Declaration made pursuant to article 5(1) of annex IX to the Convention and to article 4(4) of the Agreement):

[E] Article 5 (1) of Annex IX of [the said] Convention provides that the instrument of formal confirmation of an international organization shall contain a declaration specifying the matters governed by the Convention in respect of which competence has been transferred to the organization by its member States which are Parties to the Convention.

Article 4(4) of [this Agreement] provides that formal confirmation by an international organization shall be in accordance with Annex IX of the Convention.

[F] The European Communities were established by the Treaties of Paris (ECSC) and of Rome (EEC and Euratom), signed on 18 April 1951 and 25 March 1957 respectively. After being ratified by the Signatory States, the Treaties entered into force on 25 July 1952 and 1 January 1958. They have been amended by the Treaty on European Union, which was signed in Maastricht on 7 February 1992, and most recently by the Accession Treaty signed in Corfu on 24 June 1994, which entered into force on 1 January 1995.

[G] The current Members of the Communites are the Kingdom of Belgium, the Kingdom of Denmark, the Federal Republic of Germany, the Hellenic Republic, the Kingdom of Spain, the French Republic, Ireland, the Italian Republic, the Grand Duchy of Luxembourg, the Kingdom of the Netherlands, the Republic of Austria, the Portuguese Republic, the Republic of Finland, the Kingdom of Sweden and the United Kingdom of Great Britain and Northern Ireland.

[H] [This Convention and Agreement] shall apply, with regard to the competences transferred to the European Community, to the territories in which the Treaty establishing the European Community is applied and under the conditions laid down in that Treaty, in particular Article 227 thereof.

[I] The declaration is not applicable to theterritories of Member States in which the said Treaty does not apply and is without prejudice to such acts or positions as may be adopted under the Convention and the Agreement by the Member States concerned on behalf of and in the interests of those territories.

[J] In accordance with the provisions referred to above, this declaration indicates the competence that the Members States have transferred to the Community under the Treaties in matters governed by the Convention and the Agreement.

[K] The scope and the exercise of such Community competence are, by their nature, subject to continuous development, and the Community will complete or amend this declaration, if necessary, in accordance with article 5(4) of Annex IX to the Convention.

[L] The Community has exclusive competence for certain matters and shares competence with its Member States for certain other matters.

1. Matters for which the Community has exclusive competence:

The Community points out that its Member Sates have transferred competence to it with regard to the conservation and management of sea fishing resources. Hence in this field it is for the Community to adopt the relevant rules and regulations (which are enforced by the Member States) and, within its competence, to enter into external undertakings with third States or competent international organizations. This competence applies to waters under national fisheries jurisdiction and to the high seas. Nevertheless, in respect of measures relating to the exercise of jurisdiction over vessels, flagging and registration of vessels and the enforcement of penal and administrative sanctions, competence rests with the Member States whilst respecting Community law. Community law also provides for administrative sanctions.

By virtue of its commercial and customspolicy, the Community has competence in respect of those provisions of Parts X and XI of the Convention and of the Agreement of 28 July 1994 which are related to international trade.

2. Matters for which the Community shares competence with its Member States:

With regard to fisheries, for a certain number of matters that are not directly related to the conservation and management of sea fishing resources, for example research and technological development and development cooperation, there is shared competence.

With regard to the provisions on maritime transport, safety of shipping and the prevention of marine pollution contained inter alia in Parts II, III, V, VII and XII of the Convention, the Community has exclusive competence only to the extent that such provisions of the Convention or legal instruments adopted in implementation thereof affect common rules established by the Community. When Community rules exist but are not affected, in particular in cases of Community provisions establishing only minimum standards, the Member States have competence, without prejudice to the competence of the Community to act in this field.

A list of relevant Community acts appears in the Appendix. The extent of Community competence ensuing from these acts must be assessed by reference to the precise provisions of each measure, and in particular, the extent to which these provisions establish common rules.

With regard to the provisions of Parts XIII and XIV of the Convention, the Community's competence relates mainly to the promotion of coopeation on research and technological development with non-member countries and international organizations. The activities carried out by the Community here complement the activities of the Member States. Competence in this instance is implemented by the adoption of the programmes listed in the Appendix.

3. Possible impact of other Community policies:

Mention should also be made of the Community's policies and activities in the fields of control of unfair economic practices, government procurement and industrial competitiveness as well as in the area of development aid. These policies may also have some relevance to the Convention and the Agreement, in particular with regard to certain provisions of Parts VI and XI of the Convention."

Finland[55]

Declaration:

"As regards those parts of the Convention which deal with innocent passage through the territorial sea, it is the intention of the Government of Finland to continue to apply the present régime to the passage of foreign warships and other government-owned vessels used for non-commercial purposes through the Finnish territorial sea, that régime being fully compatible with the Convention."

Declaration:

"It is the understanding of the Government of Finland that the exception from the transit passage régime in straits provided for in article 35 (c) of the Convention is applicable to the strait between Finland

---

[55] *Also see* the reservation entered by the European Community, *supra.*

(the Aland Islands) and Sweden. Since in that strait the passage is regulated in part by a long-standing international convention in force, the present legal régime in that strait will remain unchanged after the entry into force of the Convention."

Declaration:

"In accordance with article 287 of the Convention, Finland chooses the International Court of Justice and the International Tribunal for the Law of the Sea as means for settlement of disputes concerning the interpretation or application of the Convention as well as of the Agreement relating to the Implementation of its Part XI.

Finland recalls that, as a Member State of the European Community, it has transferred competence to the Community in respect of certain matters governed by the Convention. A detailed declaration on the nature and extent of the competence transferred to the European Community will be made in due course in accordance with the provisions of Annex IX of the Convention."

France[56]

Declaration:

"1. The provisions of the Convention relating to the status of the different maritime spaces and to the legal régime of the uses and protection of the marine environment confirm and consolidate the general rules of the law of the sea and thus entitle the French Republic not to recognize as enforceable against it any foreign laws or regulations that are not in conformity with those general rules.

2. The provisions of the Convention relating to the area of the sea-bed and ocean floor beyond the limits of national jurisdiction show considerable deficiencies and flaws with respect to the exploration and exploitation of the said area which will require rectification through the adoption by the Preparatory Commission of draft rules, regulations and procedures to ensure the establishment and effective functioning of the International Sea-Bed Authority.

To this end, all efforts must be made within the Preparatory Commission to reach general agreement on any matter of substance, in accordance with the procedure set out in rule 37 of the rules of procedure of the Third United Nations Conference on the Law of the Sea.

---

[56] *Also see* the reservation entered by the European Community, *supra.*

3. With reference to article 140, the signing of the Convention by France shall not be interpreted as implying any change in its position in respect of resolution 1514 (XV).

4. The provisions of article 230, paragraph 2, of the Con- vention shall not preclude interim or preventive measures against the parties responsible for the operation of foreign vessels, such as immobilization of the vessel. They shall also not preclude the imposition of penalties other than monetary penalties for any willful and serious act which causes pollution."

Declaration:

"1. France recalls that, as a Member State of the European Community, it has transferred competence to the Community in certain areas covered under the Convention. A detailed statement of the nature and scope of the areas of competence transferred to te European Community will be made in due course in accordance with the provisions of Annex IX of the Convention.

2. France rejects declarations or reservations that are contrary to the provisions of the Convention. France also rejects unilateral measures or measures resulting from an agreement between States which would have effects contrary to the provisions of the Convention.

3. With reference to the provisions of article 298, paragraph 1, France does not accept any of the procedures provided for in Part XV, section 2, with respect to the following disputes:

Disputes concerning the interpretation or application of articles 15, 74 and 83 relating to sea boundary delimitations, or those involving historic bays or titles;

Disputes concerning military activities, including military activities by government vessels and aircraft engaged in non-commercial service, and disputes concerning law enforcement activities in regard to the exercise of sovereign rights or jurisdiction excluded from the jurisdiction of a court or tribunal under article 297, paragraph 2 or 3;

Disputes in respect of which the Security Council of the United Nations is exercising the functions assigned to it by the Charter of the United Nations, unless the Security Council decides to remove the matter from its agenda or calls upon the parties to settle it by the means provided for in this Convention."

Gabon

Declaration:

"[...] the Government of the Republic of Gabon pursuant to article 298, paragraph 1 of the Convention, does not accept any of the procedures provided for in section 2 of Part XV of the said Convention with respect to the categories of disputes referred to in paragraph 1 (a) of article 298."

Germany[57]

Statement:

"[A] [58] The Federal Republic of Germany recalls that, as a Member of the European Community, it has transferred competence to the Community in respect of certain matters governed by the Convention. A detailed declaration on the nature and extent of the competence transferred to the European Community will be made in due course in accordance with the provisions of Annex IX of the Convention.

[B] For the Federal Republic of Germany the link between Part IX of the United Nations Convention on the Law of the Sea of 10 December 1982 and the Agreement of 28 July 1994 relating to the implementation of Part XI of the United Nations Convention on the Law of the Sea as foreseen in article 2 (1) of that Agreement is fundamental.

[C] In the absence of any other peaceful means, which would be given preference by the Government of the Federal Republic of Germany, that Government considers it useful to choose one of the following means for the settlement of disputes concerning the interpretation or application of the two Conventions, as it is free to do under article 287 of the Convention on the Law of the Sea, in the following order:

1. the International Tribunal for the Law of the Sea established in accordance with Annex VI;
2. An arbitral tribunal constituted in accordance with Annex VII;
3. the International Court of Justice.

---

[57] *Also see* the reservation entered by the European Community, *supra*.
[58] Paragraph numbers added for the reader's reference. They do not constitute a part of the communication.

[D] Also in the absence of any other peaceful means, the Government of the Federal Republic of Germany hereby recognizes as of today the validity of special arbitration for any dispute concerning the interpretation or application of the Convention on the Law of the Sea relating to fisheries, protection and preservation of the marine environment, marine scientific research and navigation, including pollution from vessels and by dumping.

[E] With reference to similar declarations made by the Government of the Federal Republic of Germany during the Third United Nations Conference on the Law of the Sea, the Government of the Federal Republic of Germany, in the light of declarations already made or yet to be made by States upon signature, ratification of or accession to the Convention on the Law of the Sea declares as follows:

[1] Territorial Sea, Archipelagic Waters, Straits

[i] The provisions on the territorial sea represent in general a set of rules reconciling the legitimate desire of coastal States to protect their sovereignty and that of the international community to exercise the right of passage. The right to extend the breadth of the territorial sea up to 12 nautical miles will significantly increase the importance of the right of innocent passage through the territorial sea for all ships including warships, merchant ships and fishing vessels; this is a fundamental right of the community of nations.

[ii] None of the provisions of the Convention, which in so far reflect existing international law, can be regarded as entitling the coastal State to make the innocent passage of any specific category of foreign ships dependent on prior consent or notification.

[iii] A prerequisite for the recognition of the coastal State's right to extend the territorial sea is the régime of transit passage through straits used for international navigation. Article 38 limits the right of transit passage only in cases where a route of similar convenience exists in respect of navigational and hydrographical characteristics, which include the economic aspect of shipping.

[iv] According to the provisions of the Convention, archipelagic sea-lane passage is not dependent on the designation by the archipelagic States of specific sea-lanes or air routesin so far as there are existing routes through the archipelago normally used for international navigation.

[2] Exclusive Economic Zone

[i] In the exclusive economic zone, which is a new concept of international law, coastal States will be granted precise resource-related rights and jurisdiction. All other States will continue to enjoy the high seas freedoms of navigation and overflight and of all other internationl lawful uses of the sea. These uses will be exercised in a peaceful manner, and that is, in accordance with the principles embodied in the Charter of the United Nations.

[ii] The exercise of these rights can therefore not be construed as affecting the security of the coastal State or affecting its rights and obligations under international law. Accordingly, the notion of a 200-mile zone of general rights of sovereignty and jurisdiction of the coastal State cannot be sustained either in general international law or under the relevant provisions of the Convention.

[iii] In articles 56 and 58 a careful and delicate balance has been struck between the interests of the coastal State and the freedoms and rights of all other States. This balance includes the reference contained in article 58, paragraph 2, to articles 88 to 115 which apply to the exclusive economic zone in so far as they are not incompatible with Part V. Nothing in Part V is incompatible with article 89 which invalidates claims of sovereignty.

[iv] According to the Convention, the coastal State does not enjoy residual rights in the exclusive economic zone. In particular, the rights and jurisdiction of the coastal State in such zone do not include the rights to obtain notification of military exercises or manoeuvres or to authorize them.

[v] Apart from artificial islands, the coastal State enjoys the right in the exclusive economic zone to authorize, construct, operate and use only those installations and structures which have economic purposes.

[3] The High Seas

As geographically disadvantaged State with important interests in the traditional uses of the seas, the Federal Republic of Germany remains committed to the established principle of the freedom of the high seas. This principle, which has governed all uses of the sea for centuries, has been affirmed and in various fields, adapted to new requirements in the provisions of the Convention, which will therefore have to be interpreted to the furthest extent possible in accordance with that traditional principle.

[4] Land-Locked States

As to the regulation of the freedom of transit enjoyed by land-locked States, transit through the territory of transit States must not interfere with the sovereignty of these States. In accordance with article 125, paragraph 3, the rights and facilities provided for in Part X in no way infringe upon the sovereignty and legitimate interests of transit States. The precise content of the freedom of transit has in each single case to be agreed upon by the transit State and the land-locked State concerned. in the absence of such agreement concerning the terms and modalities for exercising the right of access of persons and goods to transit through the territory of the Federal Republic of Germany is only regulated by national law, in particular with regard to means and ways of transport and the use of traffic infrastructure.

[5] Marine Scientific Research

[i] Although the traditional freedom of research suffered a considerable erosion by the Convention, this freedom will remain in force for States, international organizations and private entities in some maritime areas, e.g., the sea-bed beyond the continental shelf and the high seas. However, the exclusive economic zone and the continental shelf, which are of particular interest to marine scientific research, will be subject to a consent régime, a basic element of which is the obligation of the coastal State under article 246, paragraph 3, to grant its consent in normal circumstances. In this regard, promotion and creation of favourable conditions for scientific research, as postulated in the Convention, are general principles governing the application and interpretation of all relevant provisions of the Convention.

[ii] The marine scientific research régime on the continental shelf beyond 200 nautical miles denies the coastal State the discretion to withhold consent under article 246, paragraph 5 (a), outside areas it has publicly designated in accordance with the prerequisitestipulated in paragraph 6. Relating to the obligation, to disclose information about exploitation or exploratory operations in the process of designation is taken into account in article 246, paragraph 6, which explicitly excluded details from the information to be provided."

Declaration by the German Democratic Republic:

"The German Democratic Republic declares that it accepts an arbitral tribunal as provided for in article 287, paragraph 1(c), which is to be constituted in accordance with Annex VII, as competent for the settlement of disputes concerning the interpretation or application of this

Convention, which cannot be settled by the States involved by recourse to other peaceful means of dispute settlement agreed between them.

The German Democratic Republic further declares that it accepts a special arbitral tribunal as provided for in article 287, paragraph 1(d), which is to be constituted in accordance with Annex VIII, as competent for the settlement of disputes concerning the in terpretation or application of articles of this Convention relating to fisheries, the protection and preservation of the marine environment, marine scientific research and navigation, including pollution from ships and through dumping.

The German Democratic Republic recognizes the competence, provided for in article 292 of the Convention, of the International Tribunal for the Law of the Sea in matters relating to the prompt release of vessels and crews.

The German Democratic Republic declares, in accordance with article 298 of the Convention, that it does not accept any compulsory procedures entailing binding decisions

- in disputes relating to sea boundary delimitations,
- in disputes relating to military activities and
- in disputes concerning which the United Nations Security Council exercises the functions assigned to it by the Charter of the United Nations."

Declaration by the German Democratic Republic:

"The German Democratic Republic reserves the right, in connection with the ratification of the Convention on the Law of the Sea, to make declarations and statements pursuant to article 310 of the Convention and to present its views on declarations and statements made by other States when signing, ratifying or acceding to the Convention."

Communciation by the Federal Republic of Germany:

[Requesting modification of the statement previously reading: "A *special* arbitral [...] article *VIII*]

Objection by the Czech Republic:

"The Government of the Czech Republic having considered the declaration of the Federal Republic of Germany of 14 October 1994 pertaining to the interpretation of the provisions of Part X of the [Convention], which deals with the right of access of land-locked States to and from the sea and freedom of transit, states that the [applicable] declaration of the Federal Republic of Germany cannot be interpreted with regard to the Czech Republic in contradiction with the provisions of Part X of the Convention."

Greece[59]

Interpretative declaration upon signature and upon ratification:

"The present declaration concerns the provisions of Part III `on straits used for international navigation' and more especially the application in practice of articles 36, 38, 41 and 42 of the Convention on the Law of the Sea.

In areas where there are numerous spread out islands that form a great number of alternative straits which serve in fact one and the same route of international navigation, it is the understanding of Greece, that the coastal state concerned has the responsibility to designate the route or routes, in the said alternative straits, through which ships and aircrafts of third countries could pass under transit passage régime, in such a way as on the one hand the requirements of international navigation and overflight are satisfied, and on the other hand the minimum security requirements of both the ships and aircrafts in transit as well as those of the coastal state are fulfilled."

Declaration upon ratification:

"1. In ratifying the United Nations Convention on the Law of the Sea, Greece secures all the rights and assumes all the obligations deriving from the Convention.

Greece shall determine when and how it shall exercise these rights, according to its national strategy. This shall not imply that Greece renounces these rights in any way.

2. Greece wishes to reiterate the interpretative declaration on straits which it deposited at the time of the Convention's adoption and at the time of its signature.

3. Pursuant to article 287 of the United Nations Convention on the Law of the Sea, the Government of the Hellenic Republic hereby choose, the International Tribunal for the Law of the Sea established in accordance with annex VI of the Convention as the means for the

---

[59] *Also see* the reservation entered by the European Community, *supra*.

settlement of diconcerning the interpretation or application of the Convention.

4. Greece, as a State member of the European Union, has given the latter jurisdiction with respect to certain issues relating to the Convention. Following the deposit by the European Union of its instrument of formal confirmation, Greece will make a special declaration specifying in detail the issues dealt with in the Convention for which it has transferred jurisdiction to the European Union.

5. Greece's ratification of the United Nations Convention on the Law of the Sea does not imply that it recognizes the former Yugoslav Republic of Macedonia and does not, therefore, constitute the establishment of treaty relations with the latter."

Communciation from Turkey [in connection with the Final Act]:

"1. The signature and ratification of the Convention by Greece and the subsequent declaration in this regard shall neither prejudice nor affect the existing rights and legitimate interests of Turkey with respect to maritime jurisdiction areas in the Aegean. Turkey fully reserves her rights under international law.

Turkey wishes to state that she will not acquiesce in any claim or attempt designed to upset the long-standing status quo in this respect, that would deprive Turkey of her existing rights and interests. Any unilateral act in this respect that would constitute an abuse of the provisions of the Convention would entail totally unacceptable consequences. Turkey has registered her opposition in this regard actively and persistently from the very outset.

2. In view of the interpretative statement of Greece concerning the provisions of the Convention on the Law of the Sea on the `Straits used for International Navigation', Turkey wishes to reiterate her statement of 15 November 1982, contained in document A/CONF.62/WS/34, which remains fully valid at present and reads as follows:

'In connection with the views expressed by the Greek delegation in the written statement contained in document A/CONF.62/WS/26 of May 1982 the Delegation of Turkey wishes to make the following statement:
The scope of the regime of straits used for international navigation and the rights and duties of States bordering straits are clearly defined in the provisions contained in Part III of the Convention on the Law of the Sea. With the limited exceptions provided in articles 35, 36, 38, paragraph 1 and

45, all straits used for international navigation are subject to the regime of transit passage.

In the written statement referred to above Greece is attempting to create a separate category of straits, i.e. spread out islands that form a great number of alternative straits which is not envisaged in the Convention nor in international law. Thereby Greece wishes to retain the power to exclude some of the straits which link the Aegean Sea to the Mediterranean from the regime of transit passage. Such arbitrary action is not permissible under the Convention nor under the rules and principles of international law.

It seems that Greece, failing in the Conference in its efforts to ensure the application of the regime of archipelagic States to the islands of the continental States, is now trying to circumvent the provisions of the Convention by a unilateral and arbitrary statement of understanding.

The reference in the Greek written statement to article 36 is of particular concern as it is an indication of Greece's intention to exercise discretionary powers not only over straits, but also over high seas.

With regard to the air routes, the Greek statement is contrary to the International Civil Aviation Organization (ICAO) rules according to which air routes are established by ICAO regional meetings with the consent of all interested parties and approved by the ICAO Council.

In view of the above considerations, the Delegation of Turkey finds the Greek views expressed in the document A/CONF.62/WS/26 legally unfounded and totally unacceptable.'

3. Turkey reserves its right to make further declarations as may be required under the circumstances in the future."

Communciation from Greece in reply:

"Turkey has neither signed nor acceded to the [Convention]. It is, therefore, clear the above-mentioned notification cannot have any legal effect, whatsoever.

With regard to the substance of the Turkish notification, Greece rejects all the allegations therein and would like to make the following observations, in this connection:

The purpose of the Greek statement is to interpret certain provisions of the Convention in full accordance with the spirit and the true meaning of the Convention. It is clear, therefore, that Greece neither wishes nor intends, in any way whatsoever, to create any separate category of straits used for international navigation, nor does she intend to circumvent the provisions of the Convention, in any manner.

Greece observes, in particular, that the reference of Turkey to art. 36 is misleading, since the part of the high seas referred to in that article constitutes simply an element of the straits in question. Therefore, reference of Greece to this article in no way can be interpreted as an intention to exercise any discretionary powers over the high seas.

Regarding the allegation that Greece violates ICAO rules and regulations, Greece states emphatically that she respects all the rules and regulations established within the ICAO framework. It must be noted, in this respect, that the institution of transit passage is new and, for the time being, it does not influence the ICAO rules and regulations. In view of this, Greece does not see how her statement could interfere with the ICAO international air routes, in any way.

The Turkish allegations amount to a direct and unequivocal threat by a non-party to the Convention, addressed to a party thereto, with the obvious purpose of compelling Greece to abstain from exercising legitimate rights deriving from international law.

Finally, Greece notes that Turkey makes in her statement repeatedly reference to the provision of the United Nations Law of the Sea, 1982, attempting to draw legal conclusions. Greece interprets these references as an indication that Turkey – a non signatory to the Convention – daccepts its provisions as reflecting general customary law."

Guatemala

Declaration:

"[Guatemala] declares, that:

(a) approval of the Convention by the Congress of the Republic of Guatemala shall under no circumstances affect the rights of Guatemala over the territory of Belize, including the islands, cays and islets, or its historical rights over Bahía de Amatique, and

(b) accordingly, the territorial sea and maritime zones cannot be delimited until such time as the existing dispute is resolved."

Objection by Belize:

"Belize cannot accept any declaration or statement made by a State which is not in conformity with articles 309 and 310 of the Convention.

Article 309 prohibits reservations or exceptions unless expressly permitted by other articles of the Convention. Under article 310, declarations or statements made by a State cannot exclude or modify the legal effect of the provisions of the Convention in their application to that State.

Belize considers that declarations and statements not in conformity with articles 309 and 310 of the Convention include, *inter alia*, those which are not compatible with the dispute resolution mechanism provided in Part XV of the Convention as well as those which purport to subordinate the interpretation or application of the Convention to national laws and regulations, including constitutional provisions.

The recent declaration made by the Government of Guatemala on ratification of the Convention is inconsistent with the aforesaid articles 309 and 310 in the following respects:

(a) Any alleged `rights' over land territory referred to in paragraph (a) of the declaration are outside the scope of the Convention, so that part of the declaration does not fall within the range permitted by article 310.

(b) With regard to the alleged `historical rights' over Bahia de Amatique, the declaration purports to preclude the application of the Convention, in particular article 310 which defines bays, and Part XV which enjoins that State Parties shall settle any disputes between them concerning the interpretation or application of the Convention in accordance with the procedure prescribed therein.

(c) With regard to paragraph (b) of the Guatemalan declaration that 'the territorial sea and maritime zones cannot be delimited until such time as the existing dispute is resolved', article 74 of the Convention requires States with opposite or adjacent coasts to delimit their respective Exclusive Economic Zones by agreement or, if no agreement can be reached within a reasonable time, by recourse to the dispute settlement mechanism under Part XV of the Convention. As for the delimitation of territorial sea, article 15 of the Convention provides that States with opposite or adjacent coast may not extend their respective territorial seas beyond the median line unless they so agree. To the extent that Guatemala is purporting to make a reservation as to, or to exclude or modify the effect of the aforesaid articles 15 or 74, or Part XV of the Convention, the declaration is inconsistent with articles 309 and 310 of the Convention.

For the reasons given above, the Government of Belize hereby categorically rejects as unfounded and misconceived the Guatemala declaration *in toto* ."

Guinea

Declaration upon signature:

"The Government of the Republic of Guinea reserves the right to interpret any article of the Convention in the context and taking due account of the sovereignty of Guinea and of its territorial integrity as it applies to the land, space and sea."

Guinea-Bissau

Declaration:

"As regards article 287 on the choice of a procedure for the settlement of disputes concerning the interpretation or application of the United Nations Convention on the Law of the Sea, [Guinea-Bissau] does not accept the jurisdiction of the International Court of Justice and consequently will not accept that jurisdiction with respect to articles 297 and 298."

Honduras

Declaration:

"In accordance with article 287, paragraph 1, of the United Nations Convention on the Law of the Sea, the State of Honduras chooses the International Court of Justice as the means for the settlement of disputes of any kind concerning the interpretation or application of the said Convention.

Notwithstanding the foregoing, the State of Honduras reserves the possibility of considering any other means of peaceful settlement, including the International Tribunal for the Law of the Sea, as agreed on a case-by-case basis."

Hungary[60]

Declaration:

"[...] the Government of the Republic of Hungary makes the following declaration in relation to Article 287 of the United Nations Convention on the Law of the Sea adopted in Montego Bay on 10 December 1982:

In accordance with the Article 287 of the said Convention the Government of the Republic of Hungary shall choose the following means for the settlement of disputes concerning the interpretation or application of the Convention in the following order:

1. The International Tribunal for the Law of the Sea,
2. The International Court of Justice,
3. A special tribunal constructed in accordance with Annex VIII for all of the categories of disputes specified therein."

Iceland

"Under article 298 of the Convention the right is reserved [by Iceland] that any interpretation of article 83 shall be submitted to conciliation under Annex V, Section 2 of the Convention."

India

Declaration:

"(a) The Government of the Republic of India reserves the right to make at the appropriate time the declarations provided for in articles 287 and 298, concerning the settlement of disputes.

(b) The Government of the Republic of India understands that the provisions of the Convention do not authorize other States to carry out in the exclusive economic zone and on the continental shelf military exercises or manoeuvres, in particular those involving the use of weapons or explosives without the consent of the coastal State."

Objection by Italy [omitted][61]

---

[60] *Also see* the reservation entered by the European Community, *supra.*
[61] See objection entered in connection to the declaration by Brazil.

Iran

Interpretive declaration upon signature:

"In accordance with article 310 of the Convention on the Law of the Sea, the Government of the Islamic Republic of Iran seizes the opportunity at this solemn moment of signing the Convention, to place on the records its "understanding" in relation to certain provisions of the Convention. The main objective for submitting these declarations is the avoidance of eventual future interpretation of the following articles in a manner incompatible with the original intention and previous positions or in disharmony with national laws and regulations of the Islamic Republic of Iran. It is [...] the understanding of the Islamic Republic of Iran that:

1) Notwithstanding the intended character of the Convention being one of general application and of law making nature, certain of its provisions are merely product of *quid pro quo* which do not necessarily purport to codify the existing customs or established usage (practice) regarded as having an obligatory character. Therefore, it seems natural and in harmony with article 34 of the 1969 Vienna Convention on the Law of Treaties, that only states parties to the Law of the Sea Convention shall be entitled to benefit from the contractual rights created therein.

The above considerations pertain specifically (but not exclusively) to the following:

-- The right of Transit passage through straits used for international navigation (Part III, Section 2, article 38).
-- The notion of "Exclusive Economic Zone" (Part V).
-- All matters regarding the International Seabed Area and the Concept of "Common Heritage of mankind" (Part XI).

2) In the light of customary international law, the provisions of article 21, read in association with article 19 (on the Meaning of Innocent Passage) and article 25 (on the Rights of Protection of the Coastal States), recognize (though implicitly) the rights of the Coastal States to take measures to safeguard their security interests including the adoption of laws and regulations regarding, *inter alia*, the requirements of prior authorization for warships willing to exercise the right of innocent passage through the territorial sea.

3) The right referred to in article 125 regarding access to and from the sea and freedom of transit of Land-locked States is one which is derived from mutual agreement of States concerned based on the principle of reciprocity.

4) The provisions of article 70, regarding "Right of States with Special Geographical Characteristics" are without prejudice to the *exclusive right* of the Coastal States of enclosed and semi-enclosed maritime regions (such as the Persian Gulf and the Sea of Oman) with large population predominantly dependent upon relatively poor stocks of living resources of the same regions.

5) Islets situated in enclosed and semi-enclosed seas which potentially can sustain human habitation or economic life of their own, but due to climatic conditions, resource restriction or other limitations, have not yet been put to development, fall within the provisions of paragraph 2 of article 121 concerning "Regime of Islands", and have, therefore, full effect in boundary delimitation of various maritime zones of the interested Coastal States.

Furthermore, with regard to "Compulsory Procedures Entailing Binding Decisions" the Government of the Islamic Republic of Iran, while fully endorsing the Concept of settlement of all international disputes by peaceful means, and recognizing the necessity and desirability of settling, in an atmosphere of mutual understanding and cooperation, issues relating to the interpretation and application of the Convention on the Law of the Sea, at this time will not pronounce on the choice of procedures pursuant to articles 287 and 298 and reserves its positions to be declared in due time."

Iraq

Declaration upon signature:

"Pursuant to article 310 of the present Convention and with a view to harmonizing Iraqi laws and regulations with the provisions of the Convention, the Republic of Iraq has decided to issue the following statement:

1. The present signature in no way signifies recognition of Israel and implies no relationship with it.

2. Iraq interprets the provisions applying to all types of straits set forth in Part III of the Convention as applying also to navigation between islands situated near those straits if the shipping lanes leaving or entering those straits and defined by the competent international organization lie near such islands."

Communciation from Israel

"The Government of the State of Israel has noted that declarations made by Iraq and Yemen upon signing the Convention contain explicit statements of a political character in respect of Israel.

In the view of the Government of the State of Israel, this Convention is not the proper place for making such political pronouncements.

Furthermore, the Government of the State of Israel objects to all reservations, declarations and statements of a political nature in respect of States, made in connection with the signing of the Final Act of the Convention, which are incompatible with the purposes and objects of this Convention.

Such reservations, declarations and statements cannot in any way affect whatever obligations are binding upon the above-mentioned States under general international law or under particular conventions.

The Government of the State of Israel will, insofar as concerns the substance of the matter, adopt towards the Governments of the States in question, an attitude of complete reciprocity."

Ireland[62]

Declaration:

"Ireland recalls that, as a member of the European Community, it has transferred competence to the Community in regard to certain matters which are governed by the Convention. A detailed declaration on the nature and extent of the competence transferred to the European Community will be made in due course in accordance with the provisions of Annex IX of the Convention."

---

[62] *Also see* the reservation entered by the European Community, *supra*.

Israel

Declaration upon signature [in connection with the Final Act]

"This signature of this Final Act in no way implies recognition in any manner whatsoever of the group calling itself the Palestine Liberation Organization or of any rights whatsoever conferred upon it within the framework of any of the documents attached to this Final Act, and is subject to the statements of the Delegation of Israel at the 163rd, 182nd, 184th and 190th meetings of the Conference and document A/CONF.62/WS/33."

Italy[63]

Declaration upon signature and upon ratification:

"Upon signing the United Nations Convention on the Law of the Sea of 10 December 1982, Italy wishes to state that in its opinion part XI and annexes III and IV contain considerable flaws and deficiencies which require rectification through the adoption by the Preparatory Commission of the International Sea-Bed Authority and the International Tribunal for the Law of the Sea of appropriate draft rules, regulations and procedures.

Italy wishes also to confirm the following points made in its written statement dated 7 March 1983:

-- according to the Convention, the Coastal State does not enjoy residual rights in the exclusive economic zone. In particular, the rights and jurisdiction of the Coastal State in such zone do not include the right to obtain notification of military exercises or manoeuvres or to authorize them.

Moreover, the rights of the Coastal State to build and to authorize the construction operation and the use of installations and structures in the exclusive economic zone and on the continental shelf is limited only to the categories of such installations and structures as listed in art. 60 of the Convention.

-- None of the provisions of the Convention, which corresponds on this matter to customary International Law, can be regarded as entitling the Coastal State to make innocent passage of particular categories of foreign ships dependent on prior consent or notification."

---

[63] *Also see* the reservation entered by the European Community, *supra*.

Declaration upon ratification:

"Upon depositing its instrument of ratification Italy recalls that, as Member State of the European Community, it has transferred competence to the Community with respect to certain matters governed by the Convention. A detailed declaration on the nature and extension of the competence transferred to the European Community will be made in due course in accordance with the provisions in Annex IX of the Convention.

Italy has the honour to declare, under paragraph 1(a) of article 298 of the Convention, that it does not accept any of the procedures provided for in section 2 of Part XV with respect to disputes concerning the interpretation of articles 15, 74 and 83 relating to sea boundary delimitations as well as those involving historic bays or titles.

In any case, the present declarations should not be interpreted as entailing acceptance or rejection by Italy of declarations concerning matters other than those considered in it, made by other States upon signature or ratification.

Italy reserves the right to make further declarations relating to the Convention and to the Agreement."

Declaration:

"In implementation of article 287 of the United Nations Convention on the Law of the Sea, the Government of Italy has the honour to declare that, for the settlement of disputes concerning the application or interpretation of the Convention and of the Agreement adopted on 28 July 1994 relating to the Implementation of Part XI, it chooses the International Tribunal for the Law of the Sea and the International Court of Justice, without specifying that one has precedence over the other.

In making this declaration under article 287 of the Convention on the Law of the Sea, the Government of Italy is reaffirming its confidence in the existing international judicial organs. In accordance with article 287, paragraph 4, Italy considers that it has chosen 'the same procedure' as any other State Party that has chosen the International Tribunal for the Law of the Sea or the International Court of Justice."

Kiribati

Declaration:

"In exercise of the right conferred by Article 310 of the Convention, the Republic of Kiribati, upon accession to the United Nations Convention on the Law of the Sea (UNCLOS), declares that in accepting the provisions of Part IV of Article 47 of the said Convention, wishes to highlight its concerns relating to the formula used for drawing archipelagic baselines.

Part IV calculations for archipelagic waters do not allow a baseline to be drawn around all the islands of each of the three Groups of islands that make up the Republic of Kiribati. These Group of islands are spread over an expanse of over three million square kilometres of ocean, and the existing formula as spelt out in Part IV of the Convention, will divide Kiribati's three island groups into three distinct exclusive zone waters and international waters.

The Government of Kiribati wishes to propose that the formula used for drawing archipelagic baselines be revisited in the future to take into consideration the above-mentioned concerns of Kiribati.

Accession by Kiribati to the UN Convention on the Law of the Sea does not in any way prejudice its status as an archipelagic state or its legal rights to declare all or part of its maritime territory as archipelagic waters under the said Convention."

Kuwait

Understanding:

"The ratification by Kuwait of the said Convention does not mean in any way a recognition of Israel nor that treaty relations will arise with Israel."

Communciation from Israel [omitted][64]

---

[64] *See* substantially similar communication from Israel in connection with the declaration of Iraq.

Latvia[65]

Declaration:

"In accordance with paragraph 1 of the Article 287 of the United Nations Convention on the Law of the Sea the Republic of Latvia declares that it chooses the following means for the settlement of dispute concerning the interpretation or application of this Convention:

1) The International Tribunal for the Law of the Sea established in accordance with Annex VI of the Convention,
2) The International Court of Justice."

Lithuania[66]

Declaration:

"[...] in accordance with paragraph 1 of Article 287 of the Convention, the Republic of Lithuania chooses the following means for the settlement of dispute concerning the interpretation or application of this Convention:

a) The International Tribunal for the Law of the Sea established in accordance with Annex VI;
b) The International Court of Justice."

Luxembourg[67]

Declaration upon signature:

"The Government of the Grand Duchy of Luxembourg has decided to sign the United Nations Convention on the Law of the Sea because it represents, in the context of the law of the sea, a major contribution to the codification and progressive development of international law.

Nevertheless, in the view of the Government of Luxembourg, certain provisions of Part XI and Annexes III and IV of the Convention are marred by serious shortcomings and defects which, moreover, explain why it was not possible to reach a consensus on the text at the last

---

[65] *Also see* the reservation entered by the European Community, *supra.*
[66] *Also see* the reservation entered by the European Community, *supra.*
[67] *Also see* the reservation entered by the European Community, *supra.*

session of the Third Conference on the Law of the Sea, held in New York in April 1982.

These shortcomings and defects concern, in particular, the mandatory transfer of technology and the cost and financing of the future Sea-Bed Authority and the first mine site of the Enterprise. They will have to be rectified by the rules, regulations and procedures to be drawn up by the Preparatory Commission. The Government of Luxembourg recognizes that the work remaining to be done is of great importance and hopes that it will be possible to reach agreement on the modalities for operating a sea-bed mining régime that will be generally acceptable and therefore conducive to promoting the activities of the international zone of the sea-bed.

As the representatives of France and the Netherlands pointed out two years ago, [the Government] wishes to make it abundantly clear that, notwithstanding its decision to sign the Convention today, the Grand Duchy of Luxembourg is not here and now determined to ratify it.

It will take a separate decision on this point, at a later date, which will take account of what the Preparatory Commission has accomplished to make the international régime of the sea-bed acceptable to all.

[The Government] also wishes to recall that Luxembourg is a member of the European Economic Community and, by virtue thereof, has transferred to the Community powers in certain ars covered by the Convention. Detailed declarations on the nature and extent of the powers transferred will be made in due course, in accordance with the provisions of Annex IX of the Convention.

Like other members of the Community, the Grand Duchy of Luxembourg also reserves its position on all declarations made at the final session of the Third United Nations Conference on the Law of the Sea, at Montego Bay, that may contain elements of interpretation concerning the provisions of the United Nations Convention on the Law of the Sea."

Malaysia

Declaration:

"1. The Malaysian Government is not bound by any domestic legislation or by any declaration issued by other States upon signature or ratification of this Convention. Malaysia reserves the right to state its positions concerning all such legislations or declarations at the appropriate time, in particular the maritime claims of any other State having signed or ratified the Convention, where such claims are inconsistent with the relevant principles of international laws and the provisions of the Convention on the Law of the Sea and which are prejudicial to the sovereign rights and jurisdiction of Malaysia in its maritime areas.

2. The Malaysian Government understands that the provisions of article 301 prohibiting 'any threat or use of force against the territorial integrity of any State, or in other manner inconsistent with the principles of international law embodied in the Charter of the United Nations' apply in particular to the maritime areas under the sovereignty or jurisdiction of the coastal state.

3. The Malaysian Government also understands that the provisions of the Convention do not authorize other States to carry out military exercises or manoeuvres, in particular those involving the use of weapon or explosives in the exclusive economic zone without the consent of the coastal state.

4. In view of the inherent danger entailed in the passage of nuclear-powered vessels or vessels carrying nuclear material or other material of a similar nature and in view of the provision of article 22, paragraph 2, of the Convention on the Law of the Sea concerning the right of the coastal State to confine the passage of such vessels to sea lanes designated by the State within its territorial sea, as well as that of article 23 of the Convention, which requires such vessels to carry documents and observe special precautionary measures as specified by international agreements, the Malaysian Government, with all of the above in mind, requires the aforesaid vessels to obtain prior authorization of passage before entering the territorial sea of Malaysia until such time as the international agreements referred to in article 23 are concluded and Malaysia becomes a party thereto. Under all circumstances, the flag State of such vessels shall assume all responsibility for any loss or damage resulting from the passage of such vessels within the territorial sea of Malaysia.

5. The Malaysian Government also wishes to reiterate the statement relating to article 233 of the Convention in its application to the Straits of Malacca and Singapore which has been annexed to a letter dated 28th April 1982 transmitted to the President of UNCLOS III and as contained in Document A/CONF.62/L 145, UNCLOS III Off. Rec., vol. XVI, p. 250-251.

6. The ratification of the Convention by the Malaysian Government shall not in any manner affect its rights and obligations under any agreements and treaties on maritime matters entered into to which the Malaysian Government is a party.

7. The Malaysian Government interprets article 74 and article 83 to the effect that in the absence of agreement on the delimitation of the exclusive economic zone or continental shelf or other maritime zones, for an equitable solution to be achieved, the boundary shall be the median line, namely a line every point of which is equidistant from the nearest points of the baselines from which the breadth of the territorial sea of Malaysia and of such other States is measured.

Malaysia is also of the view that in accordance with the provisions of the Convention, namely article 56 and article 76, if the maritime area is less or to a distance of 200 nautical miles from the baselines, the boundary for continental shelf and exclusive economic zone shall be on the same line (identical).

8. The Malaysian Government declares, without prejudice to article 303 of the Convention of the Law of the Sea, that any objects of an archeological and historical nature found within the maritime areas over which it exerts sovereignty or jurisdiction shall not be removed, without its prior notification and consent."

Mali

Declaration upon signature:

"On signing the United Nations Convention on the Law of the Sea, the Republic of Mali remains convinced of the interdependence of the interests of all peoples and of the need to base international co-operation on, in particular, mutual respect, equality, solidarity at the international, regional and sub-regional levels, and positive good-neighbourliness between States.

It thus reiterates its statement of 30 April 1982, reaffirming that the United Nations Convention on the Law of the Sea, in the negotiation and adoption of which the Government of Mali participated in good faith, constitutes a perfectible international legal instrument.

Nevertheless, Mali's signature of the said Convention is without prejudice to any other instrument concluded or to be concluded by the Republic of Mali with a view to improving its status as a geographically disadvantaged and land-locked State. It is likewise without prejudice to the elements of any position which the Government of Mali may deem it necessary to take with regard to any question of the Law of the Sea pursuant to article 310.

In any case, the present signature has no effect on the course of Mali's foreign policy or on the rights it derives from its sovereignty under its Constitution or the Charter of the United Nations and any other relevant rule of international law."

Malta [68]

Declaration:

"[A] [69] The ratification of the United Nations Convention on the Law of the Sea is a reflection of Malta's recognition of the many positive elements it contains, including its comprehensiveness, and its role in the application of the concept of the common heritage of mankind.

[B] At the same time, it is realised that the effectiveness of the regime established by the Convention depends to a great extent on the attainment of its universal acceptance, not least by major maritime States and those with technology which are most   affected by the regime.

[C] The effectiveness of the provisions of Part IX on 'enclosed or semi-enclosed seas', which provide for cooperation of States bordering such seas, like the Mediterranean, depends on the acceptance of the Convention by the States concerned. To this end, the Government of Malta encourages and actively supports all efforts at achieving this universality.

[D] The Government of Malta interprets articles 69 and 70 of the Convention as meaning that access to fishing in the exclusive economic zone of third States by vessels of developed land-locked and geographically disadvantaged States is dependent upon the prior granting of access by the coastal States in question to the nationals of other States which have habitually fished in the said zone.

[E] The baselines as established by Maltese legislation for the delimitation of the territorial sea, and related areas, for the archipelago of the islands of Malta and which incorporate the island of Filfla as one of the points from which baselines are drawn, are fully in line with the relevant provisions of the Convention.

---

[68] *Also see* the reservation entered by the European Community, *supra.*
[69] Paragraph numbers added for the reader's reference. They do not constitute a part of the communication.

[F] The Government of Malta interprets article 74 and article 83 to the effect that in the absence of agreement on the delimitation of the exclusive economic zone or the continental shelf or other maritime zones, for an equitable solution to be achieved, the boundary shall be the median line, namely a line every point of which is equidistant from the nearest points of the baselines from which the breadth of the territorial waters of Malta and of such other States is measured.

[G] The exercise of the right of innocent passage of warships through the territorial sea of other States, should also be perceived to be a peaceful one. Effective and speedy means of communication are easily available, and make the prior notification of the exercise of the right of innocent passage of warships, reasonable and not incompatible with the Convention. Such notification is already required by some States. Malta reserves the right to legislate on this point.

[H] Malta is also of the view that such a notification requirement is needed in respect of nuclear-powered ships or ships carrying nuclear or other inherently dangerous or noxious substances. Furthermore, no such ships shall be allowed within Maltese internal waters without the necessary authorisation.

[I] Malta is of the view that the sovereign immunity contemplated in article 236, does not exonerate a State from such obligation, moral or otherwise, in accepting responsibility and liability for compensation and relief in respect of damage caused by pollution of the marine environment by any warship, naval auxiliary, other vessels or aircraft owned or operated by the State and used on government non-commercial service.

[J] Legislation and regulations concerning the passage of ships through Malta's territorial sea are compatible with the provisions of the Convention. At the same time, the right is reserved to develop further this legislation in conformity with the Convention as may be required.

[K] Malta declares itself in favour of establishing sea-lanes and special regimes for foreign fishing vessels transversing its territorial sea.

[L] Note is taken of the statement by the European Community made at the time of signature of the Convention regarding the fact that its Member States have transferred competence to it with regard to certain aspects of the Convention. In view of Malta's application to join the European Community, it is understood that this will also become applicable to Malta on membership.

[M] The Government of Malta does not consider itself bound by any of the declarations which other States may have made, or will make, upon signing or ratifying the Convention, reserving the right, as necessary, to determine its position with regard to each of them at the appropriate time. In particular, ratification of the Convention does not imply automatic recognition of maritime or territorial claims by any signatory or ratifying State."

Mexico

Declaration:

"In accordance with the terms of article 287 of the United Nations Convention on the Law of the Sea, the Government of Mexico declares that it chooses, in no order of preference, one of the following means for the settlement of disputes concerning the interpretation or application of the Convention:

1. The International Tribunal for the Law of the Sea established in accordance with annex VI;
2. The International Court of Justice;
3. A special arbitral tribunal constituted in accordance with annex VIII for one or more of the categories of disputes specified therein."

Declaration:

"The Government of Mexico declares that, pursuant to article 298 of the Convention, it does not accept the procedures provided for in part XV, section 2, with respect to the following categories of disputes:

1. Disputes relating to sea boundary delimitations, or those involving historic bays or titles, pursuant to paragraph 1 (a) of article 298;
2. Disputes concerning military activities and the other activities referred to in paragraph 1 (b) of article 298.

Moldova

Declaration:

"As a country without seashore and geographically disadvantaged bordering a sea poor in living resources, Republic of Moldova affirms the necessity to develop international cooperation for the exploitation of the living resources of the economic zones, on the basis of just and equitable agreements that should ensure the access of the countries from this category to the fishing resources in the economic zones of other regions or sub regions."

Montenegro

Declaration upon succession:

"1. Proceeding from the right that State Parties have on the basis of article 310 of the United Nations Convention on the Law of the Sea, the [Montenegro] considers that a coastal State may, by its laws and regulations, subject the passage of foreign warships to the requirement of previous notification to the respective coastal State and limit the number of ships simultaneously passing, on the basis of the international customary law and in compliance with the right of innocent passage (articles 17-32 of the Convention).

2. [Montenegro] also considers that it may, on the basis of article 38, para.1, and article 45, para. 1(a) of the Convention, determine by its laws and regulations which of the straits used for international navigation in the territorial sea of [Montenegro] will retain the regime of innocent passage, as appropriate.

3. Due to the fact that the provisions of the Convention relating to the contiguous zone (article 33) do not provide rules on the delimitation of the contiguous zone between States with opposite or adjacent coasts, the [Montenegro] considers that the principles of the customary international law, codified in article 24, para. 3, of the Convention on the Territorial Sea and the Contiguous Zone, signed in Geneva on 29 April 1958, will apply to the delimitation of the contiguous zone between the Parties to the United Nations Convention on the Law of the Sea."

Morocco

Declaration:

"The laws and regulations relating to maritime areas in force in Morocco shall remain applicable without prejudice to the provisions of the United Nations Convention on the Law of the Sea.

The Government of the Kingdom of Morocco affirms once again that Sebta, Melilia, the islet of Al-Hoceima, the rock of Badis and the Chafarinas Islands are Moroccan territories.

Morocco has never ceased to demand the recovery of these territories, which are under Spanish occupation, in order to achieve its territorial unity.

On ratifying the Convention, the Government of the Kingdom of Morocco declares that ratification may in no way be interpreted as recognition of that occupation.

The Government of the Kingdom of Morocco does not consider itself bound by any national legal instrument or declaration that has been made or may be made by other States when they sign or ratify the Convention and reserves the right to determine its position on any such instruments or declarations at the appropriate time.

The Government of the Kingdom of Morocco reserves the right to make, at the appropriate time, declarations pursuant to articles 287 and 298 relating to the settlement of disputes."

Objection by Spain:

"Spain would like to make the following declarations in respect of the declaration made by Morocco on 31 May 2007 upon its ratification of the United Nations Convention on the Law of the Sea:

(i) The autonomous cities of Ceuta and Melilla, the Peñón de Alhucemas, the Peñón Vélez de la Gomera, and the Chafarinas Islands are an integral part of the Kingdom of Spain, which exercises full and total sovereignty over said territories, as well as their marine areas, in accordance with the United Nations Convention on the Law of the Sea.

(ii) The Moroccan laws and regulations on marine areas are not opposable to Spain except insofar as they are compatible with the United Nations Convention on the Law of the Sea, nor do they have any effect on the sovereign rights or jurisdiction that Spain exercises, or may exercise, over its own marine areas, as defined in accordance with the Convention and other applicable international provisions."

Netherlands[70]

Declaration [I]:

"The Kingdom of the Netherlands hereby declares that, having regard to article 287 of the Convention, it accepts the jurisdiction of the International Court of Justice in the settlement of disputes concerning the interpretation and application of the Convention with State Parties to the Convention which have likewise accepted the said jurisdiction."

Declaration [II]:

"The Kingdom of the Netherlands objects to any declaration or statement excluding or modifying the legal effect of the provisions of the United Nations Convention on the Law of the Sea.

This is particularly the case with regard to the following matters:

I. Innocent passage in the territorial sea

The Convention permits innocent passage in the territorial sea for all ships, including foreign warships, nuclear-powered ships and ships carrying nuclear or hazardous waste, without any prior consent or notification, and with due observance of special precautionary measures established for such ships by international agreements.

II. Exclusive economic zone

1. Passage through the Exclusive Economic Zone

Nothing in the Convention restricts the freedom of navigation of nuclear-powered ships or ships carrying nuclear or hazardous waste in the Exclusive Economic Zone, provided such navigation is in accordance with the applicable rules of international law. In particular, the Convention does not authorize the coastal state to make the navigation of such ships in the EEZ dependent on prior consent or notification.

---

[70] *Also see* the reservation entered by the European Community, *supra*. The declarations were made only on behalf of the Kingdom in Europe, but extended to the Netherlands Antilles on 13 February 2009.

2. Military exercises in the Exclusive Economic Zone

The Convention does not authorize the coastal state to prohibit military exercises in its EEZ. The rights of the coastal state in its EEZ are listed in article 56 of the Convention, and no such authority is given to the coastal state. In the EEZ all states enjoy the freedoms of navigation and overflight, subject to the relevant provisions of the Convention.

3. Installations in the Exclusive Economic Zone

The coastal state enjoys the right to authorize, operate and use installations and structures in the EEZ for economic purposes. Jurisdiction over the establishment and use of installations and structures is limited to the rules contained in article 56 paragraph 1, and is subject to the obligations contained in article 56 paragraph 2, article 58 and article 60 of the Convention.

4. Residual rights

The coastal state does not enjoy residual rights in the EEZ. The rights of the coastal state in its EEZ are listed in article 56 of the Convention, and can not be extended unilaterally.

III. Passage through Straits

Routes and sea lanes through straits shall be established in accordance with the rules provided for in the Convention. Considerations with respect to domestic security and public order shall not affect navigation in straits used for international navigation. The application of other international instruments to straits is subject to the relevant articles of the Convention.

IV. Archipelagic States

The application of Part IV of the Convention is limited to a state constituted wholly by one or more archipelagos, and may include other islands. Claims to archipelagic status in contravention of article 46 are not acceptable.

The status of archipelagic state, and the rights and obligations deriving from such status can only be invoked under the conditions of Part IV of the Convention.

V. Fisheries

The Convention confers no jurisdiction on the coastal state with respect to the exploitation, conservation and management of living marine resources other than sedentary species beyond the Exclusive Economic Zone.

The Kingdom of the Netherlands considers that the conservation and management of straddling fish stocks and highly migratory species should, in accordance with articles 63 and 64 of the Convention, take place on the basis of international cooperation in appropriate sub-regional and regional organizations.

VI. Underwater cultural heritage

Jurisdiction over objects of an archaeological and historical nature found at sea is limited to articles 149 and 303 of the Convention.

The Kingdom of the Netherlands does however consider that there may be a need to further develop, in international cooperation, the international law on the protection of underwater cultural heritage.

VII. Baselines and delimitation

A claim that the drawing of baselines or the delimitation of maritime zones is in accordance with the Convention will only be acceptable if such lines and zones have been established in accordance with Convention.

VIII. National Legislation

As a general rule of international law, as stated in articles 27 and 46 of the Vienna Convention on the Law of Treaties, states may not rely on national legislation as a justification for a failure to implement the Convention.

IX. Territorial Claims

Ratification by the Kingdom of the Netherlands does not imply recognition or acceptance of any territorial claim made by a State Party to the Convention.

X. Article 301

Article 301 must be interpreted, in accordance with the Charter of the United Nations, as applying to the territory and the territorial sea of a coastal state.

XI. General Declaration

The Kingdom of the Netherlandsreserves the right to make further declarations relative to the Convention and to the Agreement, in response to future declarations and statements."

Declaration [III]:

"Upon depositing its instrument of ratification the Kingdom of the Netherlands recalls that, as Member State of the European Community, it has transferred competence to the Community with respect to certain matters governed by the Convention. A detailed declaration on the nature and extent of the competence transferred to the European Community will be made in due course in accordance with the provisions in annex IX of the Convention."

Declaration [IV]:

"The Kingdom of the Netherlands hereby declares that, having regard to Article 287 of the Convention, it accepts the jurisdiction of the International Court of Justice in the settlement of disputes concerning the interpretation and application of the Convention with States Parties to the Convention which have likewise accepted the said jurisdiction."

Objection:

"The Kingdom of the Netherlands objects to any declaration or statement excluding or modifying the legal effect of the provisions of the United Nations Convention on the Law of the Sea.
This is particularly the case with regard to the following matters:

I. Innocent passage in the territorial sea

The Convention permits innocent passage in the territorial sea for all ships, including foreign warships, nuclear-powered ships and ships carrying nuclear or hazardous waste, without any prior consent or notification, and with due observance of special precautionary measures established for such ships by international agreements.

II. Exclusive economic zone

1. Passage through the Exclusive Economic Zone

Nothing in the Convention restricts the freedom of navigation of nuclear-powered ships or ships carrying nuclear or hazardous waste in the Exclusive Economic Zone, provided such navigation is in accordance with the applicable rules of international law. In particular, the Convention does not authorize the coastal state to make the navigation of such ships in the EEZ dependent on prior consent or notification.

2. Military exercises in the Exclusive Economic Zone

The Convention does not authorize the coastal state to prohibit military exercises in its EEZ. The rights of the coastal state in its EEZ are listed in article 56 of the Convention, and no such authority is given to the coastal state. In the EEZ all states enjoy the freedoms of navigation and overflight, subject to the relevant provisions of the Convention.

3. Installations in the Exclusive Economic Zone

The coastal state enjoys the right to authorize, operate and use installations and structures in the EEZ for economic purposes. Jurisdiction over the establishment and use of installations and structures is limited to the rules contained in article 56, paragraph 1, and is subject to the obligations contained in article 56, paragraph 2, article 58 and article 60 of the Convention.

4. Residual rights

The coastal state does not enjoy residual rights in the EEZ. The rights of the coastal state in its EEZ are listed in article 56 of the Convention, and cannot be extended unilaterally.

III. Passage through straits

Routes and sealanes through straits shall be established in accordance with the rules provided for in the Convention. Considerations with respect to domestic security and public order shall not affect navigation in straits used for international navigation. The application of other international instruments to straits is subject to the relevant articles of the Convention.

IV. Archipelagic States

The application of Part IV of the Convention is limited to a state constituted wholly by one or more archipelagos, and may include other islands. Claims to archipelagic status in contravention of article 46 are not acceptable.

The status of archipelagic state, and the rights and obligations deriving from each status, can only be invoked under the conditions of part IV of the Convention.

V. Fisheries

The Convention confers no jurisdiction on the coastal state with respect to the exploitation, conservation and management of living marine resources other than sedentary species beyond the Exclusive Economic Zone.

The Kingdom of the Netherlands considers that the conservation and management of straddling fish stocks and highly migratory species should, in accordance with articles 63 [and] 64 of the Convention, take place on the basis of international cooperation in appropriate subregional and regional organizations.

VI. Underwater cultural heritage

Jurisdiction over objects of an archaeological and historical nature found at sea is limited to articles 149 and 303 of the Convention.

The Kingdom of the Netherlands does however consider that there may be a need to further develop, in international cooperation, the international law on the protection of underwater cultural heritage.

VII. Baselines and delimitation

A claim that the drawing of baselines of the delimitation of maritime zones is in accordance with the Convention will only be acceptable if such lines and zones have been established in accordance with the Convention.

VIII. National legislation

As a general rule of international law, as stated in articles 27 and 46 of the Vienna Convention on the law of Treaties, states may not rely on national legislation as a justification for a failure to implement the Convention.

IX. Territorial claims

Ratification by the Kingdom of the Netherlands does not imply recognition or acceptance of any territorial claim made by a State Party to the Convention.

X. Article 301

Article 301 must be interpreted, in accordance with the Charter of the United Nations, as applying to the territory and the territorial sea of a coastal state.

XI. General declaration

The Kingdom of the Netherlands reserves its right to make further declarations relative to the Convention and to the Agreement, in response to future declarations and statements."

Nicaragua

Declaration upon signature:

"In accordance with article 310, Nicaragua declares that such adjustments of its domestic law as may be required in order to harmonize it with the Convention will follow from the process of constitutional change initiated by the revolutionary State of Nicaragua, it being understood that the Convention and the Resolutions adopted on 10 December 1982 and the Annexes to the Convention constitute an inseparable whole.

For the purposes of articles 287 and 298 and of other articles concerning the interpretation and application of the Convention, the Government of Nicaragua shall, if and as the occasion demands, exercise the right conferred by the Convention to make further supplementary or clarificatory declarations."

Declaration upon ratification:

"In accordance with article 310 of the United Nations Convention on the Law of the Sea, the Government of Nicaragua hereby declares:

1. That it does not consider itself bound by any of the declarations or statements, however phrased or named, made by other States when signing, accepting, ratifying or acceding to the Convention and that it

reserves the right to state its position on any of those declarations or statements at any time.

2. That ratification of the Convention does not imply recognition or acceptance of any territorial claim made by a State party to the Convention, nor automatic recognition of any land or sea border.

In accordance with article 287, paragraph 1, of the Convention, Nicaragua hereby declares that it accepts only recourse to the International Court of Justice as a means for the settlement of disputes concerning the interpretation or application of the Convention.

Nicaragua hereby declares that it accepts only recourse to the International Court of Justice as a means for the settlement of the categories of disputes set forth in subparagraphs (a), (b) and (c) of paragraph 1 of article 298 of the Convention."

Norway

Declaration [I]:

"According to article 309 of the Convention, no reservations or exceptions other than those expressly permitted by its provisions may be made. A declaration pursuant to its article 310 can not have the effect of an exception or reservation for the State making it. Consequently, the Government of the Kingdom of Norway declares that it does not consider itself bound by declarations pursuant to article 310 of the Convention that are or will be made by other States or international organizations. Passivity with respect to such declarations shall be interpreted neither as acceptance nor rejection of such declarations. The Government reserves Norway's right at any time to take a position on such declarations in the manner deemed appropriate."

Declaration [II]:

"The Government of the Kingdom of Norway declares pursuant to article 287 of the Convention that it chooses the International Court of Justice for the settlement of disputes concerning the interpretation or application of the Convention."

Declaration [III]:

"The Government of the Kingdom of Norway declares pursuant to article 298 of the Convention that it does not accept an arbitral tribunal constituted in accordance with Annex VII of any of the categories of disputes mentioned in article 298."

Oman

Declaration upon signature:

"It is the understanding of the Government of the Sultanate of Oman that the application of the provisions of articles 19, 25, 34, 38 and 45 of the Convention does not preclude a coastal State from taking such appropriate measures as are necessary to protect its interest of peace and security."

Declaration upon ratification:

"Pursuant to the provisions of article 310 of the Convention and further to the earlier declaration by the Sultanate of Oman dated 1 June 1982 concerning the establishment of straight baselines at any point on the coastline of the Sultanate of Oman and the lines enclosing waters within inlets and bays and waters between islands and the coast-line, in accordance with article 2(c) of Royal Decree No. 15/81 and in view of the desire of the Sultanante of Oman to bring its laws into line with the provisions of the Convention, the Sultanate of Oman issues the following declarations:

Declaration No. 1, on the territorial sea

1. The Sultanate of Oman determines that its territorial sea, in accordance with article 2 of Royal Decree No. 15/81 dated 10 February 1981, extends 12 nautical miles in a seaward direction, measured from the nearest point of the baselines.

2. The Sultanate of Oman exercises full sovereignty over its territorial sea, the space above the territorial sea and its bed and subsoil, pursuant to the relevant laws and regulations of the Sultanate and in conformity with the provisions of this Convention concerning the principle of innocent passage.

Declaration No. 2, on the passage of warships throughout Omani territorial waters

Innocent passage is guaranteed to warships through Omani territorial waters, subject to prior permission. This also applies to submarines, on condition that they navigate on the surface and fly the flag of their home state.

Declaration No. 3, on the passage of nuclear-powered ships and the like through Omani territorial waters

With regard to foreign nuclear-powered ships and ships carrying nuclear or other substances that are inherently dangerous or harmful to health or the environment, the right of innocent passage, subject to prior permission, is guaranteed to the types of vessel, whether or not warships, to which the descriptions apply. This right is also guaranteed to submarines to which the descriptions apply, on condition that they navigate on the surface and fly the flag of their home State.

Declaration No. 4, on the contiguous zone

The contiguous zone extends for a distance of 12 nautical miles measured from the outer limit of the territorial waters and the Sultanate of Oman exercises the same prerogatives over it as are established by the Convention.

Declaration No. 5, on the exclusive economic zone

1. The Sultanate of Oman determines that its exclusive economic zone, in accordance with article 5 of Royal Decree No. 15/81 dated 10 February 1981, extends 200 nautical miles in a seaward direction, measured from the baselines from which the territorial sea is measured.

2. The Sultanate of Oman possesses sovereign rights over its economic zone and also exercises jurisdiction over that zone as provided for in the Convention. It further declares that, in exercising its rights and performing its duties under the Convention in the exclusive economic zone, it will have due regard to the rights and duties of other States and will act in a manner compatible with the provisions of the Convention.

Declaration No. 6, on the continental shelf

The Sultanate of Oman exercises over its continental shelf sovereign rights for the purpose of exploring it and exploiting its natural resources, as permitted by geographical conditions and in accordance with this Convention.

Declaration No. 7, on the procedure chosen for the settlement of disputes under the Convention

Pursuant to article 287 of the Convention, the Sultanate of Oman declares its acceptance of the jurisdiction of the International Tribunal for the Law of the Sea, as set forth in annex VI to the Convention, and the jurisdiction of the International Court of Justice, with a view to the settlement of any dispute that may arise between it and another State concerning the interpretation or application of the Convention."

Pakistan

Declaration:

"i) The Government of the Islamic Republic of Pakistan shall, at an appropriate time, make declarations provided for in articles 287 and 298 relating to the settlement of disputes.

ii) The Law of the Sea Convention, while dealing with transit through the territory of the transit State, fully safeguards the sovereignty of the transit State. Consequently, in accordance with article 125 of the rights and facilities of transit to the land locked State ensures that it shall not in any way infringe upon the sovereignty and the legitimate interest of the transit State. The precise content of the freedom of transit consequently, in each case, has to be agreed upon by the transit State and the land locked State concerned. In the absence of such an agreement concerning the terms and modalities for exercising the right of transit, through the territory of the Islamic Republic of Pakistan shall be regulated only by national laws of Pakistan.

iii) It is the understanding of the Government of the Islamic Republic of Pakistan that the provisions of the Convention on the Law of the Sea do not in any way authorize the carrying out in the Exclusive Economic Zone and in the Continental Shelf of any coastal State military exercises or manoeuvres by other States, in particular where the use of weapons or explosives are involved, without the consent of the coastal State concerned."

Palau

Declaration:

"The Government of the Republic of Palau declares under paragraph 1(a) of Article 298 of the 1982 United Nations Convention on the Law of the Sea that it does not accept compulsory procedures entailing binding decisions relating to the delimitation and/or interpretation of maritime boundaries."

Panama

Declaration:

"[Panama] declares that it has exclusive sovereignty over the 'historic Panamanian bay' of the Golfo de Panamá, a well-marked geographic configuration the coasts of which belong entirely to the Republic of Panama. It is a large indentation or inlet to the south of the Panamanian isthmus, where sea-waters superjacent to the seabed and subsoil cover the area between latitudes 70 28' 00" North and 70 31' 00" North and longitudes 70 59' 53" and 78 11' 40", both west of Greenwich, these being the positions of Punta Mala and Punta Jaqué, respectively, west and east of the entrance of the Golfo de Panamá. This large indentation penetrates fairly deep into the Panamanian isthmus. The width of its entrance, from Punta Mala to Punta de Jaqué, is some 200 kilometres and it penetrates inland a distance of 165 kilometres (measured from the imaginary line joining Punta Mala and Punta Jaqué to the mouths of the Rio Chico east of Panama City).

Given its present and potential resources, the historic bay of the Golfo de Panamá is a vital necessity for the Republic of Panama, both in terms of security and defence (this had been the case since time immemorial) and in economic terms, as its marine resources have been utilized since ancient times by the inhabitants of the Panamanian isthmus.

It is oblong in shape, with a coast outline that roughly resembles a calf's head, and its coastal perimeter, which measures some 668 kilometres, is under the maritime control of Panama. According to this delimitation, the historic bay of the Golfo de Panama has an area of approximately 30,000 km 2 .

The Republic of Panama declares that, in the exercise of its sovereign and territorial rights and in compliance with its duties, it will act in a manner compatible with the provisions of the Convention and reserves the right to issue further statements on the Convention if necessary.

Philippines

Declaration made upon signature and confirmed upon ratification:

"1. The signing of the Convention by the Government of the Republic of the Philippines shall not in any manner impair or prejudice the sovereign rights of the Republic of the Philippines under and arising from the Constitution of the Philippines;

2. Such signing shall not in any manner affect the sovereign rights of the Republic of the Philippines as successor of the United States of America, under and arising out of the Treaty of Paris between Spain and the United States of America of December 10, 1898, and the Treaty of Washington between the United States of America and Great Britain of January 2, 1930;

3. Such signing shall not diminish or in any manner affect the rights and obligations of the contracting parties under the Mutual Defense Treaty between the Philippines and the United States of America of August 30, 1951, and its related interpretative instruments; nor those under any other pertinent bilateral or multilateral treaty or agreement to which the Philippines is a party;

4. Such signing shall not in any manner impair or prejudice the sovereignty of the Republic of the Philippines over any territory over which it exercises sovereign authority, such as the Kalayaan Islands, and the waters appurtenant thereto;

5. The Convention shall not be construed as amending in any manner any pertinent laws and Presidential Decrees or Proclamations of the Republic of the Philippines; the Government of the Republic of the Philippines maintains and reserves the right and authority to make any amendments to such laws, decrees or proclamations pursuant to the provisions of the Philippine Constitution;

6. The provisions of the Convention on archipelagic passage through sea lanes do not nullify or impair the sovereignty of the Philippines as an archipelagic state over the sea lanes and do not deprive it of authority to enact legislation to protect its sovereignty, independence, and security;

7. The concept of archipelagic waters is similar to the concept of internal waters under the Constitution of the Philippines, and removes straits connecting these waters with the economic zone or high sea from the rights of foreign vessels to transit passage for international navigation;

8. The agreement of the Republic of the Philippines to the submission for peaceful resolution, under any of the procedures provided in the Convention, of disputes under Article 298 shall not be considered as a derogation of Philippine sovereignty."

Objection by Australia:

"Australia considers that [the] declaration made by the Republic of the Philippines is not consistent with article 309 of the Law of the Sea Convention, which prohibits the making of reservations, nor with article 310 which permits declarations to be made 'provided that such declarations or statements do not purport to exclude or to modify the legal effects of the provisions of this Convention in their application to that State'.

The declaration of the Republic of the Philippines asserts that the Convention shall not affect the sovereign rights of the Philippines arising from its Constitution, its domestic legislation and any treaties to which the Philippines is a party. This indicates, in effect, that the Philippines does not consider that it is obliged to harmonise its law with the provisions of the Convention. By making such an assertion, the Philippines is seeking to modify the legal effect of the Convention's provisions.

This view is supported by the specific reference in the declaration to the status of archipelagic waters. The declaration states that the concept of archipelagic waters in the Convention is similar to the concept of internal waters held under former constitutions of the Philippines and recently reaffirmed in article 1 of the New Constitution of the Philippines in 1987. It is clear, however, that the Convention distinguishes the two concepts and that different obligations and rights are applicable to archipelagic waters from those which apply to internal waters. In particular, the Convention provides for the exercise by foreign ships of the rights of innocent passage and of archipelagic sea lanes passage in archipelagic waters.

Australia cannot, therefore, accept that the statement of the Philippines has any legal effect or will have any effect when the Convention comes into force and considers that the provisions of the Convention should be observed without being made subject to the restrictions asserted in thedeclaration of the Republic of the Philippines."

Declaration by the Philippines in reply:

"The Philippines declaration was made in conformity with article 310 of the United Nations Convention on the Law of the Sea. The declaration consists of interpretative statements concerning certain provisions of the Convention.

The Philippine Government intends to harmonize its domestic legislation with the provisions of the Convention.

The necessary steps are being undertaken to enact legislation dealing with archipelagic sea lanes passage and the exercise of Philippine sovereign rights over archipelagic waters, in accordance with the Convention.

The Philippine Government, therefore, wishes to assure the Australian Government and the States Parties to the Convention that the Philippines will abide by the provisions of the said Convention."

Obejction by Belarus:

"The Byelorussian Soviet Socialist Republic considers that the statement which was made by the Government of the Philippines upon signing the United Nations Convention on the Law of the Sea and confirmed subsequently upon ratification of that Convention in essence contains reservations and exceptions to the said Convention, contrary to the provisions of article 309 thereof. The statement by the Government of the Philippines is also inconsistent with article 310 of the Convention, under which any declarations or statements made by a State when signing, ratifying or acceding to the Convention are admissible only 'provided that such declarations or statements do not purport to exclude or to modify the legal effect of the provisions of this Convention in their application to that State'.

The Government of the Philippines in its statement repeatedly emphasizes its intention to continue to be governed in ocean affairs not by the Convention or by obligations thereunder, but by its national laws and previously concluded agreements, which are not in conformity with the provisions of the Convention. The Philippine side therefore declines to harmonize its national legislation with the provisions of the

Convention and fails to perform one of its most fundamental obligations thereunder – to comply with the régime of archipelagic waters, which provides for the right of archipelagic passage of foreign ships and aircraft through or over such waters.

For the above reasons, the Byelorussian Soviet Socialist Republic cannot recognize the validity of the statement by the Government of the Philippines and regards it as having no legal force in the light of the provisions of the Convention.

The Byelorussian Soviet Socialist Republic believes that if the similar statements which were likewise made by certain other States when signing the Convention and which are inconsistent with the provisions thereof also occur at the stage of ratification or accession, th result could be to undermine the object and importance of the Convention and to prejudice that major instrument of international law.

In view of the foregoing, the Permanent Mission of the Byelorussian Soviet Socialist Republic to the United Nations believes that it would be appropriate for the Secretary-General of the United Nations, in accordance with article 319, paragraph 2(a), of the Convention, to carry out a study of a general nature relating to the universal application of the provisions of the Convention and, *inter alia*, to the issue of harmonizing the national laws of States parties with the Convention. The findings of such a study should be incorporated in the report of the Secretary-General to the General Assembly at its fortieth session under the agenda item entitled 'Law of the sea'."

Objection by Bulgaria:

"The People's Republic of Bulgaria is seriously concerned by the actions of a number of States which, upon signature or ratification of the United Nations Convention on the Law of the Sea, have made reservations conflicting with the Convention itself or have enacted national legislation which excludes or modifies the legal effect of the provisions of this Convention in their application to those States. Such actions contravene article 310 of the United Nations Convention on the Law of the Sea and are at variance with the norms of customary international law and with the explicit provision of article 18 of the Vienna Convention on the Law of Treaties.

Such a tendency undermines the purport and meaning of the Convention on the Law of the Sea, which establishes a universal and uniform regime for the use of the oceans and seas and their resources. In the note verbale of the Ministry for Foreign Affairs of the People's Republic of Bulgaria to the Embassy of the Philippines in Belgrade, [...] the Bulgarian Government has rejected as devoid of legal force the statement made by the Philippines upon signature, and confirmed upon ratification, of the Convention.

The People's Republic of Bulgaria will oppose in the future as well any attempts aimed at unilaterally modifying the legal regime, established by the United Nations Convention on the Law of the Sea."

Objection by China [omitted][71]

Objection by the Czech Republic[72]

"[The Czechoslovak Socialist Republic] wishes to draw the Secretary-General's attention to the concern of the Czechoslovak Socialist Republic about the fact that certain States made upon signature of the United Nations Convention on the Law of the Sea declarations which are incompatible with the Convention and which, if reaffirmed upon ratification of the Convention by those States, would constitute a violation of the obligations to be assumed by them under the Convention. Such approach would lead to a breach of the universality of the obligations embodied in the Convention, to the disruption of the legal regime established thereunder and, in the long run, even to the undermining of the Convention as such.

A concrete example of such declaration as referred to above is the understanding made upon signature and reaffirmed upon ratification of the Convention by the Philippines which was communicated to Member States by notification [...] dated 22 May 1984.

The Czechoslovak Socialist Republic considers that this understanding of the Philippines

-- is inconsistent with Article 309 of the Convention on the Law of the Sea because it contains, in essence, reservations to the provisions of the Convention;

-- contravenes Article 310 of the Convention which stipulates that declarations can be made by States upon signature or ratification of or accession to the Convention only provided that they 'do not purport to exclude or to modify the legal effect of the provisions of this Convention';

---

[71] *See* Spratley Islands dispute *supra* under China. Listing this dispute under China is for the reader's ease of reference and is not intended to constribute an opinion as to the sovereignty over the disputed islands.

[72] Entered by the former Czechoslovak Socialist Republic. *Also see* the reservation entered by the European Community, *infra*.

-- indicates that in spite of having ratified the Convention, the Philippines intends to follow its national laws and previous agreements rather than the obligations under the Convention, not only taking no account of whether those laws and agreements are in harmony with the Convention but even, as proved in paragraphs 6 and 7 of the Philippine understanding, deliberately contravening the obligations set forth therein.

Given the above-mentioned circumstances, the Czechoslovak Socialist Republic cannot recognize the above-mentioned understanding of the Philippines as having any legal effect.

In view of the significance of the matter, the Czechoslovak Socialist Republic considers it necessary that the problem of such declarations made upon signature or ratification of the Convention which endanger the universality of the Convention and the unified mode of its implementation be dealt with by the Secretary-General in his capacity as depositary of the Convention and that the Member States of the United Nations be informed thereof."

Objection of Russia[73]

"The Union of Soviet Socialist Republics considers that the statement made by the Philippines upon signature, and then confirmed upon ratification, of the United Nations Convention on the Law of the Sea in essence contains reservations and exceptions to the Convention, which is prohibited under article 309 of the Convention. At the same time, the statement of the Philippines is incompatible with article 310 of the Convention, under which a State, when signing or ratifying the Convention, may make declarations or statements only 'provided that such declarations or statements do not purport to exclude or to modify the legal effect of the provisions of this Convention in their application to that State'.

The discrepancy between the Philippine statement and the Convention can be seen, *inter alia*, from the affirmation by the Philippines that 'The concept of archipelagic waters is similar to the concept of internal waters under the Constitution of the Philippines, and removes straits connecting these waters with the economic zone or high sea from the rights of foreign vessels to transit passage for international navigation'.

Moreover, the statement emphasizes more than once that, despite its ratification of the Convention, the Philippines will continue to be guided in matters relating to the sea, not by the Convention and the obligations

---

[73] Entered by the former USSR.

under it, but by its domestic law and by agreements it has already concluded which are not in line with the Convention. Thus, the Philippines not only is evading the harmonization of its legislation with the Convention but also is refusing to fulfil one of its most fundamental obligations under the Convention namely, to respect the régime of archipelagic waters, which provides that foreign ships enjoy the right of archipelagic passage through, and foreign aircraft the right of overflight over, such waters.

In view of the foregoing, the USSR cannot recognize as lawful the statement of the Philippnes and considers it to be without legal effect in the light of the provisions of the Convention.

Furthermore, the Soviet Union is gravely concerned by the fact that, upon signing the Convention, a number of other States have also made statements of a similar type conflicting with the Convention. If such statements are also made later on, at the ratification stage or upon accession to the Convention, the purport and meaning of the Convention, which establishes a universal and uniform régime for the use of the oceans and seas and their resources, could be undermined and this important instrument of international law impaired.

Taking into account the statement of the Philippines and the statements made by a number of other countries upon signing the Convention, together with the statements that might possibly be made subsequently upon ratification of and accession to the Convention, the Permanent Mission of the USSR considers that it would be appropriate for the Secretary-General of the United Nations to conduct, in accordance with article 319, paragraph 2(a), a study of a general nature on the problem of ensuring universal application of the provisions of the Convention, including the question of the harmonization of the national legislation of States with the Convention. The results of such a study should be included in the report of the Secretary-General to the United Nations General Assembly at its fortieth session under the agenda item entitled 'Law of the sea'."

Objection by Ukraine

"The Ukrainian Soviet Socialist Republic believes that the statement which was made by the Government of the Republic of the Philippines when signing the United Nations Convention on the Law of the Sea and subsequently confirmed upon ratification thereof contains elements which are inconsistent with articles 309 and 310 of the Convention. In accordance with those articles, statements which a State may make upon signature, ratification or accession should not purport 'to exclude or to modify the legal effect of the provisions of this Convention in their application to that State' (art. 310). Such exceptions or reservations are legitimate only when they are 'expressly permitted by other articles of this Convention' (art. 309). Article 310 also emphasizes that statements may be made by a State 'with a view, *inter alia*, to the harmonization of its laws and regulations with the provisions of this Convention'.

However, the statement by the Government of the Republic of the Philippines not only provides no evidence of the intention to harmonize the laws of that State with the Convention, but on the contrary has the purpose, as implied particularly in paragraphs 2, 3 and 5 of the statement, of granting precedence over the Convention to domestic legislation and international agreements to which the Republic of the Philippines is a party. For example, this applies, *inter alia*, to the Mutual Defense Treaty between the Philippines and the United States of America of 30 August 1951.

Furthermore, paragraph 5 of the statement not only grants priority over the Convention to the pertinent laws of the Republic of the Philippines which are currently in force, but also reserves the right to amend such laws in future pursuant only to the Constitution of the Philippines, and consequently without harmonizing them with the provisions of the Convention. Paragraph 7 of the statement draws an analogy between internal waters of the Republic of the Philippines and archipelagic waters and contains a reservation, which is inadmissible in the light of article 309 of the Convention, depriving foreign vessels of the right of transit passage for international navigation through the straits connecting the archipelagic waters with the economic zone or high sea. This reservation is evidence of the intention not to carry out the obligation under the Convention of parties thereto to comply with the régime of archipelagic waters and transit passage and to respect the rights of other States with regard to international navigation and overflight by aircraft. Failure to comply with this obligation would seriously undermine the effectiveness and significance of the United Nations Convention on the Law of the Sea.

It follows from the above that the statement by the Government of the Republic of the Philippines has the purpose of establishing unjustified exceptions for that State and in fact of modifying the legal effect of important provisions of the Convention as applied thereto. In view of this, the Ukrainian Soviet Socialist Republic cannot regard the [said] statement as having legal force. Such statements can only be described as harmful to the unified international legal régime for seas and oceans which is being established under the United Nations Convention on the Law of the Sea.

In the opinion of the Ukrainian Soviet Socialist Republic, the harmonization of national laws with the Convention would be facilitated by an examination within the framework of the United Nations

Secretariat of the uniform and universal application of the Convention and the preparation of an appropriate study by the Secretary-General."

Objection by Vietnam [omitted][74]

Poland [none][75]

Portugal[76]

Declaration:

1. Portugal reaffirms, for the purposes of delimitation of the territorial sea, the continental shelf and the exclusive economic zone, its rights under domestic law in respect of the mainland and of the archipelagos and the islands incorporated therein;

2. Portugal declares that, within a 12-nautical mile zone contiguous to its territorial sea, it will take such control measures as it deems to be necessary, in accordance with the provisions of article 33 of this Convention;

3. Pursuant to the provisions of [this Convention], Portugal enjoys sovereign rights and jurisdiction over an exclusive economic zone of 200 nautical miles from the baseline from which the breadth of the territorial sea is measured;

4. The maritime boundary lines between Portugal and the States whose coasts are opposite or adjacent to its own coasts are those which historically have been established on the basis of international law;

5. Portugal expresses its understanding that Resolution III of the Third United Nations Conference on the Law of the Sea shall fully apply to the non-self-governing Territory of East Timor, of which it remains the administering Power, under the United Nations Charter and the relevant Resolutions of the General Assembly and of the Security Council. Accordingly the application of the Convention, in particular a

---

[74] *See* Spratley Islands dispute *supra* under China. Listing this dispute under China is for the reader's ease of reference and is not intended to constribute an opinion as to the sovereignty over the disputed islands.

[75] *Also see* the reservation entered by the European Community, *supra*.

[76] *Also see* the reservation entered by the European Community, *supra*.

delimitation, if any, of the maritime areas of the territory of East Timor, shall take into consideration the rights of its people under the Charter and the said Resolutions, and, furthermore, the responsibilities incumbent upon Portugal as administering Power of the Territory of East Timor;

6. Portugal declares that, without prejudice to the provisions of article 303 of [this Convention] and to the application of other legal instruments of international law regarding the protection of the underwater archaeological heritage, any objects of a historical or archaeological nature found in the maritime zones under its sovereignty or jurisdiction may be removed only after prior notice to and subject to the consent of the competent Portuguese authorities.

7. Ratification by Portugal of this Convention does not imply the automatic recognition of any maritime or land boundary;

8. Portugal does not consider itself bound by the declarations made by other States and it reserves its position as regards each declaration to be expressed in due time;

9. Bearing in mind the available scientific information and with a view to the protection of the environment and of the sustained growth of economic activities based on the sea, Portugal will, preferably through international co-operation and taking into account the precautionary principle, carry out control activities beyond the areas under national jurisdiction;

10. For the purposes of article 287 of the Convention, Portugal declares that, in the absence of non-judicial means for the settlement of disputes arising out of the application of this Convention, it will choose one of the following means for the settlement of disputes:

a) The International Tribunal for the Law of the Sea, established in pursuance of Annex VI;
b) The International Court of Justice;
c) An arbitral tribunal, constituted in accordance with Annex VII;
d) A special arbitral tribunal, constituted in accordance with Annex VIII;

11. In the absence of other peaceful means for the settlement of disputes Portugal will in accordance with Annex VIII to the Convention,

choose the recourse to a special arbitral tribunal in so far as the application of the provisions of this Convention, or the interpretation thereof, to the matters relating to fisheries, protection and preservation of marine living resources and marine environment, scientific research, navigation and marine pollution are concerned;

12. Portugal declares that, without prejudice to the provisions contained in Section 2, Part XV of this Convention, it does not accept the compulsory procedures referred to in Section 1 of the said Part, with respect to one or more of the categories specified in article 298 (a) (b) (c) of this Convention;

13. Portugal Notes that, as a Member State of the European community, it has transferred to the Community competence over a few matters governed by this Convention. A detailed declaration will be submitted in due time, specifying the nature and extent of the matters in respect of which it has transferred competence to the Community, in accordance with the provisions of Annex IX to the Convention.

Qatar

Declaration upon signature:

"The State of Qatar declares that its signature of the Convention on the Law of the Sea shall in no way imply recognition of Israel or any dealing with Israel or, lead to entry with Israel into any of the relations governed by the Convention or entailed by the implementation of the provisions thereof."

Communication from Israel [omitted][77]

Korea, Republic of

Declaration:

"1. In accordance with paragraph 1 of Article 298 of the Convention, the Republic of Korea does not accept any of the procedures provided for in section 2 of Part XV of the Convention with respect to all the

---

[77] *See* substantially similar communication from Israel in connection with the declaration by Iraq.

categories of disputes referred to in paragraph 1(a), (b) and (c) of Article 298 of the Convention.

2. The present declaration shall be effective immediately.

3. Nothing in the present declaration shall affect the right of the Republic of Korea to submit a request to a court or tribunal referred to in Article 287 of the Convention to be permitted to intervene in the proceedings of any dispute between other States Parties, should it consider that it has an interest of a legal nature which may be affected by the decision in that dispute."

Romania[78]

Declaration upon signature and upon ratification:

"1. As a geographically disadvantaged country bordering a sea poor in living resources, Romania reaffirms the necessity to develop international cooperation for the exploitation of the living resources of the economic zones, on the basis of just and equitable agreements that should ensure the access of the countries from this category to the fishing resources in the economic zones of other regions or subregions.

2. Romania reaffirms the right of coastal States to adopt measures to safeguard their security interests, including the right to adopt national laws and regulations relating to the passage of foreign warships through their territorial sea.

The right to adopt such measures is in full conformity with articles 19 and 25 of the Convention, as it is also specified in the Statement by the President of the United Nations Conference on the Law of the Sea in the plenary meeting of the Conference on April 26, 1982.

3. Romania states that according to the requirements of equity as it results from articles 74 and 83 of the Convention on the Law of the Sea the uninhabited islands and without economic life can in no way affect the delimitation of the maritime spaces belonging to the main land coasts of the coastal States."

---

[78] *Also see* the reservation entered by the European Community, *supra*.

Russia

Declaration upon signature:[79]

"1. The Union of Soviet Socialist Republics declares that, under article 287 of the United Nations Convention on the Law of the Sea, it chooses an arbitral tribunal constituted in accordance with Annex VII as the basic means for the settlement of disputes concerning the interpretation or application of the Convention. It opts for a special arbitral tribunal constituted in accordance with Annex VIII for the consideration of matters relating to fisheries, the protection and preservation of the marine environment, marine scientific research, and navigation, including pollution from vessels and dumping. It recognizes the competence of the International Tribunal for the Law of the Sea, as provided for in article 292, in matters relating to the prompt release of detained vessels and crews.

2. The Union of Soviet Socialist Republics declares that, in accordance with article 298 of the Convention, it does not accept the compulsory procedures entailing binding decisions for the consideration of disputes relating to sea boundary delimitations, disputes concerning military activities, or disputes in respect of which the Security Council of the United Nations is exercising the functions assigned to it by the Charter of the United Nations."

Declaration upon ratification: [80]

"The Russian Federation declares that, in accordance with article 298 of the United Nations Convention on the Law of the Sea, it does not accept the procedures, provided for in section 2 of Part XV of the Convention, entailing binding decisions with respect to disputes concerning the interpretation or application of articles 15, 74 and 83 of the Convention, relating to sea boundary delimitations, or those involving historic bays or titles; disputes concerning military activities, including military activities by government vessels and aircraft, and disputes concerning law-enforcement activities in regard to the exercise of sovereign rights or jurisdiction; and disputes in respect of which the Security Council of the United Nations is exercising the functions assigned to it by the Charter of the United Nations.

---

[79] Entered by the USSR.
[80] Entered by the Russian Federation.

The Russian Federation, bearing in mind articles 309 and 310 of the Convention, declares that it objects to any declarations and statements made in the past or which may be made in future when signing, ratifying or acceding to the Convention, or made for any other reason in connection with the Convention, that are not in keeping with the provisions of article 310 of the Convention. The Russian Federation believes that such declarations and statements, however phrased or named, cannot exclude or modify the legal effect of the provisions of the Convention in their application to the party to the Convention that made such declarations or statements, and for this reason they shall not be taken into account by the Russian Federation in its relations with that party to the Convention."

São Tomé and Príncipe

Declaration upon signature:

"I. The signing of the Convention by the Government of the Democratic Republic of Sao Tome and Principe will in no way affect or prejudice the sovereign rights of the Democratic Republic of Sao Tome and Principe embodied in and flowing from the Constitution of Sao Tome and Principe;

II. The Government of the Democratic Republic of Sao Tome and Principe reserves the right to adopt laws and regulations relating to the innocent passage of foreign warships through its territorial sea or its archipelagic waters and to take any other measures aimed at safeguarding its security;

III. The Government of the Democratic Republic of Sao Tome and Principe considers that the provisions of the Convention relating to archipelagic waters, the territorial sea and the exclusive economic zone are compatible with the legislation of the Republic of Sao Tome and Principe as regards its sovereignty and its jurisdiction over the maritime space adjacent to its coasts;

IV. The Government of the Democratic Republic of Sao Tome and Principe considers that, in accordance with the provisions of the Convention, where the same stock area adjacent thereto, the States fishing for such stocks in the adjacent area are under an obligation to agree with the coastal State upon the measures necessary for the conservation of the stock or stocks of associated species;

V. The Government of the Democratic Republic of Sao Tome and Principe, in accordance with the relevant provisions of the Convention, reserves the right to adopt laws and regulations to ensure the conservation of highly migratory species and to co-operate with the States whose nationals harvest these species in order to promote the optimum utilization thereof."

Saudi Arabia

Declaration:

1. The Government of the Kingdom of Saudi Arabia is not bound by any domestic legislation or by any declaration issued by other States upon signature or ratification of this Convention. The Kingdom reserves the right to state its position concerning all such legislation or declarations at the appropriate time. In particular, the Kingdom's ratification of the Convention in no way constitutes recognition of the maritime claims of any other State having signed or ratified the Convention, where such claims are inconsistent with the provisions of the Convention on the Law of the Sea and are prejudicial to the sovereign rights and jurisdiction over its maritime areas.

2. The Government of the Kingdom of Saudi Arabia is not bound by any international treaty or agreement which contains provisions that are inconsistent with the Convention on the Law of the Sea and prejudicial to the sovereign rights and jurisdiction of the Kingdom in its maritime areas.

3. The Government of the Kingdom of Saudi Arabia considers that the application of the provisions of part IX of the Convention concerning the cooperation of States bordering enclosed or semi-enclosed areas is subject to the acceptance of the Convention by all the States concerned.

4. The Government of the Kingdom of Saudi Arabia considers that the provisions of the Convention relating to the application of the system of transit passage through straits used for international navigation which connect one part of the high seas or an exclusive economic zone with another part of the high seas or an exclusive economic zone also apply to navigation between islands adjacent or contiguous to such straits, particularly where the sea lanes used for entrance to or exit from the strait, as designated by the competent international organization, are situated near such islands.

5. The Government of the Kingdom of Saudi Arabia considers that innocent passage does not apply to its territorial sea where there is a route to the high seas or an exclusive economic zone which is equally suitable as regards navigational and hydrographical features.

6. In view of the inherent danger entailed in the passage of nuclear-powered vessels and vessels carrying nuclear or other material of a similar nature and in view of the provision of article 22, paragraph 2, of [this Convention] concerning the right of coastal State to confine the passage of such vessels to sea lanes designated by that State within its territorial sea, as well as that of article 23 of the Convention which requires such vessels to carry documents and observe special precautionary measures as specified by international agreements, the Kingdom of Saudi Arabia, with all the above in mind, requires the aforesaid vessels to obtain prior authorization of passage before entering the territorial sea of the Kingdom until such time as the international agreements referred to in article 23 are concluded and the Kingdom becomes a party thereto. Under all circumstances the flag State of such vessels shall assume all responsibility for any loss or damage resulting from the innocent passage of such vessels within the territorial sea of the Kingdom of Saudi Arabia.

7. The Kingdom of Saudi Arabia shall issue its internal procedures for the maritime areas subject to its sovereignty and jurisdiction, so as to affirm the sovereign rights and jurisdiction and guarantee the interests of the Kingdom in those areas."

Serbia

Declaration upon succession:[81]

"1. Proceeding from the right that State Parties have on the basis of article 310 of the United Nations Convention on the Law of the Sea, the [Yugoslavia] considers that a coastal State may, by its laws and regulations, subject the passage of foreign warships to the requirement of previous notification to the respective coastal State and limit the number of ships simultaneously passing, on the basis of the international customary law and in compliance with the right of innocent passage (articles 17-32 of the Convention).

---

[81] Entered by the Federal Republic of Yugoslavia.

2. [Yugoslavia] also considers that it may, on the basis of article 38, para. 1, and article 45, para. 1(a) of the Convention, determine by its laws and regulations which of the straits used for international navigation in the territorial sea of [Yugoslavia] will retain the regime of innocent passage, as appropriate.

3. Due to the fact that the provisions of the Convention relating to the contiguous zone (article 33) do not provide rules on the delimitation of the contiguous zone between States with opposite or adjacent coasts, [Yugoslavia] considers that the principles of the customary international law, codified in article 24, para. 3, of the Convention on the Territorial Sea and the Contiguous Zone, signed in Geneva on 29 April 1958, will apply to the delimitation of the contiguous zone between the Parties to the United Nations Convention on the Law of the Sea."

Slovenia [82]

Declaration [I]:

"Proceeding from the right that State Parties have on the basis of article 310 of the United Nations Convention on the Law of the Sea, the Republic of Slovenia considers that its Part V Exclusive Economic Zone, including the provisions of article 70 Right of Geographically Disadvantaged States, forms part of the general customary international law."

Declaration [II]:

"The Republic of Slovenia does not consider itself to be bound by the declaratory statement on the basis of article 310 of the Convention, given by the former SFR of Yugoslavia."

Declaration [III]:

"The Government of the Republic of Slovenia declares pursuant to article 287 of the Convention that it chooses an arbitral tribunal constituted in accordance with Annex VII for the settlement of disputes concerning the interpretation or application of the Convention."

---

[82] *Also see* the reservation entered by the European Community, *supra.*

Declaration [IV]:

"The Government of the Republic of Slovenia declares pursuant to article 298 of the Convention that it does not accept an arbitral tribunal constituted in accordance with Annex VII of any of the categories disputes mentioned in article 298."

South Africa

Declaration:

"The Government of the Republic of South Africa shall, at the appropriate time, make declarations provided for in articles 287 and 298 of the Convention relating to the settlement of disputes."

Declaration upon signature [withdrawn upon ratification]

"Pursuant to the provisions of Article 310 of the Convention the South African Government declares that the signature of this Convention by South Africa in no way implies recognition by South Africa of the United Nations Council for Namibia or its competence to act on behalf of South West Africa/Namibia."

Spain[83]

Declaration upon signature:

"1. The Spanish Government, upon signing this Convention, declares that this act cannot be interpreted as recognition of any rights or situations relating to the maritime spaces of Gibraltar which are not included in article 10 of the Treaty of Utrecht of 13 July 1713 between the Spanish and British Crowns. The Spanish Government also considers that Resolution III of the Third United Nations Conference on the Law of the Sea is not applicable in the case of the Colony of Gibraltar, which is undergoing a decolonization process in which only the relevant resolutions adopted by the United Nations General Assembly apply.

---

[83] *Also see id.*

2. It is the Spanish Government's interpretation that the régime established in Part III of the Convention is compatible with the right of the coastal State to issue and apply its own air regulations in the air space of the straits used for international navigation so long as this does not impede the transit passage of aircraft.

3. With regard to article 39, paragraph 3, it takes the word 'normally' to mean 'except in cases of *force majeure* or distress'.

4. With regard to Article 42, it considers that the provisions of paragraph 1(b) do not prevent it from issuing, in accordance with international law, laws and regulations giving effect to generally accepted international regulations.

5. The Spanish Government interprets articles 69 and 70 of the Convention as meaning that access to fishing in the economic zones of third States by the fleets of developed land-locked and geographically disadvantaged States is dependent upon the prior granting of access by the coastal States in question to the nationals of other States who have habitually fished in the economic zone concerned.

6. It interprets the provisions of Article 221 as not depriving the coastal State of a strait used for international navigation of its powers, recognized by international law, to intervene in the case of the casualties referred to in that artcle.

7. It considers that Article 233 must be interpreted, in any case, in conjunction with the provisions of Article 34.

8. It considers that, without prejudice to the provisions of Article 297 regarding the settlement of disputes, Articles 56, 61 and 62 of the Convention preclude considering as discretionary the powers of the coastal State to determine the allowable catch, its harvesting capacity and the allocation of surpluses to other States.

9. Its interpretation of Annex III, Article 9, is that the provisions thereof shall not obstruct participation, in the joint ventures referred to in paragraph 2, of the States Parties whose industrial potential precludes them from participating directly as contractors in the exploitation and resources of the Area."

Declaration upon ratification:

"1. The Kingdom of Spain recalls that, as a member of the European Union, it has transferred competence over certain matters governed by the Convention to the European Community. A detailed declaration will be made in due course as to the nature and extent of the competence transferred to the European Community, in accordance with the provisions of Annex IX of the Convention.

2. In ratifying the Convention, Spain wishes to make it known that this act cannot be construed as recognition of any rights or status regarding the maritime space of Gibraltar that are not included in article 10 of the Treaty of Utrecht of 13 July 1713 concluded between the Crowns of Spain and Great Britain. Furthermore, Spain does not consider that Resolution III of the Third United Nations Conference on the Law of the Sea is applicable to the colony of Gibraltar, which is subject to a process of decolonization in which only relevant resolutions adopted by the United Nations General Assembly are applicable.

3. Spain understands that:

a) The provisions laid down in Part III of the Convention are compatible with the right of a coastal State to dictate and apply its own regulations in straits used for international navigation, provided that this does not impede the right of transit passage.

(b) In article 39, paragraph 3(a), the word 'normally' means 'unless by *force majeure* or by distress'.

(c) The provisions of article 221 shall not deprive a State bordering a strait used for international navigation of its competence under international law regarding intervention in the event of the casualties referred to in that article.

4. Spain interprets that:

(a) Articles 69 and 70 of the Convention mean that access to fisheries in the exclusive economic zone of third States by the fleets of developed landlocked or geographically disadvantaged States shall depend on whether the relevant coastal States have previously granted access to the fleets of States which habitually fish in the relevant exclusive economic zone.

(b) With regard to article 297, and without prejudice to the provisions of that article in respect of settlement of disputes, articles 56, 61 and 62 of the Convention do not allow of an interpretation whereby the rights of the coastal State to determine permissible catches, its capacity for exploitation and the allocation of surpluses to other States may be considered discretionary.

5. The provisions of article 9 of Annex III shall not prevent States Parties whose industrial potential does not enable them to participate directly as contractors in the exploitation of the resources of the zone from participating in the joint ventures referred to in paragraph 2 of that article.

6. In accordance with the provisions of article 287, paragraph 1, Spain chooses the International Court of Justice as the means for the settlement of disputes concerning the interpretation or application of the Convention.

Declaration:

"Pursuant to article 287, paragraph 1, the Government of Spain declares that it chooses the International Tribunal for the Law of the Sea and the International Court of Justice as means for the settlement of disputes concerning the interpretation or application of the Convention.

The Government of Spain declares, pursuant to the provisions of article 298, para. 1(a) of the Convention, that it does not accept the procedures provided for in part XV, section 2, with respect to the settlement of disputes concerning the interpretation or application of articles 15, 74 and 83 relating to sea boundary delimitations, or those involving historic bays or titles."

Objection by the UK

"[(a) – (c) omitted]

(d) *Gibraltar*

With regard to point 2 of the declaration made upon ratification of the convention by the Government of Spain, the Government of the United Kingdom has no doubt about the sovereignty of the United Kingdom over Gibraltar, including its territorial waters. The Government of the United Kingdom, as the administering authority of Gibraltar, has extended the United Kingdom's accession to the Convention and ratification of the Agreement to Gibraltar. The

Government of the United Kingdom, therefore, rejects as unfounded point 2 of the Spanish declaration."

Sudan

Declaration in plenary and upon signature:

"[1] [84] In accordance with article 310 of the Convention, the Sudanese Government will make such declarations as it deems necessary in order to clarify its position regarding the content of certain provisions of this instrument.

[2] [The Sudan] wishes to reiterate [the statement by the President of the Conference] in plenary meeting during the Third United Nations Conference on the Law of the Sea, on 26 April 1982, concerning article 21, in which deals with the laws and regulations of the coastal State relating to innocent passage: namely, that the withdrawal of the amendment submitted at the time by a number of States did not prejudge the right of coastal States to take all necessary measures, particularly in order to protect their security, in accordance with article 19 on the meaning of the term 'innocent passage' and article 25 on the rights of protection of the coastal State.

[3] The Sudan also wishes to state that, according to its interpretation, the definition of the term 'geographically disadvantaged States' given in article 70, paragraph 2, applies to all the parts of the Convention in which this term appears.

[4] The fact that [the Sudan] is signing this Convention and the Final Act of the Conference in no way means that [it] recognizes any State whatsoever which it does not recognize or with which it has no relations."

---

[84] Paragraph numbering in the original.

Sweden[85]

Declaration upon signature:

"As regards those parts of the Convention which deal with innocent passage through the territorial sea, it is the intention of the Government of Sweden to continue to apply the present régime for the passage of foreign warships and other government-owned vessels used for non-commercial purposes through the Swedish territorial sea, that régime being fully compatible with the Convention.

It is also the understanding of the Government of Sweden that the Convention does not affect the rights and duties of a neutral State provided for in the Convention concerning the Rights and Duties of Neutral Powers in case of Naval Warfare (XIII Convention), adopted at The Hague on 18 October 1907."

Declaration upon signature and upon ratification:

"It is the understanding of the Government of Sweden that the exception from the transit passage régime in straits, provided for in Article 35 (c) of the Convention is applicable to the strait between Sweden and Denmark (Oresund) as well as to the strait between Sweden and Finland (the Aland islands). Since in both those straits the passage is regulated in whole or in part by long-standing international conventions in force, the present legal régime in the two straits will remain unchanged."

Declaration upon ratification:

"The Government of the Kingdom of Sweden hereby chooses, in accordance with article 287 of the Convention, the International Court of Justice for the settlement of disputes concerning the interpretation or application of the Convention and the Agreement Implementing Part XI of the Convention.

The Kingdom of Sweden recalls that as a Member of the European Community, it has transferred competence in respect of certain matters governed by the Convention. A detailed declaration on the nature and extent of the competence transferred to the European Community will be made in due course in accordance with the provisions of Annex IX of the Convention."

---

[85] *Also see* the reservation entered by the European Community, *supra*.

Tanzania

Declaration:

"The United Republic of Tanzania declares that is chooses the International Tribunal for the Law of the Sea for the settlement of disputes concerning the interpretation or application of the Convention."

Trinidad and Tobago

Declaration:

" [...] [The] Minister of Foreign Affairs of the Republic of Trinidad and Tobago, do hereby declare under paragraph 1(a) of article 298 of the United Nations Convention on the Law of the Sea done at Montego Bay on the tenth day of December one thousand nine hundred and eighty-two, that the Republic of Trinidad and Tobago does not accept any of the procedures provided for in Part XV, section 2 of the Convention with respect to the categories of disputes concerning the interpretation or application of articles 15, 74 and 83 relating to sea boundary delimitations as well as those involving historic bays or titles."

Declaration:

"The Republic of Trinidad and Tobago [...] declare[s] that in the absence of or failing any other peaceful means, The Republic of Trinidad and Tobago chooses the following means in order of priority for the settlement of disputes concerning the interpretation or application of the United Nations Convention on the Law of the Sea:

> a. The International Tribunal for the Law of the Sea established in accordance with Annex VI;
> b. The International Court of Justice."

Tunisia

Declaration 1:

"The Republic of Tunisia, on the basis of resolution 4262 of the council of the League of Arab States, dated 31 March 1983, declares that its accession to the United Nations Convention on the Law of the Sea does not imply recognition of or dealings with any States which the Republic of Tunisia does not recognize or have dealings with."

Declaration 2:

"The Republic of Tunisia, in accordance with the provisions of article 311, and, in particular, paragraph 6 thereof, declares its adherence to the basic principles relating to the common heritage of mankind and that it will not be a party to any agreement in derogation thereof. The Republic of Tunisia calls upon all States to avoid any unilateral measure or legislation of this kind that would lead to disregard of the provisions of the Convention or to the exploitation of the resources of the seabed and ocean floor and the subsoil thereof outside of the legal régime of the seas and oceans provided for in this convention and in the other legal instruments pertaining thereto, in particular resolution I and resolution II."

Declaration 3:

"The Republic of Tunisia, in accordance with the provisions of article 298 of the United Nations Convention on the Law of the Sea, declares that it does not accept the procedures provided for in Part XV, section 2, of the said Convention with respect to the following categories of disputes:

> (a) (i) disputes concerning the interpretation of application of articles 15, 74 and 83 relating to sea boundary delimitations, or those involving historic bays or titles, provided that a State having made such a declaration shall, when such a dispute arises subsequent to the entry into force of this Convention and where no agreement within a reasonable period of time is reached in negotiations between the parties, at the request of any party to the dispute, accept submission of the matter to conciliation under Annex V, section 2; and provided furher that any dispute that necessarily involves the concurrent consideration of any unsettled dispute concerning sovereignty or other rights over continental or insular land territory shall be excluded from such submission;

> (ii) after the conciliation commission has presented its report, which shall state the reasons on which it is based, the parties shall negotiate an agreement on the basis of that report; if these negotiations do not result in an agreement, the parties shall, by mutual consent, submit the question to one of the

procedures provided for in section 2, unless the parties otherwise agree;

(iii) this subparagraph does not apply to any sea boundary dispute finally settled by an arrangement between the parties, or to any such dispute which is to be settled in accordance with a bilateral or multilateral agreement binding upon those parties;

(b) disputes concerning military activities, including military activities by government vessels and aircraft engaged in non-commercial service, and disputes concerning law enforcement activities in regard to the exercise of sovereign rights or jurisdiction excluded from the jurisdiction of a court or tribunal under article 297, paragraph 2 or 3;

(c) disputes in respect of which the Security Council of the United Nations is exercising the functions assigned to it by the Charter of the United Nations, unless the Security council decides to remove the matter from its agenda or calls upon the parties to settle it by the means provided for in this Convention."

Declaration 4:

"The Republic of Tunisia, in accordance with the provisions of article 310 of the United Nations Convention on the Law of the Sea, declares that its legislation currently in force does not conflict with the provisions of this Convention. However, laws and regulations will be adopted as soon as possible in order to ensure closer harmony between the provisions of the Convention and the requirements for completing Tunisian legislation in the maritime sphere."

Declaration [5]:

"In accordance with the provisions of article 287 of the United Nations Convention on the Law of the Sea, the Government of Tunisia declares that it accepts, in order of preference, the following means for the settlement of disputes relating to the interpretation or implementation of the above-mentioned Convention:

a) - The International Tribunal for the Law of the Sea
b) - An Arbitral Tribunal established in accordance with Annex VII.

Communication

"In [the] declaration [above], articles 74 and 83 of the Convention are interpreted to mean that, in the absence of any agreement on delimitation of the exclusive economic zone, the continental shelf or other maritime zones, the search for an equitable solution assumes that the boundary is the median line, in other words, a line every point of which is equidistant from the nearest points on the baselines from which the breadth of the territorial waters is measured.

The Tunisian Government believes that such an interpretation is not in the least consistent with the spirit and letter of the provisions of these articles, which do not provide for automatic application of the median line with regard to delimitation of the exclusive economic zone or the continental shelf."

Ukraine

Declaration upon signature:

"1. The Ukrainian Soviet Socialist Republic declares that, in accordance with article 287 of the United Nations Convention on the Law of the Sea, it chooses as the principal means for the settlement of disputes concerning the interpretation or application of this Convention an arbitral tribunal constituted in accordance with Annex VII. For the consideration of questions relating to fisheries, protection and preservation of the marine environment, marine scientific research and navigation, including pollution from vessels and by dumping, the Ukrainian SSR chooses a special arbitral tribunal constituted in accordance with Annex VIII. The Ukrainian SSR recognizes the competence, as stipulated in article 292, of the International Tribunal for the Law of the Sea in respect of questions relating to the prompt release of detained vessels or their crews.

2. The Ukrainian Soviet Socialist Republic declares, in accordance with article 298 of the Convention, that it does not accept compulsory procedures, involving binding decisions, for the consideration of disputes relating to sea boundary delimitations, disputes concerning military activities and disputes in respect of which the Security Council of the United Nations is exercising the functions assigned to it by the Charter of the United Nations."

Declaration upon ratification:

"1. Ukraine declares that, in accordance with article 287 of the United Nations Convention on the Law of the Sea of 1982, it chooses as the principal means for the settlement of disputes concerning the interpretation or application of this Convention an arbitral tribunal constituted in accordance with Annex VII. For the consideration of disputes concerning the interpretation or application of the Convention in respect of questions relating to fisheries, protection and preservation of the marine environment, marine scientific research and navigation, including pollution from vessels and by dumping, Ukraine chooses a special arbitral tribunal constituted in accordance with Annex VIII.

Ukraine recognises the competence, as stipulated in article 292 of the Convention, of the International Tribunal for the Law of the Sea in respect of questions relating to the prompt release of detained vessels or their crews.

2. Ukraine declares, in accordance with article 298 of the Convention, that it does not accept, unless otherwise provided by specific international treaties of Ukraine with relevant States, the compulsory procedures entailing binding decisions for the consideration of disputes relating to sea boundary delimitations, disputes involving historic bays or titles, and disputes concerning military activities.

3. Ukraine declares, taking into account articles 309 and 310 of the Convention, that it objects to any statements or declarations, irrespective of when such statements or declarations were or may be made, that may result in a failure to interpret the provisions of the Convention in good faith, or are contrary to the ordinary meaning of terms in the context of the Convention or its object and purpose.

4. As a geographically disadvantaged country bordering a sea poor in living resources, Ukraine reaffirms the necessity to develop international cooperation for the exploitation of the living resources of economic zones, on the basis of just and equitable agreements that should ensure the access to fishing resources in the economic zones of other regions and sub-regions."

United Kingdom[86]

Declaration [I] upon signation:

"*Extent*

[This] instrument of accession [...] extend[s] to:

The United Kingdom of Great Britain and Northern Ireland
The Bailiwick of Jersey
The Bailiwick of Guernsey
The Isle of Man
Anguilla
Bermuda
British Antarctic Territory
British Indian Ocean Territory
British Virgin Islands
The Cayman Islands
Falkland Islands
Gibraltar
Montserrat
Pitcairn, Henderson, Ducie and Oeno Islands
St. Helena and Dependencies
South Georgia and South Sandwich Islands
Turks and Caicos Islands."

Declaration [II]:

"*(a) General*

The United Kingdom cannot accept any declaration or statement made or to be made in the future which is not in conformity with articles 309 and 310 of the Convention. Article 309 of the Convention prohibits reservations and exceptions (except those expressly permitted by other articles of the Convention). Under article 310 declarations and statements made by a State cannot exclude or modify the legal effect of the provisions of the Convention in their application to the State concerned.

The United Kingdom considers that declarations and statements not in conformity with articles 309 and 310 include, *inter alia*, the following:

– Those which relate to baselines not drawn in conformity with the Convention;

---

[86] *Also see* the reservation entered by the European Community, *supra*.

– Those which purport to require any form of notification or permission before warships or other ships exercise the right of innocent passage or freedom of navigation or which otherwise purport to limit navigational rights in ways not permitted by the Convention;

– Those which are incompatible with the provisions of the Convention relating to straits used for international navigation, including the right of transit passage;

– Those which are incompatible with the provisions of the Convention relating to archipelagic states or waters, including archipelagic baselines and archipelagic sea lanes passage;

– Those which are not in conformity with the provisions of the Convention relating to the exclusive economic zone or the continental shelf, including those which claim coastal state jurisdiction over all installations and structures in the exclusive economic zone or on the continental shelf, and those which pur- port to require consent for exercises or manoeuvres (including weapons exercises) inthose areas;

– Those which purport to subordinate the interpretation or application of the Convention to national laws and regulations, including constitutional provisions.

(b) *European Community*

The United Kingdom recalls that, as a Member of the European Community, it has transferred competence to the Community in respect of certain matters governed by the Convention. A detailed declaration on the nature and extent of the competence to the European Community will be made in due course in accordance with the provisions of Annex IX of the Convention.

[(c) – (d) omitted]"[87]

Declaration [III]:

"In accordance with article 287, paragraph 1, of the [said Convention], the Kingdom of Great Britain and Northern Ireland chooses the International Court of Justice for the settlement of disputes concerning the interpretation or application of the Convention.

---

[87] See declaration entered by Argentina and the objection by the UK and see declaration entered by Spain and the objection by the UK.

The International Tribunal for the Law of the Sea is a new institution, which the United Kingm hopes will make an important contribution to the peaceful settlement of disputes concerning the law of the sea. In addition to those cases where the Convention itself provides for the compulsory jurisdiction of the Tribunal, the United Kingdom remains ready to consider the submission of disputes to the Tribunal as may be agreed on a case-by-case basis."

Declaration [IV]:

"[...] the United Kingdom of Great Britain and Northern Ireland does not accept any of the procedures provided for in section 2 of Part XV of the Convention with respect to the categories of disputes referred to in paragraph 1(b) and (c) of article 298."

Uruguay

Declaration upon signature and upon ratification:

"(A) The provisions of the Convention concerning the territorial sea and the exclusive economic zone are compatible with the main purposes and principles underlying Uruguayan legisla- tion in respect of Uruguay's sovereignty and jurisdiction over the sea adjacent to its coast and over its bed and sub-soil up to a limit of 200 miles.

(B) The legal nature of the exclusive economic zone as defined in the Convention and the scope of the rights which the Convention recognizes to the coastal State leave room for no doubt that it is a *'sui generis'* zone of national jurisdiction different from the territorial sea and that it is not part of the high seas.

(C) Regulation of the uses and activities not provided for expressly in the Convention (residual rights and obligations) relating to the rights of sovereignty and to the jurisdiction of the coastal State in its exclusive economic zone falls within the competence of that State, provided that such regulation does not prevent enjoyment of the freedom of international communication which is recognized to other States.

(D) In the exclusive economic zone, enjoyment of the freedom of international communication in accordance with the way it is defined and in accordance with other relevant provisions of the Convention excludes any non-peaceful use without the consent of the coastal State for instance, military exercises or other activities which may affect the rights or interests of that State and it also excludes the threat or use of force against the territorial integrity, political independence, peace or security of the coastal State.

(E) This Convention does not empower any State to build, operate or utilize installations or structures in the exclusive economic zone of another State, neither those referred to in the Convention nor any other kind, without the consent of the coastal State.

(F) In accordance with all the relevant provisions of the Convention, where the same stock or stocks of associated species occur both within the exclusive economic zone and in an area beyond and adjacent to the zone, the States fishing for such stocks in the adjacent area are duty bound to agree with the coastal State upon the measures necessary for the conservation of these stocks or associated species.

(G) When the Convention enters into force, Uruguay will apply, with respect to other States Parties, the provisions established by the Convention and by Uruguayan legislation, on the basis of reciprocity.

(H) Pursuant to the provisions of article 287, Uruguay declares that it chooses the International Tribunal for the Law of the Sea for the settlement of such disputes relating to the interpretation or application of the Convention as are not subject to other procedures, without prejudice to its recognition of the jurisdiction of the International Court of Justice and of such agreements with other States as may provide for other means for peaceful settlement.

(I) Pursuant to the provisions of article 298, Uruguay declares that it will not accept the procedures provided for in Part XV, section 2 of the Convention, in respect of disputes concerning law enforcement activities in regard to the exercise of sovereign rights or jurisdiction excluded from the jurisdiction of a court or tribunal under article 297, paragraphs 2 and 3.

(J) Reaffirms that, as stated in article 76, the continental shelf is the natural prolongation of the territory of the coastal State to the outer edge of the continental margin."

Objection by Italy [omitted][88]

---

[88] *See* objection by Italy to the reservation entered by Brazil *supra*.

Venezuela

Declaration upon signature [in connection with the Final Act]

"Venezuela is signing the Final Act on the understanding that it is merely noting the work of the Conference without making any value judgement about its results. Its signing does not signify, nor can it be construed as signifying, any change in its position with regard to articles 15, 74, 83 and 121, paragraph 3, of the Convention. For the reasons stated by the delegation of Venezuela at the plenary meeting on 30 April 1982, those provisions are unacceptable to Venezuela, which is therefore not bound by them and is not prepared to agree to be bound by them in any way."

Vietnam

Declaration:

"The Socialist Republic of Vietnam, by ratifying the 1982 UN Convention on the Law of the Sea, expresses its determination to join the international community in the establishment of an equitable legal order and in the promotion of maritime development and cooperation.

The National Assembly reaffirms the sovereignty of the Socialist Republic of Vietnam over its internal waters and territorial sea; the sovereign rights and jurisdiction in the contiguous zone, the exclusive economic zone and the continental shelf of Vietnam, based on the provisions of the Convention and principles of international law and calls on other countries to respect the above-said rights of Vietnam.

The National Assembly reiterates Vietnam's sovereignty over the Hoang Sa and Truong Sa archipelagoes and its position to settle those disputes relating to territorial claims as well as other disputes in the Eastern Sea through peaceful negotiations in the spirit of equality, mutual respect and understanding, and with due respect of international law, particularly the 1982 UN Convention on the Law of the Sea, and of the sovereign rights and jurisdiction of the coastal states over their respective continental shelves and exclusive economic zones; the concerned parties should, while exerting active efforts to promote negotiations for a fundamental and long-term solution, maintain stability on the basis of the status quo, refrain from any act that may further complicate the situation and from the use of force or threat of force.

The National Assembly emphasizes that it is necessary to identify between the settlement of dispute over the Hoang Sa and Truong Sa archipelagoes and the defense of the continental shelf and maritime zones falling under Vietnam's sovereignty, rights and jurisdiction, based on the principles and standards and specified in the 1982 UN Convention on the Law of the Sea.

The National Assembly entitles the National Assembly's Standing Committee and the Government to review all relevant national legislation to consider necessary amendments in conformity with the 1982 UN Convention on the Law of the Sea, and to safeguard the interest of Vietnam.

The National Assembly authorizes the Government to undertake effective measures for the management and defense of the continental shelf and maritime zones of Vietnam."

Yemen

Declaration by the People's Republic of Yemen:

"1. The People's Democratic Republic of Yemen will give precedence to its national laws in force which require prior permission for the entry or transit of foreign warships or of submarines or ships operated by nuclear power or carrying radioactive materials

2. With regard to the delimitation of the maritime borders between the People's Democratic Republic of Yemen and any State having coasts opposite or adjacent to it, the median line basically adopted shall be drawn in a way such that every point of it is equidistant from the nearest points on the baselines from which the breadth of the territorial sea of any State is measured. This shall be applicable to the maritime borders of the mainland territory of the People's Democratic Republic of Yemen and also of its islands."

Declaration by the Yemen Arab Republic:

"1. The Yemen Arabic Republic adheres to the rules of general international law concerning rights to national sovereignty over coastal territorial waters, even in the case of the waters of a strait linking two seas.

2. The Yemen Arab Republic adheres to the concept of general international law concerning free passage as applying exclusively to merchant ships and aircraft; nuclear-powered craft, as well as warships and warplanes in general, must obtain the prior agreement of the Yemen

Arab Republic before passing through its territorial waters, in accordance with the established norm of general international law relating to national sovereignty.

3. The Yemen Arab Republic confirms its national sovereignty over all the islands in the Red Sea and the Indian Ocean which have been its dependencies since the period when the Yemen and the Arab countries were a Turkish administration.

4. The Yemen Arab Republic declares that its signature of the Convention on the Law of the Sea is subject to the provisions of this declaration and the completion of the constitutional procedures in effect.

The fact that we have signed the said Convention in no way implies that we recognize Israel or are entering into relations with it.

Objection by Ethiopia

"Paragraph 3 of the declaration relates to claims of sovereignty over unspecified islands in the Red Sea and the Indian Ocean which clearly is outside the purview of the Convention. Although the declaration, not constituting a reservation as it is prohibited by article 309 of the Convention, is made under article 310 of same and as such is not governed by articles 19-23 of the Vienna Convention on the Law of Treaties providing for acceptance of and objections to reservations, nevertheless, the Provisional Military Government of Socialist Ethiopia wishes to place on record that paragraph 3 of the declaration by the Yemen Arab Republic cannot in any way affect Ethiopia's sovereignty over all the islands in the Red Sea forming part of its national territory."

Communication from Israel [omitted][89]

---

[89] *See* communication from Israel in connection with the declaration by Iraq.

**Notifications made under Annex V, Art.1, and Annex VII, Art. 2
(List of conciliators and arbitrators)**

State Party	Conciliator or Arbitrator	Notification
Australia	Sir Gerard Brennan AC KBE	19 Aug 1999
Australia	Mr. Henry Burmester QC	19 Aug 1999
Australia	Prof. Ivan Shearer AM	19 Aug 1999
Austria	Prof. Dr. Gerhard Hafner	9 Jan 2008
Austria	Prof. Dr. Gerhard Loibl	9 Jan 2008
Austria	Amb. Dr. Helmut Tichy	9 Jan 2008
Austria	Amb./Judge Dr. Helmut Türk	9 Jan 2008
Brazil	Walter de Sá Leitão	10 Sep 2001
Chile	Helmut Brunner Nöer	18 Nov 1998
Chile	Rodrigo Díaz Albónico	18 Nov 1998
Chile	Carlos Martínez Sotomayor	18 Nov 1998
Chile	Eduardo Vío Grossi	18 Nov 1998
Chile	José Miguel Barros Franco	18 Nov 1998
Chile	María Teresa Infante Caffi	18 Nov 1998
Chile	Edmundo Vargas Carreño	18 Nov 1998
Chile	Fernando Zegers Santa Cruz	18 Nov 1998
Costa Rica	Carlos Fernando Alvarado Valverde	15 Mar 2000
Cyprus	Amb. Andrew Jacovides	23 Feb 2007
Czech Rep.	Dr. Vladimír Kopal	18 Dec 1996
Estonia	Mrs. Ena Lillipuu	
Estonia	Mr. Heiki Lindpere	
Finland	Prof. Kari Hakapää	
Finland	Prof. Martti Koskenniemi	
Finland	Justice Gutav Möller	
Finland	Justice Pekka Vihervuori	25 May 2001
France	Daniel Bardonnet	4 Feb 1998
France	Pierre-Marie Dupuy	4 Feb 1998
France	Jean-Pierre Queneudec	4 Feb 1998
France	Laurent Lucchini	4 Feb 1998
Germany	Dr. Renate Platzoeder	25 Mar 1996
Indonesia	Prof. Dr. Hasjim Djalal, M.A.	3 Aug 2001
Indonesia	Dr. Etty Roesmaryati Agoes, SH, LLM	3 Aug 2001
Indonesia	Dr. Sudirman Saad, D.H., M.Hum.	3 Aug 2001
Indonesia	Lt. Comm. Kresno Bruntoro, SH, LLM	3 Aug 2001
Italy	Prof. Umberto Leanza	21 Sep 1999

Italy	Amb. Luigi Vittorio Ferraris	21 Sep 1999
Italy	Amb. Giuseppe Jacoangeli	21 Sep 1999
Italy	Prof. Tullio Scovazzi	21 Sep 1999
Japan	Amb./Judge Hisashi Owada	28 Sep 2000
Japan	Amb. Prof. Chusei Yamada	28 Sep 2000
Japan	Prof. Em. Dr. Soji Yamamoto	28 Sep 2000
Japan	Prof. Dr. Nisuke Ando	28 Sep 2000
Japan	Prof. Em. Dr. Soji Yamamoto	2 May 2006
Japan	Amb. Chusei Yamada	2 May 2006
Mexico	Amb. Alberto Székely Sánchez	9 Dec 2002
Mexico	Dr. Alonso Gómez Robledo Verduzco	9 Dec 2002
Mexico	Frig. Capt. JN. LD.DEM. Agustín Rodríguez Malpica Esquivel	9 Dec 2002
Mexico	Frig. Lt. SJN.LD. Juan Jorge Quiroz Richards	9 Dec 2002
Mexico	Amb. José Luis Vallarta Marrón	9 Dec 2002
Mexico	Dr. Alejandro Sobarzo	9 Dec 2002
Mexico	Joel Hernández García	9 Dec 2002
Mexico	Dr. Erasmo Lara Cabrera	9 Dec 2002
Mongolia	Prof. Rüdiger Wolfrum	
Mongolia	Prof. Jean-Pierre Cot	22 Feb 2005
Netherlands	Prof. E. Hey	9 Feb 1998
Netherlands	Prof. A. Soons	9 Feb 1998
Netherlands	A. Bos	9 Feb 1998
Netherlands	Prof. Dr. Barbara Kwiatkowska	29 May 2002
Norway	Judge Carsten Smith	22 Nov 1999
Norway	Judge Karin Bruzelius	22 Nov 1999
Norway	Hans Wilhelm Longva	22 Nov 1999
Norway	Amb. Per Tresselt	22 Nov 1999
Poland	Mr. Janusz Symonides	14 May 2004
Poland	Mr. Stanislaw Pawlak	14 May 2004
Poland	Mrs. Maria Dragun-Gertner	14 May 2004
Russia	Vladimir S. Kotliar	26 May 1997
Russia	Prof. Kamil A. Bekyashev	4 Mar 1998
Russia	Mr. Alexander N. Vylegjanin	17 Jan 2003
Slovakia	Dr. Marek Smid	
Slovakia	Judge Dr. Peter Tomka	9 July 2004
Spain	Amb. José Antonio de Yturriaga Barberán	23 Jun 1999
Spain	Amb. José Manuel Lacleta Muños	7 Feb 2002
Spain	Amb. José Antonio de Yturriaga	7 Feb 2002

	Barberán	
Spain	Amb. Juan Antonio Yáñez-Barnuevo García	7 Feb 2002
Spain	Aurelio Pérez Giralda	7 Feb 2002
Spain	Judge José Antonio Pastor Ridruejo	7 Feb 2002
Spain	Prof./Judge Julio D. González Campos	7 Feb 2002
Sri Lanka	Hon. M.S. Aziz, P.C.	17 Jan 1996
Sri Lanka	C. W. Pinto	17 Sept 2002
Sudan	Sayed/Shawgi Hussain	8 Sept 1995
Sudan	Dr. Ahmed Elmufti	8 Sept 1995
Sudan	Dr. Abd Elrahman Elkhalifa	8 Sept 1995
Sudan	Sayed/Eltahir Hamadalla	8 Sept 1995
Sudan	Prof. Elihu Lauterpacht CBE QC	8 Sept 1995
Sudan	Sir Arthur Watts KCMG QC	8 Sept 1995
Sweden	Dr. Marie Jacobsson	2 June 2006
Sweden	Prof. Dr. Said Mahmoudi	2 June 2006
Trinidad and Tobago	Judge Mr. Justice Cecil Bernard	17 Nov 2004
United Kingdom	Prof. Christopher Greenwood	19 Feb 1998
United Kingdom	Prof. Elihu Lautherpacht CBE QC	19 Feb 1998
United Kingdom	Sir Arthur Watts KCMG QC	19 Feb 1998
United Kingdom	Judge David Anderson, CMG	14 Sept 2005

Made in the USA
Middletown, DE
24 August 2023

37299057R00215